Social Youth Entrepreneurship

Social Youth Entrepreneurship

THE POTENTIAL FOR YOUTH AND COMMUNITY TRANSFORMATION

Melvin Delgado

Westport, Connecticut
London

Library of Congress Cataloging-in-Publication Data

Delgado, Melvin.
  Social youth entrepreneurship: the potential for
    youth and community transformation / Melvin Delgado
    p. cm.
  Includes bibliographical references and indexes.
  ISBN 0–275–97619–X (alk. paper)
    1. Youth—Services for—United States. 2. Youth with social disabilities—Employment—
  United States. 3. Young adult-owned business enterprises—United States. 4. School-to-
  work transition—United States. 5. Youth development—United States. 6. Community
  development—United States. I. Title
  HV1431.D4395   2004
  362.7—dc22   2004047974

British Library Cataloguing in Publication Data is available.

Library of Congress Catalog Card Number: 2004047974
ISBN: 0–275–97619–X

First published in 2004

Praeger Publishers, 88 Post Road West, Westport, CT 06881
An imprint of Greenwood Publishing Group, Inc.
www.praeger.com

Printed in the United States of America

The paper used in this book complies with the
Permanent Paper Standard issued by the National
Information Standards Organization (Z39.48–1984).

10   9   8   7   6   5   4   3   2   1

To Denise, Laura, and Barbara

Contents

Acknowledgments   ix

PART I   SETTING THE CONTEXT   1

Chapter 1   Setting the Context for Social Youth
            Entrepreneurship   3

Chapter 2   What Is Youth Development?   19

Chapter 3   Emerging Paradigms and Youth Development   41

Chapter 4   The Challenges for Marginalized Youth   55

PART II   THE WORLD OF CAREER, WORK, AND SOCIAL
          ENTREPRENEURSHIP   75

Chapter 5   Transition from School to Career: Challenges,
            Obstacles, and Possibilities   77

Chapter 6   Entrepreneurship: The Foundation for Social Youth
            Entrepreneurship   97

Chapter 7   Social Youth Entrepreneurship: Definition, Values,
            Goals, Elements, and Approaches/Considerations   107

PART III   CASE EXAMPLES FROM THE FIELD   133

Chapter 8   Food from the 'Hood, Los Angeles   135

Chapter 9   Young Aspirations/Young Artists (YA/YA),
            New Orleans   151

PART IV   LESSONS LEARNED AND RECOMMENDATIONS   167

Chapter 10   Summary of Lessons from the Field   169

Chapter 11   Implications for Youth and Career Development:
             Field Practice, Professional Education, and Research/
             Scholarship   177

References   185

Name Index   209

Subject Index   217

Acknowledgments

No book is capable of being written without the active support and encouragement of countless numbers of individuals, and this is certainly the case with this book. First, I need to thank and acknowledge the continued support of Dean Peebles-Wilkins, Boston University School of Social Work. She has steadfastly understood the importance of youth, particularly those of color, to the health and welfare of this country and actively supported scholarship in this area. Natalie Collins, research assistant, was involved in all facets of this book and was the field interviewer in the two case studies highlighted in this book. The staff of Food from the 'Hood took time out from their busy schedules to participate in the case study. A very special thanks goes to Monique Hunter, executive director. YA/YA staff are also thanked for their openness and support. A special thanks goes to Jana Napoli, Tarrie Alexis, Ann Schneiders, and Rondell Crier.

PART I

Setting the Context

CHAPTER 1

Setting the Context for Social Youth Entrepreneurship

OVERVIEW

Youth are often referred to by adults as being complex to understand. Yet, are they any more complex than any other age group? I do not think so. Unfortunately, unlike adults, youth rarely have an opportunity to share their opinions or have the power to shape public opinion about themselves; this power is always in the hands of adults. Adults, having been youth at some point in their lives, are the so-called national experts on youth. This bias permeates much of how youth profiles and perceptions are shaped in this and countless other countries in the world and, as a result, shapes society's efforts to address youth needs and concerns. The ultimate results of this bias, needless to say, are disastrous, with society shortchanging the potential contributions of youth (Walker, 2001).

Youth policies in the United States have often been characterized as fragmented, disconnected, contradictory, inadequate, antiquated, misguided, and last, but certainly not least, harmful (Academy for Educational Development, 1995). The primary systems mandated to serve youth often coexist as if in parallel universes and rarely engage in discourse or partnerships. Consequently, youth—particularly those who are further marginalized by society because of some physical trait, socioeconomic class, or sexual orientation—are not served well in this country.

Grossberg (1994, p. 34) argues that youth as a group are important in this society, yet they are also feared: "Youth is a material problem; it is body—the individual body and the social body of generations—that has to be properly inserted into the dominant organization of spaces and places, into the dominant systems of economic and social relationships. As a body, it has to be located in its own proper places and its movements have to be surveyed and constrained. And as a body, its gendered and racial identities have to be neatly defined, its behavior regulated and its sexuality policed." These contradictory views complicate the creation of comprehensive policies and programs that seek to meet the needs of youth without disregarding their vitality and strengths.

We live in a society that worships yet fears youth at the same, or at least what they symbolize. Youth represent energy, sexuality, hope, fun, potential, future, and freedom from responsibilities. They also represent or symbolize awkwardness, insecurity, fear, powerlessness, and economic expenses. These contradictions, unfortunately, are very often acted out in this nation's policies, or lack thereof, involving youth and thus make comprehensive and purposeful interventions difficult if not impossible (*Private/Public Ventures*, 2000, p. 1): "The last several decades have witnessed a growing skepticism in America about the capacity of social programs—especially publicly funded social programs—to address the problems and prospects of American youth. This skepticism is especially strong once youth reach the pre-teen years and beyond. Thus interest in early childhood programs continues and grows—while support for teenage employment programs declines and dwindles. The body politic seems to be in the process of deciding that a young person's life course is set in concrete after the onset of puberty."

There is no denying that youth are a significant presence in this nation's psyche and fabric. A nation's failure to successfully nurture and enhance the competencies of youth spells doom for the future of that country. One does not have to be psychic or a strategic thinker by trade to predict this outcome. A shift in viewpoints or paradigms is in order to shape effectively a more positive outcome. A view that casts youth as social capital enhances their wealth, and the importance of protecting society's investment in them and their future payoff represents such a shift in thinking (Pittman, Irby & Ferber, 2000). This shift is particularly critical and welcomed when speaking about youth of color in this society. When discussing youth of color, not surprisingly, negative perceptions far outweigh the positive, further compounding the problem of this nation's development of programs and policies targeting them, and viewing them as capital (Cheshire & Kawamoto, 2003; Olive, 2003; Rodriguez, Morrobel & Villarruel, 2003; Swanson, Spencer, 'Angelo, Harpalani & Spencer, 2002; Taylor et al., 2002).

The twenty-first century promises to present this country with innumerable challenges, some of which cannot be imagined at this time. However, the methods by which the country responds to the needs of all of its youth will undoubtedly appear as both challenges and rewards. The challenges facing today's youth have received considerable attention in the public and private sectors over the last 10 years (Besharov, 1999; Furstenberg, Cook, Eccles, Elder & Sameroff, 1999; National Research Council, 1993; Way, 1998). It seems that very few public figures in this country are prepared to extol the virtues of youth. Instead it is easier and more politically advantageous to comment on their negatives qualities.

This propensity translates into a correspondingly negative-focused legislation such as increased waivers of youth into adult courts and prisons, particularly those who are low-income and of color (Anderson, 1998; Elikann, 1996, 1999). The investment of funds into building upon the assets of youth, too, is not as easy or as advantageous as allocating funds to punish them or to try to rectify their deficits and shortcomings. Sadly, it is easier for society to place a dollar figure on the costs of youth failure than on the financial benefits of turning youth into productive members of society such as teachers, scientists, social workers, or artists, instead of becoming prison numbers.

It is rare for a few weeks to pass without a newspaper or television story addressing current and projected labor force issues. The foci of most of these stories invariably touch upon the concerns of government officials or big employers as they decry the poor quality (competencies, work habits, and motivation) of this nation's workforce and raise alarm about this country's lack of competitiveness on a global scale. A specific focus of this alarm, too, is recent high school graduates. Public education reform, in many ways, is responding to these criticisms and concerns about the preparation of youth to assume worker roles. Unfortunately, those who have dropped out of school are rarely noticed, and it is almost as if they dropped off the face of the earth when they left school.

It certainly is not unusal to hear a yearly "call to arms" in this country focused on highlighting how entry-level employees lack communication skills, positive work habits, and problem-solving skills. These widely held perceptions on the part of employers, when combined with an ever-increasing set of expectations, do not speak well for the country or the communities from which entry-level employees originate. The tendency for society to blame the victim, so to speak, is quite evident and does not bode well for the search for a comprehensive and lasting strategy to make youth socially responsible and productive as adults.

Retention of workers, too, is often a challenge since as the result of businesses downsizing or better opportunities for employment in other sectors, employees will no longer start and finish their careers with one employer (Neumark, 2000). Thus, the importance of transferable skills increases dramatically in the twenty-first century and so does having a workforce with an ability to shift loyalty from employer to employer and sector to sector. Youth must be able to build upon their existing knowledge base in order to successfully navigate the vicissitudes inherent in future workforce demands (Newman, 1999). Youth from marginalized urban communities must also navigate the rigors of their communities as they seek to succeed in school and the world of career.

Newman's (1999) book entitled *No Shame in My Game: The Working Poor in the Inner City* presents a compelling case for the importance of a work ethic within marginalized urban communities of color. However, these workers (youth as well as adults) struggle to support themselves and their families with jobs that offer little advancement, few benefits, low wages, and are unhealthy (psychologically and physically). This picture of working-class America illustrates the need for an in-depth understanding of the social forces hindering upward economic mobility for communities of color. Like Newman, Moss and Tilly's (2001) book entitled *Stories Employers Tell*, in turn, highlights how employer discrimination systematically marginalizes workers of color, and how biased perceptions have profound consequences for labor-market experiences. The presence of discriminatory employment policies is a subject that many employers generally refuse to acknowledge and address; yet discrimination is a significant factor in how people of color view their employment prospects.

Observers, not surprisingly, have been quick to point out that the future prosperity of this nation is dependent upon the quality of its workforce. Youth are a critical dimension of this current and projected workforce. The Committee for Economic Development (1997, p. v) summed up this challenge quite well: "The United States should provide opportunities for all young persons entering its workforce to develop productive careers. But the nation's schools fail to equip many of our youth with appropriate skills; the job market often fails to link them to long-term, advancement-oriented employment; and their communities often provide few role models of adult employment success. These problems are particularly acute in severely distressed neighborhoods in the nation's largest cities." The Committee for Economic Development (1997) draws attention to the multifaceted and complex nature of the problem. Solutions that are narrowly conceptualized are doomed either to fail or to result in very limited short-term gains.

Is it possible for a nation to progress and achieve its potential with a significant portion of its population and potential workforce underutilized or not utilized at all? Any serious and sustainable effort to meet these challenges requires that a nation be willing and able to have a political will to commit resources for long-term changes. Short-term solutions, although politically attractive, are doomed to failure. This nation is very quick to declare war on various social problems such as crime, drugs, and poverty. This metaphor, unfortunately, has not translated into any sustained and comprehensive initiatives. A youth productive workforce participation will require a conscientious effort from all sectors of this country. Anything short of this would be a cruel joke on youth and a serious shortcoming for this nation's global competitiveness.

Research and development within the business community does not focus on achieving immediate profits. Instead, it needs to be viewed as a strategic investment in the future. If youth are viewed from a human capital perspective, an investment in them can be easily rationalized just as the investments that corporations make in research and development are considered part of good business practices (Mangum & Waldeck, 1997).

Stein (2000, p. 2) captures the excitement that goes with expanding youth roles within a youth-development paradigm, and viewing them as social capital, in the following statement: "The possibilities are expanding for youth and youth development in communities. Once youth are seen as assets and as having the ability to contribute, then the number of roles young people can play expands dramatically. New and exciting programs are beginning to reflect this. Not only is the development of young people furthered, but also once young people are truly welcomed as community resources, the entire network of human and social capital in communities can be enhanced for all."

However, contrary to Stein's positive and humanistic perspective, this society is not accustomed to viewing humans as capital, particularly groups that are often thought of as surplus. Capital is a concept that is usually reserved for equipment, buildings, and land. Yet no nation can survive and prosper by putting significant resources into prisons and remedial services to deal with the consequences of failed policies. Taking this concept and applying it to people, youth being one example, radically alters society's viewpoint of what resources are important for future prosperity.

The preparation of youth to successfully make the transition to adulthood and the world of career is quite complex. Some observers of youth would argue that this preparation does not start at any particular age or developmental stage. Instead, it starts the moment a child is born and accelerates with age. There are many facets to the subject. A grasp of the interplay of cultural, social, economic, political, and psychological dimensions is very much required in order to comprehend fully that context (Walker, 2001). This context is highly dynamic and makes comprehension that much more necessary and challenging. Although comprehension may be difficult, we should not refrain from accepting the challenge since the consequences of not doing so can be disastrous for a country.

The reluctance of the American political system to embrace public policy as a tool for achieving positive change seriously limits any comprehensive social and economic efforts at meeting the needs of youth (Walker, 2001, p. 2): "No one would claim that American political culture embraces public social policy as a tool of first resort for improving social conditions or solving social problems. Quite the contrary: we generally view it as a tool of last resort, when private solutions clearly do not work and when the condition or problem is serious and highly visible. The major public policy initiatives of the 1930s required a national depression to gain support; those of the 1960s and 1970s required riots. This reluctance to use social policy is our historical political culture, and rarely has it been more evident than in the last decade." This reluctance necessitates that those advocates interested in providing youth with viable options for careers in the future be innovators, public relation specialists, and astute politicians.

Any in-depth examination of the field of career and work and youth will uncover numerous terms and concepts that seek to capture the state of affairs. Kazis and Pennington (1999), for example, prefer the use of the term *school-to-career* rather than the conventional *school-to-work* term. Allen, Hogan, and Steinberg (1998), too, prefer the term *career* to that of *work*." "*School-to-career*" conveys a broad set of choices for youth and a future marked by a career, not just a job. This focus necessitates recognition of the importance of lifelong learning and societal opportunities in the making of a career. The concept of school-to-work has been referred to as a method for tracking marginalized students away from college and to the world of work (Imel, 1995).

School-to-career, in turn, emphasizes self-sufficiency as an ability to advance in a career rather than a job. It is also not unusual to see the term *community-connected learning* to substitute for *school-to-work*. Critics consider school-to-work to be a one-time transition to employment and thus synonymous with entry-level work, and quite unidimensional through emphasis on income. This book, too, will use this term in the spirit in which the above authors intended it to be used. A school-to-career perspective offers endless possibilities for youth, particularly social youth entrepreneurship goal as a viable alternative to traditional preparation for the labor market. The reader, I am sure, recognizes the importance of careers versus jobs. This difference in perceptions and expectations must also apply to youth making a transition from school to the world of adulthood.

This challenge requires a vision or paradigm that successfully addresses youth abilities and needs and channels energy and resources into initiatives. The promise of a youth-development paradigm is one such perspective (Delgado, 2002; Eccles & Appelton, 2002). This paradigm has slowly evolved in complexity and broadened to include the community in identifying the context in which youth find themselves, as a vehicle for helping them achieve, and as a target for change. Community capacity enhancement is a newer paradigm that can be used to ground initiatives to actively and systematically focus on youth assets and community context. In essence, community capacity enhancement can be achieved only if all significant sectors of the community are able to maximize their potential (Delgado, 2000a). This paradigm does not provide for exceptions to the rule.

The grounding of youth within an asset paradigm by its very nature results in initiatives that look dramatically different from those of the 1970s and 1980s, which used deficit-focused premises, assumptions, and goals. Those initiatives, in turn, were not strategic, comprehensive, and long-term in nature, and as a result, were doomed to fail. Youth-development initiatives require creation of comprehensive goals and outcomes (Eccles et al., 2002; Taylor, 2001).

The reader will be introduced to numerous concepts in the course of reading this book. Social entrepreneurship, however, may be the newest idea, although its presence in the field and professional literature can be traced to the mid-1990s. This perspective brings together several disciplines that have historically not worked together (Emerson, 1996, p. 14): "Social entrepreneurship is not social work, community economic development, or business development . . . the integration of all three . . . requires those involved to modify, expand, or cast off old ways of analysis and practice." One can certainly sense a high degree of excitement, potential rewards, and challenges when combining three rather distinct and disparate fields.

The potential of social youth entrepreneurship, therefore, goes beyond narrow boundaries and goals and focuses specifically upon a specific age group—youth. Social entrepreneurship, however, is not restricted for use with any one particular age group, gender, sexual orientation, etcetera. However, the characteristics of the group initiating this type of endeavor and sponsoring settings play influential roles in shaping how this intervention gets planned and implemented, including determining the characteristics for the marketing of services and products. Male youth, for example, would be hard pressed to develop an enterprise focused on selling cosmetics to women, although this is not uncommon in the adult world. School-based enterprises, in turn, face restrictions regarding the nature of the product and service being marketed that may not be found in a community-based organization.

Smilor (1997, p. 8) believes that social entrepreneurship has a role to play in helping communities in ways that go far beyond the creation of jobs: "The problems that plague our society are profound and complex. There are no simple solutions. Entrepreneurship is certainly not a panacea, but I am convinced that it is one effective and proven way to confer 'identity, a sense of belonging, a means of security.' In other words, it can contribute to the hopeful and renewing process of building community." Interestingly, this perspective is very often overlooked in any discussion of employment and community development. Consequently, a social youth entrepreneurship outlook holds much potential for inclusion in paradigms that stress youth assets and their responsibility to community (Lakes, 1996; Yourniss & Yates, 1997).

The potential of community to enable and benefit from social youth entrepreneurship is exciting and challenging for practitioners, academics, youth, and communities. Youth certainly are a significant sector of any community as noted by Fortier and many other scholars (2001, p. 1.): "Communities and youth leaders across the country are experiencing two powerful shifts in mindset and actions. One shift is a growing realization that the Community Building process is an essential component of efforts to create healthier communities while addressing a variety of health, social and economic issues. By building 'capacity,' communities can rely less on outside assistance and more on their own internal resources. . . . A second shift is in the community's view of young people. Today, more communities and organizations are recognizing that our youth are a great resource, capable of making significant contributions to their schools and other organizations, as well as the entire community."

Youth, as a consequence, represent an age group that can be brought together to launch an enterprise as well as a group to which an enterprise can be targeted. They can play instrumental roles in both helping themselves and their communities. Unfortunately, society has little difficulty in seeing youth as consumers rather than creators of marketable goods and services. This bias, in turn, is very often internalized by youth and thereby diminishes their belief in themselves as entrepreneurs.

Any significant shift in perspectives towards youth cannot be achieved instantaneously or without considerable debate and dialogue, nor should it be. Key political stakeholders must welcome and prepare for an inclusive process that will facilitate this outcome. This shift in perspective must be a process that examines youth within a broader labor-market context that recognizes significant structural changes that have occurred over the latter part of the twentieth century and, as a result, is willing to entertain change or reform to take into account a broader perspective of what is needed to achieve positive results.

Economic self-sufficiency, with career and work being key dimensions of this construct, however, has only recently surfaced in the professional literature even though its effects can be significant and failure to achieve this goal hinders the transition of youth to adult roles. A greater emphasis on this transition from youth-development programs will necessitate a closer working relationship between programs, schools, and the world of career. However, it would be foolhardy to think that it is possible to achieve success without also paying close attention to significant technological, economic, political, and demographic changes in this society.

Structural changes have significantly altered the world of career. New careers have emerged as a result, and old careers have disappeared. Failure to contextualize these forces will result in youth employment programs and initiatives failing, and a tendency to blame the victim. In this case, a valuable source of creativity, energy, hope, and talent is lost. Blaming youth for their failure to adapt to an ever-changing employment market is unfair. Institutions charged to prepare youth for their eventual transition to the work of adults must come forth and propose innovative ways of increasing the likelihood that youth will be successful.

No venture can guarantee that youth will be successful. Nevertheless, strategic efforts must be made to increase the chances that they will be provided with the opportunities, knowledge, and skills to be successful. The introduction of interventions using social youth entrepreneurship has the potential to transform the lives of youth. Further, a wide range of institutions such as schools and community organizations can launch these interventions; they can also be initiated outside of formal institutions.

A youth-development paradigm has slowly evolved from an almost exclusive focus on youth to a broader conception that includes families, peers, and communities. This evolution has resulted in placing youth in a central position and potentially able to wield a tremendous amount of influence in their ecology (Booth & Crouter, 2001; Fitzpatrick & LaGory, 2000). Ironically, as already noted, the American market place has been very quick to recognize youth as consumers of goods and services. However, the concept of youth as workers, potential business owners, and enterprise creators has lagged far behind the market-driven perspective. School-to-career brings a dimension to youth development that is integrally related to community as context, a vehicle for capacity enhancement, and a target for initiatives.

The centrality of community within most youth-development definitions, and particularly so in the community youth-development school of thought, opens up a wealth of opportunities for social youth entrepreneurship with a community focus to guide actions and programs. Any effort to contextualize the experiences of youth in an effort to better understand their assets and challenges will also result in initiatives seeking to alter community conditions and tap community assets. Such a community focus serves to ensure that the development of products and services has a social value base that increases the likelihood of work and business having a community benefit rather than a focus on profits without community benefits. Efforts to tie careers, education, and community building, as a result, are more commonplace in many of the nation's cities (Ellis, 1992; Rosenblum, 1998).

A social youth entrepreneurship focus fits well within a community context and expands its potential for significant community contributions and transformations. Community fulfills a variety of roles within social youth entrepreneurship initiatives, just as it does within youth-development initiatives. Community represents a viable market for the purchase of products and services; a supplier of labor; a setting within which to situate an enterprise; an ultimate beneficiary of the enterprise. When the enterprise is based within the community, other intended and unintended benefits, such as role modeling and hope, are fostered for other youth and residents. These social benefits very often go unnoticed by the entrepreneurs but are significant nevertheless.

Current movements towards revitalizing urban schools and communities can exist parallel to each other or be synergistic depending upon the specific focus and location of these efforts. Nevertheless, there is no denying the tremendous potential each of these movements possesses for youth and community transformation when the movements are combined or coordinated (Boyd, Crowson, & Gresson, 1997). The interdependence between youth development/learning and the health of families and communities blurs historical distinctions and separation of schools and communities. An ecological perspective on learning connections provides a conceptual frame through which to develop initiatives such as social youth entrepreneurship. This conceptualization enhances the potential of social youth entrepreneurship to wield considerable influence within multiple social arenas and settings.

GOALS FOR THE BOOK

Unfortunately, it is not possible to delve directly into a book solely focused on social youth entrepreneurship. The reader, I believe, needs to be exposed to the concepts of youth development, entrepreneurship, and social entrepreneurship before specifically examining social youth entrepreneurship. This book, as a result, addresses six goals that both seek to broaden the reader's understanding of youth development and social youth entrepreneurship and to ground them in the key issues and challenges to be found in this field.

These goals, not surprisingly, overlap considerably yet attempt to individually focus on specific content areas that are important unto themselves. But most important, these goals provide the reader with an understanding of history and process; they also serve as a basis for examining the potential for innovation in this area of practice. The field of social youth entrepreneurship is still in its infancy and can evolve in countless ways in the not too distant future. The six goals are as follows:

1. provide an up-to-date view of how the youth-development field has evolved and expanded into arenas that historically were not part of this field and of its potential for conceptually grounding social youth entrepreneurship;
2. emphasize the key concepts and elements of the world of social youth entrepreneurship and of career pertaining to youth who are marginalized in this society;
3. examine key demographic and career/work trends with direct implications for marginalized youth, with a particular emphasis on small community-based enterprises;
4. explore how youth-development principles, programs, and activities are currently being used in youth-development programs targeting various social entrepreneurship/career arenas—the leap from youth development to career-force development, if you wish, is not great;
5. provide concrete and in-depth case examples of social youth entrepreneurial programs that will allow them to draw their own conclusions about the value of this perspective for youth development; and
6. outline a series of recommendations and action steps that the field of youth development and graduate professional schools must address in order to play influential roles in shaping the field of youth development with a career focus.

STRUCTURE AND ORGANIZATION OF THE BOOK

It is always advisable for an introductory chapter of a book to inform readers of how the book is structured and organized. This roadmap, so to speak, prepares readers for their journey. This book consists of eleven chapters that will be divided into four sections. Each section systematically sets the foundation for the next section: Part 1, Setting the Context (four chapters); Part 2, The World of Career, Work, and Social Entrepreneurship (three chapters); Part 3, Case Examples from the Field (two chapters); and Part 4, Lessons Learned and Recommendations (two chapters).

Although it is always tempting for readers to skip certain chapters, that is not advisable. The reading of the cases studies, which many readers may prefer, will not be as useful without a conceptual grounding and an historical appreciation of how certain key constructs have shaped current-day initiatives, for example. Further, it is not possible to go straight to the chapter on social youth entrepreneurship without first reading about youth development, entrepreneurship, and social entrepreneurship. In many ways, the reading of this content can be compared with the peeling of an onion, layer by layer.

PURPOSE FOR WRITING THIS BOOK

Why write a book on youth development, career, and social entrepreneurship? Writing a book is never for the faint of heart. A considerable amount of time, energy, and resources are required. In many ways, it is a zero-sum equation. Numerous sacrifices and compromises are needed in order to accomplish this task. At minimum, no other major writing projects can occur during this period. Consequently, the subject matter must be of sufficient importance to warrant the undertaking of a writing project.

Why write this particular book? The future of youth development is very much contingent upon the field's ability to recognize opportunities to expand into areas that historically would not be considered attractive or receptive to this paradigm. Social youth entrepreneurship represents this type of advancement opportunity. The introduction of school-based enterprises, for example, has opened the door to youth-development principles and practices within schools.

Social entrepreneurs—and in the case of this book they are young—are reformers and revolutionaries with a social mission (Dees, 1998, p. 4): "They make fundamental changes in the way things are done in the social sector. Their visions are bold. They attack the underlying causes of problems, rather than simply treating the symptoms. They often reduce needs rather than just meeting them. They seek to create systematic changes and sustainable improvements in their chosen arenas, whether that is education, health care, economic development, the environment, the arts, or any other social sector field." Clearly, social youth entrepreneurs, at least based upon Dees's vision, are deserving of a book that tells their story to the world!

There is currently no book that specifically explores an entrepreneurship and career perspective on youth development, even though transition to adulthood is a central goal of most interventions, youth-development-focused or otherwise. I have written two books that specifically focus on youth development. However, neither book addressed social youth entrepreneurship and career. Such a book represents a logical next step in advancing the field of youth development and broadening its appeal to fields of practice that have historically not been associated with youth development or with each other, such as economics, community development, and social work.

From a personal point of view, I see a glaring gap in the field. School-to-career needs to be firmly anchored within a youth-development paradigm, although as the reader will find out there are other, less promising paradigms to choose from. *New Arenas for Community Social Work Practice with Urban Youth: The Use of the Arts, Humanities, and Sports* (Columbia University Press, 2000b) has a specific focus on social development and recreation as a vehicle for youth development. *New Frontiers in Youth Development in the Twenty-First Century: Revitalizing and Broadening Youth Development* (Columbia University Press, 2002) focuses on new ways youth development can transpire with an emphasis on social development and recreation.

Although both books address youth development and so does this book, the paradigm is too complex, particularly with its ever-expanding nature, for two or even several books to be sufficient for the field. The transition from school-to-career has historically been considered of great importance in both the education and human services fields. This importance has translated into numerous articles and reports on the subject. However, the application of a conceptually based youth-development perspective has only recently started to get the attention it warrants.

A book on career and social youth entrepreneurship should be a welcome addition to the literature, particularly one that purposefully seeks to bridge the divide between school, the world of career, and human services. The immense popularity of the field will no doubt continue well into this decade. This popularity will fuel the need for more books on a variety of youth-development perspectives. As universities mount new courses on youth development and/or develop degree programs, books on the subject will be needed to meet this demand. I sincerely hope that this book plays at least a small part in helping the field of youth development broaden its realm of influence and, in so doing, further enhancing its potential for youth and community transformation.

The reader will quickly discover in reading this book that there are many current and potential sources for influencing how social youth entrepreneurship is thought about and carried out in this society. Every effort will be made in the course of this book to at least touch upon these sources, although some sources will be emphasized and others will not. Nevertheless, the reader at the very least will have a solid grounding on the origins and manifestations of social youth entrepreneurship and on its role in individual and community transformation. Many issues will need to be resolved if social youth entrepreneurship is to fulfill its potential for youth, community, and society. Some of these issues will spark controversy; others will result in dialogue and significant gains.

WHO SHOULD READ THIS BOOK?

I wish I could say that everyone should read this book, particularly youth in secondary schools. However, this book is intended as a supplemental text for undergraduate and graduate courses on youth development, education, communities, business, and human service practice. The field of youth development is rich in its diversity of practitioners, scholars, activities, and settings. No one profession has cornered the market on practicing youth development, nor should any profession do so. The field's potential for achieving its lofty goals requires a multidisciplinary perspective. With social youth entrepreneurship, the fields of economics and business are added to education, recreation, social work, psychology, sociology, and rehabilitation, to list but a few of the more prominent professions involved in youth development.

Since youth development is not a profession unto itself, the boundaries of who can practice using this paradigm are very permeable. The reader may rightly be concerned that I as a social worker will consciously or unconsciously take a social work approach to the subject and thereby focus the content unnecessarily. I have endeavored not to do so. However, the reader will be the ultimate judge. The field of youth development does not need a book that narrowly seeks to influence and claim the field. Such a book would do a disservice for the field of youth development by effectively eliminating the potential contribution of other professions.

This book will also be of use to field-based practitioners in schools, particularly those with transition to work programs, youth agencies, and programs targeting at-risk youth. A book with the intention of reaching practitioners cannot be solely theoretically based. Field-based examples are essential to help illustrate how concepts can be operationalized. However, a book strictly using case studies will not do justice to the subject matter. The combination of both theory and practice examples serves as a bridge between the academic course of study and field practice. Needless to say, a book that actively sets out to appeal to a broad audience faces incredible challenges, one of which is not being able to provide sufficient depth to please any one sector.

CONCLUSION

Any book wishing to do justice to the subjects of youth, work, career, and social youth entrepreneurship must be prepared to take a broad perspective. Such a perspective is in order to contextualize youth transition from school-to-career since successful achievement of this goal is dependent upon numerous highly dynamic market supply- and-demand factors. Caution, however, must be taken not to take such a broad view that important specific details are lost. These specifics not only refer to day-to-day challenges and rewards for youth, but also put faces to statistics. Initiatives must never lose sight of the ultimate beneficiaries of programs and projects, nor lose sight of the context in which they reside. Contextualizing experiences is one way of ensuring that behavior is not individualized to the point where environment is neglected.

Caution is also needed in the excitement of putting forth a paradigm like youth development that we do not overpromise on what can be accomplished (Connell, Gambone & Smith, 2000, p. 284): "The bad news is that we have created expectations that we can produce a myriad of positive skills and psychological traits in young people outside the influences of families, schools or neighborhoods. As we sought to shift discourse around youth from fixing problems to supporting development, we also unintentionally created an expectation that youth-serving organizations can provide on their own—without involvement of families, neighbors, schools and other institutions—experiences that are necessary and sufficient for youth to reach a healthy, productive adulthood."

As already noted, this book is intended to reach a broad audience of practitioners, educators, policymakers, and academics. By embracing a youth-development paradigm, school-to-career and social youth entrepreneurship transitions are grounded in a paradigm that will only increase in significance during this decade. Transitions of any kind invariably involve challenges and rewards, and the subject of this book is no exception. Youth, particularly those who are undervalued in this society by the nature of their race, ethnicity, or socioeconomic backgrounds, are of particular importance in this book.

My entire practice and academic career has been devoted to undervalued population groups and communities, and this book, as a result, is a continuation of this interest. The reader may argue that all youth can benefit from the potential of youth development, whether it is carried out as social youth entrepreneurship or as some other type of activity. That, I believe, is true. However, marginalized youth stand to make the greatest advances as the result of youth-development initiatives, particularly those that have a significant community focus such as social youth entrepreneurship.

Finally, any book with a specific focus on youth, those who are marginalized or not, cannot help but actively seek to capture their energy, excitement, sense of fun, drive, dreams, hopes, and fears. How to balance their assets with their fears and obstacles is certainly a goal for any author. Nevertheless, I cannot shy away from embracing this goal. I certainly hope that this book meets this challenge for the reader! The reader, however, needs to play an active role while reading this book. Passive reading is fine for leisure but detrimental when it comes to learning about practice with youth. The reader must be willing to critique, develop his or her own definitions, generalize, and innovate while journeying through this book. Social youth entrepreneurship is not for every reader. The youth-development field is very broad in nature and ever expanding; this book is a testament to this vitality.

Remarkable as it may seem, my enthusiasm for the potential role that social youth entrepreneurship can play in youth and community transformation has only gotten stronger while writing this book. It is quite evident to me that the field of social youth entrepreneurship, like that of youth development, will only increase in importance and relevancy during the twenty-first century. Hopefully, the graduates of social youth entrepreneurship programs will eventually transition to creating social entrepreneurial initiatives as adults. This is not to say that every youth who participates in social youth enterprises must continue in this field. Many may just wish to build upon their successful experience and move into other fields and professions. A small percentage may just transition to adulthood and launch social enterprises that can grow beyond the confines of their community to be national in scope and influence.

Nevertheless, when the future leaders of social enterprises are studied, their origins will undoubtedly be traced back to their days in social youth entrepreneurship programs.

Chapter 2

What Is Youth Development?

INTRODUCTION

The primary goal of this chapter is to ground the reader in the subject matter that is important for the field of youth development, although the dynamic nature of youth development defies its being adequately covered in a single chapter or in one book for that matter. Social youth entrepreneurship must be grounded within a paradigm that reinforces its goals and principles, and youth development is such a paradigm. Two other broader paradigms (sustainable community development and community capacity enhancement) will also be presented as potential perspectives on social youth entrepreneurship.

However, there is little disagreement that the paradigm of youth development offers the greatest potential for influencing how social youth entrepreneurship is carried out as an initiative. Its potential for positive change is not restricted to any particular socioeconomic or ethnic/racial community, but it does have particular appeal for use within marginalized communities. This paradigm also lends itself to multidisciplinary collaboration and places youth as central actors within programs and initiatives. Further, it makes youth the ultimate beneficiaries of attention focused, not on their needs and issues, but on their assets and potential for contribution to society.

As already noted, the subject of youth development is receiving increasing attention in the fields of education and recreation as well as the helping professions, with social work being one of these professions (Delgado, 2000; Public Private Ventures, 2000; Villarruel, Perkins, Borden, & Keith, 2003). The vibrancy of youth development holds much promise for practitioners and academics with interests in viewing youth for their potential rather than their frailties and for the potential of youth development for community transformation (Astroth, 2000; Eccles et al., 2002; Pittman & Zeldin, 1994).

Nevertheless, the field of youth development must still struggle to define or, as some critics will argue, contain its boundaries if it is to be relevant in the twenty-first century. Benson and Saito (2000) go so far as to state that the field needs to set out and develop a conceptual agenda that theoretically defines the territory of youth development, developmental strengths (and how these vary by sociodemographic variables), and outcomes. Then, and only then, can we build models to show how inputs influence the development of strengths and create theories of change at the system and community levels and be in a position to launch rigorous evaluation studies.

The inclusion of social youth entrepreneurship within this paradigm—unfortunately, from the perspective of critics—only serves to further expand the boundaries of what constitutes youth development into realms that have historically not been associated with this form of practice. This broadening of the field is to be expected since youth development as a practice is still relatively new in its development and can be expected to continue to evolve in the future (Connell et al., 2000; Costello, Toles, Spielberger, & Wynn, 2000; Delgado, 2002). This evolution, however, will not occur without considerable discussion, debate, and advancement in research that will allow outsiders to effectively measure youth and community outcomes. Further, the successful evolution of youth development will be dependent upon how effective we as advocates are at clearly defining what is meant and not meant by this paradigm and at evaluating its contributions for positive change (American Youth Policy Forum, 1997; Kibel, 2001; Zeldin & Camino, 1998).

This chapter also examines some of the major perspectives that focus on revitalizing the inner city (Boston & Ross, 1997; Jargowsky, 1997; Wilson, 1999). This content will help the reader contextualize youth development, work, career, and entrepreneurship within the major strategies being put forth on how social-economic institutions can help revitalize economically distressed communities. The importance of gainful employment or career goes far beyond individuals to include families and community-based institutions (profit and nonprofit). This chapter, in essence, is intended to orient those readers without a substantial grasp of the field of youth development to its potential for socioeconomic community transformation.

YOUTH DEVELOPMENT PARADIGM

Anyone who is familiar with the purpose of paradigms will quickly realize that paradigms can be compared to a cloud on a sunny day. We can see the cloud and it stands out quite vividly; we can describe it; and we can even track it across the sky as the wind moves it. Its beauty is self-evident, and its potential for conversation and dialogue is limitless. However, any effort at grabbing the cloud with one's hands will prove futile. Thus, when addressing the paradigm of youth development, the reader can compare this experience to the grabbing of a cloud. Paradigms, regrettably but unavoidably, are highly theoretical in nature, making them more cloudlike than hard substance and thus arduous to grasp in more ways than one. The abstract nature of paradigms, nevertheless, does not diminish their importance for influencing practice.

The paradigm of youth development, not surprisingly, is no exception and therefore is elusive to describe at best (Roth, Brooks-Gunn, Murray, & Foster, 1998). First, it is highly influenced by the context in which it operates. Youth development in urban areas of the country may look different (programs and use of activities) than it does in suburban, exurbia, and rural areas. The principles guiding youth development in these four geographical areas may be similar, but the activities may look dramatically different and so will the sociodemographic characteristics of their youth and staff. Youth development also consists of multiple approaches, core elements (cognitive, emotional, social, physical, moral, and spiritual), social domains (family, peers, school, and community), and age groups (Fassler, 1998; Quinn, 1999). There seems to be no area of youth life that the field of youth development doesn't profess to address in one form or another.

Advocates will go on to argue that youth development is simply not possible without a comprehensive and long-term commitment for change. However, comprehensive and long-term commitment based upon using a youth development paradigm is not possible without closing the gap between theory and practice as noted by Benson and Saito (2000, p. 136): "If we are to close the gap between theory and application, we need first to articulate models to guide the science of youth development and then buttress these arenas of scholarship with the necessary professional resources (e.g., multidisciplinary youth development journals, research conferences, funding)." Successfully tying theory to practice is never easy nor should it be. The process of bringing these two worlds together, so to speak, may never be finished. Yet the goal is too important to be ignored or discarded. Practice without a theoretical grounding is rarely meaningful or long lasting.

The consequences of this ambiguity, however, are quite profound as noted by Murphy in describing the importance and challenges facing youth workers (1995a, p. 1): "Youth workers, vital to the life of communities and to young people, are in diverse places, such as community centers, grass-roots youth organizations, affiliates of national youth-serving organizations, group homes, and parks and recreation departments. Unfortunately, youth workers and the organizations for which they work do not have the societal respect and support they deserve. In large part, this is because the field of youth work is poorly defined. The lack of common language to describe the goals and strategies of youth work has negative consequences for the field." It is critical for the reader, as a result, to have a high degree of grounding on its definition, trends, elements, language, arenas, and controversies. Then, and only then, can the reader be prepared to make informed assessments and opinions about the field.

Why do practitioners need a paradigm? Take that question one step back, then ask what is a paradigm and how does it relate to practice? Kuhn (1970, p. viii) defines a paradigm as "universally recognized scientific achievements that for a time provide model problems and solutions to a community of practitioners." Paradigms, by their very nature, can be elusive in detail and description yet inspirational enough to motivate action without a detailed roadmap. This combination of factors is both challenging and rewarding for practitioners and academics alike. Further, it is rare for a paradigm to enjoy universal consensus regarding its definition and boundaries. Youth development, of course, is no exception. Paradigms are created through the integration of theory and practice experiences. A paradigm, to be effective in guiding practice, must resonate for a practitioner and withstand evaluation. The ability to generalize the experience is critical for broadening its relevance to other groups and circumstances and for advancing the field.

Last, it is necessary to point out, not to the surprise of many in the field of youth development, that youth development does not occur strictly through systematized institutional interventions, and this makes the challenge of grasping this paradigm even greater for most practitioners and academics (Murphy, 1995a, p .9): "Youth development occurs in families, social networks, playgrounds with peers, and situations when no adults or peers are present. Services, supports, and opportunities are important because advantaged young people are those who have access to many places and people who provide them with necessary experiences. Youth are disadvantaged when they do not have ongoing access to developmental opportunities and supports. Therefore, for all young people, especially those we labeled disadvantaged, access to services, supports, and opportunities is the key to achieving positive developmental outcomes."

Murphy (1995a) touches upon an important aspect when noting that youth develop as the result of countless experiences. Provision of institutional support, however, takes on greater significance when these opportunities are severely limited by environmental circumstances. However, any appreciation of all of the forces, formal and informal, involved in helping youth prosper cognitively, physically, emotionally, spiritually, and morally must be flexible and broad in nature. The dynamic nature of these forces requires scholars and practitioners to contextualize youth development and to do so within a social-cultural set of expectations and behavior. The emergence of Afrocentrist practice, for example, is in part a direct response to the need to contextualize the experiences of African Americans in this country (Jeff, 1994).

Definitions and Boundaries

Readers may initially react in not so positive a manner when informed that they are required to study and grasp definitions. It is even necessary to debate.

This exercise is never embraced with wholehearted enthusiasm. Some readers may say that definitions are boring and only academics are interested in this subject matter. Some critics will even go so far as to complain that only those who are obsessional engage and enjoy developing definitions. Many others (and I am one of them) do not share this opinion, and that is why this section of the chapter exists. Definitions are never just intellectual exercises (Delgado, 2002; Murphy, 1995a; Pittman & Zeldin, 1995).

Definitions serve to ground the reader and represent the first significant step in the creation of any programmatic or research endeavor. Further, definitions also serve to embody values that wield a prodigious amount of influence on practice. Failure to have a well-established and accepted definition will ultimately doom any initiative when it comes under close scrutiny by professionals. A lack of consensus on a definition also prevents the development of initiatives that are multidisciplinary, which is what the field of youth-focused services needs.

The definition of community youth development proposed by Pennsylvania State University (2000, p. 1) illustrates the importance of a definition in helping to ground a practitioner or researcher but also highlights the illusive nature of the phenomenon being practiced or researched: "Simply put, community youth development involves creating opportunities for young people to connect to others, develop skills, and utilize those skills to contribute to their communities that, in turn, increases their ability to succeed. As with positive youth development, a community youth development orientation involves shifting away from just concentrating on problems, toward concentrating on strengths, competencies, and engagement in self-development and community development. As such, community youth development is defined as purposely creating environments that provide constructive, affirmative, and encouraging relationships that are sustained over time with adults and peers, while concurrently providing an array of opportunities that enable youth to build their competencies and become engaged as partners in their own development as well as the development of their communities."

Delgado (2002) created a definition of youth development that encompasses most recent major trends and developments related to the inclusion of positive and community prefaces that are now common in the field and will be the basis for conceptualizing youth development in this book: Youth development views youth both as partners and as central figures in interventions. These interventions systematically identify and utilize youth capacities and meet needs (social, economic, political, emotional, cognitive, and spiritual) when present. The former actively seeks to involve youth as decision makers and taps their creativity, energy, and drive. The latter acknowledges that youth are not superhuman and therefore have needs requiring the marshaling of resources targeted at them and at changing environmental circumstances (family and community) that impede their capacity enhancement.

The paradigm of youth development has recently gained increasing popularity and influence in the field of youth-related services, although it has been around in professional circles since the early 1970s (NTIS, 1971). Virtually no aspect of youth services has escaped this attention in the last decade, and it seems as if it has no permanent boundaries, similar to an ever-expanding universe (Costello et al, 2000). The fields of health (Blum, 1998; Cleland, Jemmott, & Angeles, 2001; Lerner, Ostrom, & Freel, 1997; Millstein, Petersen & Nightingale, 1993), education (Dosher, 1996; Gebreselassie & Politz, 2000), mental health (Glover, 1995), public assistance (Cohen & Greenberg, 2000; Knox, Miller, & Gennetian, 2000), juvenile justice (Bazemore & Clinton, 1997; Capowich, 1995; Schwartz, 2000; Taylor, 1997), work/career development (Ferrari, 2003; National School-to-Work Learning & Information Center, 1996; Zeldin, 1995a), and child welfare (Collins, 2001; Liederman, 1995; Sheehy, Oldham, Ansell, Correia, & Copeland, 2000) have all started to consider seriously this paradigm in the conceptualization of youth, families, and communities.

Defining a paradigm too narrowly undermines its potential for reaching out to new settings and population groups; having too broad a paradigm also seriously undermines our ability to measure our successes and identify our failures (Connell et al., 2000; Costello et al., 2000; MacDonald & Valdivieso, 2000). The field of youth development, in essence, needs to walk a very thin line in order to be specific enough to provide direction but not too narrow in its approach to limit its potential reach and lend itself to creative initiatives.

Being able to use and benefit from a youth development paradigm is very much determined by the setting and the competencies of the individual using this paradigm. Some settings, for example, do not lend themselves naturally to the use of this paradigm without significant changes to take into account the context. The application of a youth development paradigm to the juvenile justice field, for example, presents challenges for practitioners, researchers, and scholars (Schwartz, 2000; Taylor, 2002).

Systems predicated upon principles of punishment rather than rehabilitation and capacity enhancement, not surprisingly, do not lend themselves to using a youth development paradigm to achieve maximum results. This does mean, however, that some principles, elements, and activities cannot be used or adapted to fit within the contextual setting. However, the full benefits inherent in the use of a paradigm cannot possibly be achieved.

Key Underlying Goals and Principles

Goals and principles play important roles in helping individuals and organizations grasp the significance of a particular paradigm and developing a corresponding mission statement (Quinn, 1994). For the practitioner wishing detailed specificity, goals and principles may well prove disappointing, however. Mission statements, too, unfortunately, may also prove disappointing from an organizational and practice point of view.

The youth development literature generally focuses on three interweaving goals related to youth self-worth—(1) preparing youth to be contributing members of society (work and civic mindedness); (2) providing family support to assist in raising youth; and (3) satisfying developmental needs of youth (Sarver, Johnson, & Verma, 2000). Each of these goals is significant unto itself. Achievement of any of these goals is not possible without also achieving the other two goals, yet each goal requires a specific focus, strategy, and set of activities. Further, achievement of these goals requires the development of practice principles to help guide interventions in various contexts and circumstances.

Principles, in turn, fulfill two very important functions in bringing a paradigm to fruition: (1) they help bridge theory and practice, and (2) they provide guidance to organizations and practitioners in helping them navigate obstacles to carrying out their mission. These two functions are just as critical for practitioners as they are for academics, researchers, and, ultimately, youth. Principles, therefore, are essential and critical for the practice of youth development and are more than just a set of words put together to make a sentence. They hold significant meaning and purpose and serve as a vehicle for translating vision into mission!

Principles, nevertheless, are not without limitations, and these must be acknowledged and systematically addressed (Pittman et al., 1995, pp. 3–4): "(1) Principles are not relevant unless organizational staff, volunteers, and participants have had a hand in developing them and unless consensus is formed; (2) Principles always run the risk of becoming jargon. Principles take on the greatest meaning when they are stated as briefly as possible and when they are buttressed with concrete examples of how the principle translates 'into action'; (3) Principles will not be consistently used unless they are consistent with the basic beliefs, theories, or premises of the organization and staff. These basic premises are often hidden; [and] (4) Principles will not be consistently applied unless there are processes in place that require that the organization regularly assess the effectiveness of its operation, progress of its participants, and performance of its staff." Pittman and Zeldin's (1995) observations about the limitations of principles do not diminish the need to have them play significant roles in helping to translate the goals of a paradigm into real life changes, however.

Commitment to youth development does not necessarily translate into clarity about this paradigm (Murphy, 1995b). Principles, make no mistake about it, do help create clarity but only to a certain degree. Absolute clarity is impossible although it is a goal worth seeking to achieve. To abandon all hope of ever achieving absolute clarity will not advance the field in the twenty-first century. This process of seeking clarity brings its share of pain. However, this is unavoidable, and some critics would go on to argue that progress is never fully appreciated without encountering resistance and structure along the way.

The literature on youth development is replete with examples of principles that must be firmly in place in order for youth and practitioners to fully understand the potential of this paradigm for individual and community transformation. These principles, to the surprise of no one, are highly interrelated, making the sum of the parts greater than the whole. In other words, youth development principles must be purchased as a total package. Picking and choosing the most desirable and relevant ones and discarding or ignoring others makes the practice of youth development arduous at best, if not impossible.

The following five key principles reflect the collective efforts and wisdom of countless numbers of organizations, task forces, and scholars and serve as a basis for grounding social youth entrepreneurship within a youth development paradigm. These statements of principles have the potential to transform those who carry out the principles and those who are the recipients of these actions. The reader may well argue that there are many more that need to be included. I have, however, elected to focus on five that interconnect and complement each other, yet each addresses a specific realm and set of actions that capture the core elements of youth development.

Principle 1: All Youth Possess Assets and Hopes for a Better Future Regardless of the Social-Economic Circumstances They Find Themselves Within

At first sight the reader may think of this principle as rudimentary and may even question why it needs to be raised. However, I elect to start with this principle for strategic reasons. In many ways this principle represents the heart and soul of youth development and the basis from which all other principles emanate. A youth development paradigm is premised on the assumption that young people are positive resources and have a potential for productivity and a responsibility to serve their communities (Checkoway, 1994; Delgado, 2000, 2002; Hein, 2000). This principle can be broad in nature or very specific to ethnic/racial and gender factors as in the case of African American males and females (Ferguson, 1994; Stevens, 2002).

The consequences of a society viewing youth from a deficit perspective can be quite profound as noted by Michael Sherraden (as quoted in Leffert, Saito, Blyth, & Kroenke, 1996, p. 11): "It would be difficult to overstate the problem. A researcher working in an urban area, for example, can more easily obtain a million dollars to study youth purse snatching than a thousand dollars to study youth theater and dance groups. This is a misallocation of research dollars. Unfortunately, it becomes a vicious circle—the more we study problems, the more we spend on problems; and the less we study solutions, the less we spend on solutions."

This statement captures the essence of the challenge for those who seek to work with youth. Paucity of data on youth assets reflects the bias that Sheraden refers to in the above statement. Data related to positive youth behaviors such as the percentage of youth who volunteer, for example, are missing from data collection systems (MacDonald et al., 2000). These types of data not only require changes in information systems, but also a reshifting in our thinking about what types of information are important. The shift in paradigms alluded to earlier in this chapter is in order.

MacDonald and Valdivieso (2000) identified four conditions that need to occur for effectively measuring progress in youth development: (1) a broadening of the type of information we gather on youth needs; (2) adult acknowledgment that youth are experts in their own development; (3) a willingness to get over skepticism about measuring the warm and fuzzy side of youth development; and (4) the need for research methods to be practical and user-friendly. In essence, major changes regarding information gathering are needed to bring a new perspective towards youth. It would be foolish or naïve to think that these conditions can be easily changed. The accomplishment of this task may be considered radical and will meet incredible resistance.

Principle 2. Youth Development Cannot Transpire within a Vacuum by Focusing Exclusively on Youth. Their Community Must Also Play a Central Role in Influencing How Youth Development Is Conceptualized and Implemented

One of the many attractive aspects of a youth development paradigm is its duality in bringing youth together with their social environment. This paradigm, as a result, sets high expectations for change at the individual, family, and community levels. The luxury of concentrating or worrying about only the individual youth is counterproductive to the basic interests of this paradigm. However, the challenge of proving how neighborhoods enhance or undermine adolescent development, for example, is no small task (Denner, Kirby, & Coyle, 2000; Duncan & Raudenbush, 2001).

White (1999) identified five essential capacities for building communities that serve as a foundation for better appreciating the potential of youth development within a community context: (1) an abundance of social capital—a community must have a keen understanding of its assets and must present a unifying force that is stronger than any or all of its parts; (2) strong connections with the outside world—external as well as internal. Residents need to be involved in activities both inside and outside of the community. Employment appears to be a very strong factor regarding external connection and community involvement; (3) willingness and capacity to welcome and integrate newcomers. A high degree of integration of residents with various sociodemographic backgrounds increases the sense of community; (4) ability to adapt and innovate. A community's willingness to grow is very dependent upon its curiosity, acceptance of new ideas, and good use of existing resources;

and (5) capacity to collaborate. This tendency increases a community's ability to respond to crises and opportunities.

Community as a context for a youth development paradigm has its share of advocates and critics. The former, including myself, are quick to highlight the need for youth development to be anchored within a community context. Further, communities, regardless of their sociodemographic composition, have youth success stories that are well recognized by residents. Critics, on the other hand, believe that proponents of youth development within a community context do not have the requisite data to shore up their beliefs.

The construct of community, like youth development, has an endless number of definitions and has become what Poerkson (1993) has called a plastic word: it has so many meanings that it has become meaningless (Edelman, 2000). Nevertheless, there is increasing consensus in both camps that measurement of the effects on youth outcomes is only possible when the contextualization of processes is accomplished, and community must be a part of this contextualization.

Edelman (2000, p. 170) raises a voice of caution about community-based initiatives that, although not specific to youth development or social youth entrepreneurship, does have applicability nevertheless: "Certainly there are important limitations with community programs as an idea. An example is that the expectations for community-based programs are often unrealistic; they are not panaceas for social problems, nor should they replace the resources and policies that need to come from the institutional level. This can often be seen in the disparity between the rhetoric of programs that look for broad outcomes in terms of alleviating poverty, expanding employment, reducing violence, abuse, drug use, teenage pregnancy, improving school attendance and grades, and other major social and economic concerns while distributing relatively small amounts of seed money and expecting impoverished communities and volunteers to develop the organizational and financial structures that might actually affect these problems."

Four key dimensions or arenas of community-individual interactions are in order for a conceptualization of community to lend itself to a better understanding of assets-risks (Sampson, 2001; Small & Supple, 2001): (1) presence (geographical); (2) exposure (witnessing); (3) contact (encounters); and (4) duration (length of contact). The interplay between these four dimensions provides a very dynamic perspective on how community can play a mediating, enhancing, or detrimental impact on how youth develop. The scale and sustainability of youth development initiatives must take into account the experiences youth have in these four arenas (Edelman, 2000; Pittman, Irby, & Ferber, 2000).

The creation of an environment that fosters the goals of youth development and is the target of youth development must be incorporated in youth development activities (Adams, 2000; Brown, Camino, Hobson, & Knox, 2000; Denner et al., 2000). Having youth play important roles in community development remains an underappreciated and underexplored area, however (Checkoway, 1994). Armistead and Wexler (1998) specifically advocate for the merger of community and youth development through community development corporations (CDCs). CDCs are committed to a set of values that lend themselves to youth development—self-help, participation, local decision making, empowerment, and local accountability (Ferguson & Stoutland, 1999). Thus, the leap towards integrating youth development within CDC programming is not out of the question and represents an organic element of community development corporations.

Some scholars would go on to advocate the position that it is impossible to develop competent and healthy youth without developing families and communities in the process (Abbott, 1995; Burt, Resnick, & Novick, 1998; Chalk & Phillips, 1996; Connell & Kubisch, 2001; Duncan et al., 2001; Furstenberg et al., 1999; Kipke, 1999). Stein (2000, p. 1), for example, notes: "Seeing youth as resources to their communities, as people who have significant skills, and who therefore can make valuable contributions, is not a new idea, but it has gained enormous currency over the past decade." This potential for positive change, however, can only be fully realized when the field of youth development ventures into the realm of economic self-sufficiency for youth when they reach adulthood and develops vehicles (programs) for achieving the goal of successful transition from youth to adulthood.

Stein (2000) identifies a set of nine key practice factors that highlight the important role youth can play within their communities if provided with an opportunity to do so and supported: (1) youth are producers; (2) youth's cognitive abilities and energy deserve respect; (3) competencies become enhanced when youth actions are linked to public work; (4) youth can be meaningful participants in governance; (5) youth and adults can engage in reciprocal relationships; (6) cooperative action should be valued over individual action; (7) youth's public work is visible; (8) youth action needs to be connected to larger civic challenges and questions of meaning; and (9) youth actions can contribute to community and institutional change.

With youth as partners for positive change, unlimited potential for creating community well-being is possible. Further, this partnership actively builds future adult civic leaders in the process. It would be a serious mistake, however, to think of youth contributions in a narrow and very limited manner. The broader the possibilities for youth contributions the greater the ultimate contributions they can make. The possibilities for youth contributions are only limited by the imagination of adults and our willingness to allow youth to fulfill a broad range of roles.

Checkoway (1994, p. 13), although not specifically tying together youth entrepreneurship and neighborhood development, nevertheless provides a rationale for doing so in youth-centered programs: "Neighborhood-based youth initiatives simultaneously promote the positive development of young people and the neighborhoods they serve. They recognize that young people need 'real work' and 'practical learning,' and that both purposes can be served together in the same program. They thus combine 'education,' 'employment,' and 'service' in ways which enable youth to transform themselves while changing their communities."

Checkoway (1994) has merged youth assets, neighborhood development, and community service. This merger is very appealing for a variety of some obvious and not so obvious reasons. Contextualizing youthful lives by placing them within the community emphasizes the need to never lose sight of community in service to youth. However, it also serves to place youth in service to community. Further, this merger facilitates the creation of partnerships across disciplines and professions since no one discipline or profession can possibly meet all of the goals articulated by Checkoway (1994).

Social youth entrepreneurship is but one example of these three threads coming together in the twenty-first century, one that has the potential for using economic means for achieving social gains for youth and their communities. Ferrari (2003), in turn, stresses the close interrelationship between career development and community youth development.

Principle 3: The Process of Engaging and Empowering Youth Is as Important as the Ultimate Outcome or Product

The concept of empowerment has a long and very distinguished history within the United States, particularly in the human service field (Gutierrez & Lewis, 1999; Lee, 2001; Solomon, 1976). Naturally, the field of youth development has embraced empowerment goals. It seems as if no undervalued group has escaped having this concept applied to them. Nevertheless, the concept as it applies to youth brings with it many considerations that effectively undermine how empowerment is conceptualized and carried out on a daily basis. Youth, in effect, can only be empowered up to a certain point— they cannot vote, drink alcohol or smoke, and they are required to attend school up to a particular age. However, providers must be careful not to equate empowerment with the relinquishment of authority and control over a project (Huebner, 1998). Empowerment of youth refers to enabling youth and promoting their self-actualization.

From a cultural perspective, youth may not have the power or the voice to articulate their desires to parents. Some ethnic groups may actively fight against organizations empowering their children because of fears that it will undermine the family decision making process. Further, from an adult perspective, empowering youth to become decision makers can be a frightening proposition. Consequently, empowerment of youth is highly sensitive, complicated, yet essential. It becomes encumbent upon individuals in leadership positions (practitioners, academics, researchers) to find ways that youth can be empowered in this society, in their communities, and in their homes. The contextualization of empowerment is essential—one type does not fit all!

It is necessary for adults to provide for youth an atmosphere where they can exercise decision making power to determine the circumstances surrounding their participation. When, where, and how they participate and shape an initiative or activity must be firmly in the hands of youth (Zeldin, 1995). There is little argument that the pace, direction, and ultimate outcomes (learning, competencies, community transformation) is determined by youth themselves with the help of adults as partners. A developmental plan having youth exercise greater and greater control over events after requisite training is one model that offers great promise.

We live in a society where the bottom line takes on incredible importance within the education and human service fields. Any principle that actively embraces empowerment of youth must actively provide opportunities for youth to exercise power over their decisions. The empowerment of youth and communities is closely tied to the building of social capital. Enterprises that are socially driven, as a result, need to find a viable market for a service or product but must empower participants in the process of doing so.

The broadening of the learning environment beyond school settings is increasingly becoming apparent in the early part of the twenty-first century (Dryfoos, 1995). Schools place too much emphasis on formal roles of students and teachers, and this does not lend itself to preparing youth for the changing world (Heath, 2000). Project-based learning is slowly emerging as a key strategy for teaching youth. This type of vehicle for learning and teaching emphasizes hands-on problem solving, teamwork, social purpose, flexibility in roles, and the blurring of boundaries that have traditionally existed between formal organizational settings such as schools, youth agencies, and other entities in the community. Empowerment, in turn, is a natural occurrence of activities that places youth in positions of owning and shaping their actions. Interestingly, learning, too, occurs in this context.

Heath (2000, p. 10) calls project-based initiatives *joint work*: "Joint work enables participants to exhibit any special talents that they may have, as well as to talk about the process and path of success or failure. Such engagement within a task generally means commitment to seeing it through to successful outcome, and hence intention and motivations are often brought out into the open by coparticipants." Although Heath does not specifically mention empowerment, and instead emphasizes learning and participation, a different perspective identifies the process and learning associated with empowerment. Empowerment can occur individually or collectively. However, the power of peers for youth takes on added importance, and this makes project-based initiatives and learning very powerful and attractive.

Dryfoos (1995), in turn, advocates for school partnerships with community-based organizations in order for a holistic approach to student and community needs to be developed. The concept of a full-service school is receiving increasing attention and signifies the need for schools to be transformed in a way that broadens what is perceived to be a narrow view of its mission. Full-service schools are conceived as places in the community that are effectively part of the community and from which resources can be tapped to meet community needs. The potential for collaborative partnerships between these schools and community-based organizations and businesses has not been fully appreciated and maximized in this society.

Principle 4: Youth-Driven Activities Must Actively Seek to Serve Their Communities

Involving youth in civic and social aspects of communities is well accepted within the field of youth development and has been so since the very beginning of the emergence of this paradigm and form of practice (Gebreselassie et al., 2000; Lakes, 1996; Lerner, 1995; Lewis, 1992; Youniss et al., 1997). Between 1992 and 1996, the total number of American adolescents volunteering increased from 12.4 million to 13.3 million, a 7 percent increase. Adolescent volunteer hours in 1996 totaled 2.4 billion (National Collaboration for Youth, 1997). As can be seen, the idea of youth volunteering is not revolutionary. Nevertheless, youth still represent a vast untapped resource in this country. Having youth volunteer early in their lives increases the likelihood that volunteering will continue throughout their lives.

The equation of having communities support youth and youth support communities brings a multifaceted dimension to community service (Abbott, 1995; Camino, 2000; Freedman, 1993; Pittman, 2000). The interdependence of youth and their communities is quite natural, and any separation of the two or any effort to treat one as more important than the other is thereby quite artificial and doomed to fail. According to the National Collaboration for Youth (1997), youth development programs with service components must seek to address five key goals: (1) actively meet the needs of all parties involved in the endeavor, community as well as youth; (2) create and carry out clear service and learning goals for all youth who participate; (3) articulate a clear set of responsibilities for each youth and organization; (4) provide requisite support (training, supervision, recognition, and evaluation) to support the goals for community service; and (5) actively embrace the goal of reaching all sectors of a community.

Both the popular and the professional literature have highlighted the significant role youth can play in their communities (Barton, Watkins, & Jarjoura, 1997; Checkoway, 1998; Delgado, 2000a; O'Donnell, Michalak, & Ames, 1997; Lakes, 1995; Rauner, 2000; Stein, 2000; Youniss et al., 1997). Freedman (1993), for example, outlines how the concept of mentorship not only benefits urban youth but also their adult mentors and the community at large. Unfortunately, schools have only recently started to seriously consider community service as an important element of education (Delgado, 2001, 2002; Lewis, 1992).

Youth involvement in the economic fabric of community and society has not received the attention it deserves in the professional literature, and as a result this literature has not reflected the important advances being made in the field. In many ways, this field of practice is far more advanced in this area than the professional literature or the helping professions. A construct that addresses this area serves a role of bringing together in one publication the theory, trends, challenges, and opportunities for youth development and the world of work. Bringing service to community into the field of youth entrepreneurship leads to the evolution of the concept of social youth entrepreneurship.

Principle 5. Learning Is an Essential Element of Youth Development and It Can Transpire within Formal and Informal Settings

Many youth development practitioners, researchers, and scholars would argue that an emphasis on learning must permeate all elements and aspects of youth development activities for these activities to take hold and bear fruition for youth (Delgado, 2002; Dosher, 1996). Youth development programs do not have the luxury of mounting initiatives that solely focus on keeping youth safe and occupied during the time they are involved with a program.

An emphasis on learning is not restricted to this principle and can be found in various forms throughout all of the principles addressed in this section. Learning can transpire in a wide variety of settings and circumstances, although formal schooling is considered the primary source for this knowledge. However, when this system fails, what are the options? Fortunately, there are many options that can supplement or supplant, as the case may be, schools.

Abbott (1995, p. 7) notes that learning is dynamic and social in construction: "As we come to understand the dynamics of learning, we realize first that learning is essentially a social activity, and second, that learning relies upon knowledge construction more than knowledge transfer. Young people, moreover, are motivated by the wish to belong to groups that value a particular kind of knowledge; the act of learning draws people together around a common task. Conventional schooling, however, has emphasized the individual and the individual's accumulation of abstract knowledge. It can be argued that overschooling has removed the family and the local community . . . the very foundation of community existence."

Abbott's (1995) analysis of the extrication of youth from their surroundings is quite profound and has tremendous implications for any learning paradigm that stresses connectedness with community. Rogoff and Lave (2001), in turn, stress the social context for thinking and cognition development. The context for learning can be maximized. However, there are situations that lend themselves particularly well to youth learning.

Youth Assets

A youth development paradigm is firmly based upon the belief that youth represent an untapped asset in this nation. Thus, it is worthwhile to pause and provide the reader with a brief overview of how assets are thought of and a listing of the most common assets used in the field of youth development. This field has experienced a dramatic growth in scholarship and research specifically focused on youth assets (Eccles, 2002), an upsurge in attention that has placed youth assets within a broader context of family, peers, and community. This ecological approach has engendered a number of frameworks for identifying, assessing, and mobilizing youth assets. This section will touch upon only two examples to illustrate the richness of the field on this aspect since there are numerous other frameworks to choose from.

Youth assets occasionally are couched in other terms, such as strengths, resiliency, self-efficacy, coping mechanisms, protective factors, to list but four common types. The Search Institute (1999), for example, developed a comprehensive listing of 40 assets that can be classified into two major categories—external-based and internal-based (Benson, Scales, Leffert, & Roehlkepartain, 1999). However, although asset-focused scholarship identifies the world around youth as potential assets, much of the scholarship is still very much focused on youth themselves. Considerably more scholarship is needed to broaden the construct of assets beyond individual youth. The recent thrust towards placing community prominently within youth development offers much promise for the field and will necessitate creation of frameworks and scholarship that look at the environment youth interact with on a daily basis.

Relationship to Work/Career

Youth development and youth employment have been connected in the field and have had to overcome a glaring deficit in the process (Academy for Educational Development, 1995; Ferrari, 2003; Zeldin, 1995c). Unfortunately, formal schooling and the world of career/entrepreneurship have not had a long and distinguished history of working together because of the separation of the world of learning and the world of career, although schools can play an important role in facilitating this transition (Abbott, 1995).

The worlds of education and career, needless to say, need to connect in a variety of meaningful ways for youth to be successful in their transition to adulthood (American Youth Policy Forum, 2001). Gainful occupation or employment is a critical element of this transition. However, employment in a job that pays minimum wages, has limited fringe benefits and advancement opportunities, and is not intellectually challenging is not what youth development and career are all about. Preparation of youth for challenging and meaningful careers is a central goal of career initiatives utilizing a youth development paradigm as a guiding force.

A youth development paradigm can make a substantial contribution to school-to-career initiatives by countering the propensity of employment-oriented programs to disregard or minimize the developmental needs and assets of youth (Academy for Educational Development, 1995). The school-to-career field historically has had a tendency to over emphasize career-dominated knowledge and competencies, and this focus, I believe, is too narrow in scope. A youth development paradigm serves to help ground school-to-career within a broader set of factors and considerations (Zeldin, 1995c).

Murphy (1995a) specifically identifies youth employment as one of the critical outcomes of any successful youth development program. Employability is defined as "the ability and motivation to learn in school and other settings to gain the basic knowledge needed to graduate from high school; to use critical thinking, creative problem-solving, and expressive skills; and to conduct independent study" (Murphy, 1995a, p. 6). These competencies are not related to any particular job and can be considered essential elements for the world of career in the twenty-first century.

Zeldin (1995c), in turn, has focused attention on the common grounds between the school-to-work and youth development fields and concluded that the fields know very little about each other. There are many commonalties and differences between these two fields of practice. Education, particularly experiential learning, for example, does transpire in both fields. Both have missions specifically focused on youth, and both seek to prepare youth for future roles as adults. One youth advocate stated that the primary difference between these two fields is language (Academy for Educational Development, 1995, p. 1): "The dichotomy between youth development and school-to-work is an artifact of language. It is not real. The question is not whether you come together, but how you come together."

An international movement has coined the term *youth livelihood* as a means of bringing together youth that are marginalized or undervalued by society and their need to engage in viable and legal economic activities that generate incomes. *Livelihood* is defined as all of the activities that individuals know, have, and do engage in to make a living. The livelihoods perspective, originally focused on low-income youth with HIV/AIDS, seeks to: (1) provide youth salaried jobs and other avenues for earning a living; (2) provide credit, savings, and other financial services; (3) create appropriate community institutions and coalitions with the goals of advancing youth economic interests; and (4) advocate for policy and social changes that seek to improve youth livelihood prospects (In Focus, 2001).

A youth livelihood goal also merges with many youth development principles into the world of career/work/entrepreneurship. The quest for providing youth with a livelihood is akin to the subject of this book and is predicated on the importance of career and entrepreneurship. Initiatives based on livelihood goals, however, include increasing youth awareness and competencies related to avoiding risk-taking behaviors. Consequently, livelihood is not defined strictly as monetary and has an important social dimension to it. Like youth development, the construct of livelihood contextualizes youth and their experiences as well as takes into account developmental considerations. Livelihood, in addition, may well be the construct that will transcend national, geographical, and cultural boundaries and serve as a unifying construct. Such a role cannot easily be dismissed in bringing together historically considered disparate fields and professions.

Youth development or social youth entrepreneurship requires youth to be sufficiently motivated to engage in a prolonged and directed program of activities. Initiative, or the capacity for initiative, is an essential element for being successful adults in this society (Larson, 2000). Initiative, intrinsic motivation in combination with an ability to focus and concentrate for extended periods of time, is closely related to creativity, leadership, altruism, civic involvement, and problem solving (Larson, 2000). Social youth entrepreneurship, like other more conventional forms of enterprise, necessitates youth taking initiative for a venture to be successful. Thus, efforts to assess youth capacities to engage in enterprise creation require careful attention to their capacity or potential to initiate. The concept of initiative, like that of livelihood discussed earlier, can effectively bring together career and youth development.

Horton, Hutchinson, Barkman, Machtmes, and Meyers (1999) developed a five-phase model that lends itself for use in the development of social youth enterprises by stressing a developmental approach: (1) experience the activity; (2) share the experience by describing what happened; (3) process the experience to identify common themes; (4) generalize from the experience to create principles and guidelines for use in real-life situations; and (5) apply lessons learned to other spheres and situations. A developmental approach facilitates the conceptualization of an enterprise and helps predict the major goals and activities associated with each stage.

Zuckerman (2000) notes that practitioners who incorporate youth development into workforce development programs achieve higher rates of success due to accomplishing the following: (1) utilizing activities that are age- and developmental-stage appropriate; (2) creating an environment that serves to increase youth engagement; (3) engendering ongoing support and relationships with caring adults; (4) individualizing services to take into account youth aspirations, competencies, and needs; (5) fostering peer interactions; (6) stressing active and self-directed and self-paced learning; and (7) providing access and fostering long-term support and developmental activities. Thus, workforce development programs based on youth development principles result in youth benefits that far exceed generating income and obtaining and maintaining a career.

The following two program examples, one based in Baltimore and the other in New York City, illustrate how a social youth enterprise can benefit youth as well as communities. Kids on the Hill focuses on the selling of products (Youth Venture, 2002, p. 18):

By selling postcards, bumper stickers and T-shirts, Kevin, Ricky and Reco hope to bring the Baltimore community and different races together. The items they sell have positive messages and artwork designed by young people. Apart from benefiting the community it is also a good way for them to learn how to start a business. They also expect that the people who buy their products will feel good with themselves by helping children develop a project that surely keeps them busy and keeps them out of trouble. Latin Artist, in turn, sells a service that is as the name of the company indicates, art-based. Youth Venturers Jeffery and John created a for-profit air-brush art business as a means to change their neighborhood. Jeffrey and John's team of young artists volunteer their time twice a week to teach an intense schedule of art classes to children in their Brooklyn community. The goal of the business, according to Jeffrey, is to teach art skills and "keep these kids off the dangerous streets of my neighborhood. There are a lot of kids with talent that just need someone to help them out so they will gain a better view of themselves, learn some skills, and hopefully make a little money legally for their work . . . because in my neighborhood, there are too many kids selling drugs." To further involve the community, Latin Artist sponsors an annual "We Are M.A.D." (Making a Difference) street festival on their block in Williamsburg, Brooklyn.

The embrace of youth employment and development within this paradigm facilitates the creation of initiatives. Zeldin (1995a) specifically ties youth development to school-to-work transition. The National Youth Employment Coalition (1995), in its report titled *Toward a National Youth Development System: How We Can Better Serve Youth At-Risk*, merges youth employment within a youth development paradigm. The report identifies five key recommendations for using youth employment as one of the benchmarks of success on a continuum of youth development goals and challenges. In essence, youth development is never an end in itself. It is a philosophy, a process, a goal, an intervention, and an outcome.

Zuckerman (2000) specifically emphasizes the importance of workforce programs focused on the special needs of low-income urban youth. Youth from this population group very often have multiple health, social, psychological, and legal needs that effectively limit their potential to benefit from workforce programs that are narrow in scope. Brown (2000) advocates the use of a youth development approach to both address the potential of risky behavior and better prepare youth for the world of career and work. Brown (2000), in addition, identifies a series of youth development goals that particularly stand out in assisting in the transition of youth to career: (1) engaging learning environments; (2) leadership development; (3) personal challenges; (4) nurturing mentors; (5) sustained support; (6) consistent structure; and (7) incentives that promote achievement.

These goals to the informed reader are not new to the field of youth development. However, when applied to the world of career, they represent an exciting and challenging dimension to a youth development paradigm and one that breaks new ground in the evolution of that paradigm. The broadening and revitalization that occur as a result offer great potential for youth and the field of youth work within multiple arenas.

Challenges in Merging Youth Development and Social Youth Entrepreneurship

Although there is a compelling argument for merging youth development and social youth entrepreneurship, such a move is not without its challenges, and this is to be expected. There are many challenges; however, five challenges stand out in significance: (1) historically the worlds of youth development and entrepreneurship have never intersected, so documented success stories are few; (2) suspicion and misunderstanding between the occupants of these two worlds has limited exploration and collaborative projects; (3) the different languages spoken in these two worlds make effective communication, the cornerstone of any effective working relationship, arduous to achieve; (4) the youth development field's long-term view towards achieving youth goals is counter to the need for entrepreneurs to achieve profits as quickly as possible; and (5) entrepreneur programs stress the delivery of a service or product while most youth development programs may stress use of activities that are not service or product driven.

Nevertheless, these challenges are not insurmountable. Stein (2000, p. 2) more specifically ties youth development and youth entrepreneurship and highlights the complementary nature of these two perspectives towards youth: "Working with teachers and adult mentors, young people in youth-run businesses develop workplace skills and learn academic subjects while producing services and products that are valued in communities. Tens of thousands of young people participate each year. They build houses, run restaurants, and provide a wide variety of goods and services." The pervasive nature of youth enterprises makes the merger of youth development and youth entrepreneurship quite natural. Social youth entrepreneurship, too, is a natural extension and sets forth an arena for youth programming with the potential of incorporating various social goals.

The youth development field has slowly evolved over the past decade into a highly dynamic and widely accepted field of practice in this and other countries (Eccles, 2002). The past decade has also provided the field with an opportunity to identify important core elements, activities, principles, and challenges and set the stage for important advancements in the twenty-first century. In fact, there is wide recognition that the field of youth development has the potential to reach out beyond youth to involve families and communities. The emergence of social youth entrepreneurship represents both an opportunity and a challenge for the field of youth development to evolve and bring into its fold a new form of practice. This is one initiative that, incidentally, brings practitioners into contact with the world of work, career, and business.

Youth Development, Schools, and Enterprises

Ironically, the popularity of youth development as a paradigm and as a form of practice has generally found its way into most arenas within which youth travel, with the exception of the one arena in which youth spend most of their time—namely, schools (First Things First, 2000, p. 1): "Given how important educational outcomes are in the lives of youth in disadvantaged communities, it follows that public and private stakeholders will seek their improvement. But we already know from our observations of successful schools and from other youth development efforts that dramatic improvement in youth development outcomes will only come with dramatic and persistent change in the everyday lives of youth. Where does sustained opportunity to support youth development exist? In schools—where students spend six plus hours per day, five days a week, for approximately forty weeks per year."

The key elements to successful schools are not mysteries or new findings in the research field that have yet to find their way out into the practice arena. Schools are successful when the curriculum they offer and the teachers and teaching methods they employ are committed to maximizing the potential of youth, regardless of their circumstances, to succeed. These schools, in addition, take a holistic perspective on education and actively seek to be an integral part of the community they serve. Educating youth is but one element of their mission to educate and serve society. Last, successful schools manage to individualize the student and actively seek to identify and mobilize their strengths and participation in their own learning.

The paucity of schools that embrace youth development principles is alarming. If a school does embrace this paradigm, in all likelihood it will be seen in its after-school program. Why? There has been much discussion as to why American education has not embraced a paradigm that specifically addresses the primary consumers of the product it sells. Part of the answer as to why schools are slow or refuse to embrace this paradigm may be the amount of power the youth are given, and this translates directly into their power to engage in decision making. It does not mean, however, that schools have not used activities that have historically been used in youth development programs, such as peer counseling, mentorship, and student government. However, a youth development paradigm cannot be dissected by adults who will embrace some principles and discard others that are less attractive. A youth development paradigm must be embraced in its totality to be effective.

Lewis (1992) stresses the use of initiatives that provide youth with an opportunity to serve their community and themselves in the process of doing so. This type of activity (service-learning) works as a learning mechanism while providing a needed service to a community in the process. Schools, as a result, can be vehicles for the development of community-service learning programs; social youth entrepreneurship is one such example. The emergence of school-based enterprises, as will be addressed in chapter 7, illustrates how schools as institutions can engage in entrepreneurship activities with a social value base. Schools, in effect, are educational and service institutions that can be dynamic in how they view their role within society. Cookie-cutters they should not be.

CONCLUSION

This chapter was never intended to provide an exhaustive coverage of youth development. The reader wishing this depth of understanding will need to turn to a number of outstanding books currently in the field. This chapter, rather, was intended to simply ground the reader in this paradigm. The reader has no doubt developed an appreciation for the multifaceted aspects of transition programs, particularly involving a youth development paradigm. The importance of this period of time has only recently started to receive the attention it warrants. Youth who fail to successfully make this transition will in all likelihood experience long-term consequences if they do not engage in some programmatic initiatives.

Transition-to-career must be viewed and appreciated from a multifaceted perspective. The use of a paradigm that systematically and comprehensively undergirds youth-centered initiatives that take into account the importance of career will play a very influential role in shaping policy, practice, and scholarship. Paradigms that stress youth assets, participation, decision making, and potential are future oriented and help guide policymakers, teachers, and practitioners developing comprehensive initiatives that bring into consideration psychological, political, cultural, social, and economic factors. Youth are a complicated lot; however, so is every other age group. This nation's economy is also complex. How youth fit or do not fit into the economy is a subject that should be of great importance to all sectors of this nation. Failure to integrate youth into the economic fabric of the country has implications for the nation and the world.

Youth development has historically been accused of being too broad, and the last decade has witnessed it continuing to expand in scope and influence. This expansion should not serve to scare practitioners or researchers. I believe that eventually youth development advocates and critics will sit at the same table and arrive at a common definition and boundary for this paradigm. Nevertheless, this agreement should not come before the full potential of this paradigm can be appreciated and hopefully realized. The potential of youth development and many of its elements can serve as a unifying force for bringing together the world of career and other arenas. This partnership will benefit not just youth, but also their families, peers, institutions entrusted to educate and serve them, their communities, and ultimately, society.

CHAPTER 3

Emerging Paradigms and Youth Development

INTRODUCTION

The reader may well be tempted to think that there is only one real paradigm for work with youth, namely, youth development. As already noted, youth development offers tremendous advantages in helping to cast youth as assets rather than as deficits upon community and society. There are other paradigms, two in particular, that offer great promise for guiding youth-centered interventions such as social youth entrepreneurship.

Community capacity enhancement and sustainable community development will unquestionably be paradigms that will have substantial followers in the twenty-first century and that philosophically can embrace social youth entrepreneurship initiatives for youth and community transformation. Sustainable community development has an international following; community capacity enhancement is more national than international in scope and in following. These two paradigms, nevertheless, will play significant roles in addressing youth issues and needs within a community context.

Interestingly, neither of these paradigms is specifically youth-centered or age-centered, so to speak. They both focus on all age groups, and no sociodemographic group is specified as the target of an intervention. Both paradigms, in addition, take a broad view of their domain and focus on communities as the goal and vehicle for achieving change, with youth being prominent but not necessarily central in either one. Further, both paradigms lend themselves to a variety of professional interests and as a result hold much promise for collaborative undertakings that are multidisciplinary in nature.

This chapter provides the reader with a brief introduction to how these two paradigms can lend themselves to achieving many of the same goals a youth development paradigm seeks to achieve. Although this book embraces youth development as the premier paradigm, it is not the only one, and I would do a disservice to the reader by not exposing them to other asset-driven perspectives. The reader will need to decide, however, whether it is to their advantage or disadvantage to focus specifically on youth in community-based initiatives. Some settings naturally lend themselves to adopting a youth development paradigm by virtue of their mission. However, other settings, particularly those embracing a mission that cuts across age groups, may not lend themselves to a youth development paradigm in shaping their programs. These settings, as a result, can utilize a broad and encompassing paradigm in which youth are addressed along with other age groups.

ROLE AND IMPORTANCE OF PARADIGMS

The importance of paradigms in shaping educational and social intervention strategies addressing major community and national social issues goes far beyond academic circles of scholars and researchers. Paradigms by their very nature influence day-to-day practice. They not only encompass a vision, but they also do so in a manner that helps direct how this vision can be realized into goals and objectives; the latter are easily measurable. Paradigms, in addition, help guide how interventions are evaluated and the results analyzed. Youth development is such a paradigm (American Youth Policy Forum, 1997). This paradigm, however, cannot be fully understood or appreciated in a context totally devoid of other perspectives, which can be complementary or competing in some aspects. Nevertheless, there is little question that youth development overlaps with other asset-driven paradigms such as community capacity enhancement and sustainable community development.

Historically, youth were primarily viewed from a deficit perspective in this country. They constituted an age group that was either feared or considered to be a drain on the nation's resources. Youth were almost exclusively viewed as in need or as consumers of market products and services. The view of youth as possessing assets or social capital and being capable of contributing to society was held by only a few visionary scholars, policy makers, and practitioners. This perspective is even more pronounced when focused on low-income youth of color and their communities.

An inability or unwillingness to shift views has essentially doomed initiatives with a focus on youth because they have failed to engage youth as potential contributors to their futures and have neglected to build upon their assets. Some of these initiatives, in addition, have totally neglected to take into account the influence of community. This narrow perspective effectively does not meaningfully involve these youth in shaping how interventions are conceptualized and carried out. In essence, youth are voiceless and disempowered.

The emergence of various paradigms and perspectives on viewing undervalued communities through an asset or human/social capital lens, most notably sustainable community development and community capacity enhancement, has only served to further increase the viability of youth development principles and practices. It is no mistake that these two emerging paradigms place community in the center of any and all activities. The paradigm of sustainable community development, for example, further reinforces the importance of viewing youth within the broader context, with community being a key element. Economic self-sufficiency within this paradigm is viewed holistically and emphasizes the importance of investing in youth not as a potential market for goods and services but as a valuable resource in building a nation (Committee for Economic Development, 1997; Maser, 1997; Muschett, 1997).

The emergence of workforce/career-force development has not only increased the likelihood of youth-focused initiatives incorporating these goals but has also set the stage for the viability of social youth entrepreneurship with marginalized urban youth. Sustainable community development, like its economic development counterpart, for example, can only achieve success through strategic investment of resources and by identifying and protecting natural resources—human beings being considered such a resource.

Community Capacity Enhancement

The paradigm of community capacity enhancement is defined by Delgado (2000a) as the systematic identification and mobilizing of community assets as an integrated aspect of any intervention. Interventions must target residents and community in order to achieve permanent and physical changes in the environment. Assets, as a result, are not restricted to residents but can also encompass a host of types, such as history of community, location of community in relation to geographical assets (distance from downtown, bodies of water, etc.), and the availability of open public space that can be transformed in service to community.

Having a paradigm specifically focus on community as the entity for change broadens an initiative away from a focus on individual goals to community goals. This paradigm is premised on the belief that overall community change translates into individual change. This broad focus, however, must not lose sight of the ultimate beneficiaries—namely, individuals. When a community prospers and is healthy, then all individuals benefit to one degree or another; an ecological perspective reinforces the interrelationship between individual progress and community progress.

Community capacity enhancement, too, places a prodigious amount of emphasis on mobilizing indigenous assets, with youth being a critical element, to the betterment of a neighborhood or community (Delgado, 1999, 2000a, in press b). This paradigm is all encompassing. Age-specific (i.e., youth development), setting-specific (i.e., nontraditional settings), and color-specific marginalized groups (i.e., cultural competence) can all be subsumed within this paradigm. This paradigm has been applied primarily to urban areas although it can just as easily be used in rural and suburban areas. Its attractiveness for practice is due to its ability to bring together different professional disciplines and organizations with different community foci through the use of a set of principles that stress assets, participation, empowerment, decision making, and enhancement of competencies.

Elements of Community Capacity Enhancement

The relative newness of a community capacity enhancement paradigm has, not surprisingly, resulted in relatively few scholarly publications and targeted types of funding supporting programs utilizing this orientation towards practice. This paucity of activity in scholarly and funding circles is to be expected but does not detract from the importance of this paradigm for those interested in youth and other marginalized population groups and communities. The newness of the paradigm brings with it a degree of excitement to the field, and this will draw important attention from scholars and funders, not to mention practitioners.

The few publications focused on this paradigm have identified six elements that need to be present in any initiative premised on this paradigm (Delgado, 2000): (1) community participation from all sectors must be fostered, particularly stressing inter-ethnic-racial relations; (2) activities must have an element that serves to enhance community spirit as a primary or secondary goal; (3) intergenerational activities must play an important role in interventions with no age group being ignored or left behind; (4) collaborative partnerships between formal and informal institutions must occur throughout all phases of an intervention; (5) interventions must result in artifacts that actively improve the environment in additional to positively changing the lives of participants and the community; and (6) grass-roots fundraising focused on tapping community residents must be stressed as opposed to seeking outside community funding for projects.

The elements identified by Delgado (2000) highlight the broad reach of community capacity enhancement and its flexibility to take into account local circumstances. Further, these elements foster the goals of improving social relationships across disparate groups and increasing the nature and quality of participation by all residents, young and old alike. Physical transformation occurs alongside social transformation; one cannot exist without the other.

Community Capacity Enhancement, Education, and Career

The interconnectedness between individual and community in operationalizing this paradigm restricts the number of settings that can successfully teach the value of this paradigm for achieving individual and community transformation, although this situation does not have to continue. Schools, with some notable exceptions, generally do not venture out into communities in the course of educating youth, although critics would argue that the inability or unwillingness of schools to engage with the community they seek to serve is at the heart of that lacuna.

A narrow focus on students as individuals effectively decontextualizes or disconnects their experiences in life, experiences that, incidentally, are very much grounded within their communities. A similar argument has been made by how formal educational systems such as schools also neglect the families of youth. Disconnects never serve the best interests of youth, their institutions, or the community in either the short or the long run.

Community-based organizations, although geographically based within communities, rarely view education as part of their mission. Job training, however, is a notable exception. Training of residents is very different from educating residents. Funding sources for these programs wield considerable influence on the nature of the content that is covered in training workshops. Community capacity enhancement is a philosophical stance, goal, and method for achieving change. It places tremendous emphasis on the importance of process without losing sight of outcomes. This paradigm can take on various manifestations throughout the development and implementation of community-focused interventions.

Sustainable Community Development

Like most paradigms, it is rare to find one definition that is embraced by all who profess to use it in practice. Thus, various definitions of *sustainable development* exist in the field, and this can be considered quite typical and an indication of the popularity of the paradigm (Gibbs, 1994). Developmentally, it also signifies that a paradigm is still developing, so to speak, since it will take a considerable period of time before any form of consensus is reached on its definition and boundaries. The eventual emergence of a consensual definition must be a goal of advocates of this paradigm.

Brundtland (1987) defines community sustainable development as "development that meets the needs and aspirations of the present without compromising the ability of future generations to meet their own needs." Maser (1997, p. xv), in turn, defines sustainable community as "personal and social transformation into a higher level of consciousness of cause and effect and a greater responsibility to be one another's keepers through all generations." As noted in the definitions provided above, sustainable community development encompasses a philosophical perspective that stresses responsibility for actions and has a present and future orientation; it also serves as a vehicle for achieving change, both social and personal. Although youth are not specifically noted in the definitions, any paradigm that stresses the future is very much built upon youth—their needs, aspirations, and assets.

Sustainable community development can be divided into four critical, yet interrelated, sections—people, environment, economics, and technology

(Neal, 1995). Each of these sections is important unto itself. However, in reality they are inseparable, and the whole is much more powerful than the individual parts. Sustainable community development cuts across the lifespan and can systematically reach out to all age segments. Thus, the social implications of this paradigm must never be lost sight of in advocating its merits for social good.

A close relationship between sustainable community development and livelihood has emerged over the years. This emergence of the subject of economic income has focused on helping individuals and community make a living in a competitive marketplace and stressed the importance of equity, ownership of resources, participatory decision making, conflict resolution, and security as overarching goals for communities (Roy & Turner, 1996). The International Institute for Sustainable Development defines sustainable livelihood as being (Roy et al., 1996, p. 1): "concerned with people's capacities to generate and maintain their means of living, enhance their well-being, and that of future generations. These capacities are contingent upon the availability and accessibility of options which are ecological, sociocultural, economic, and political and are predicted on equity, ownership of resources, and participatory decision making. Both the notions of sustainable development and sustainable livelihoods incorporate the idea of change and uncertainty."

The literature on urban communities has generally taken a negative or deficit perspective on the subject. Urban communities have historically been refuges for many of this nation's and the world's marginalized people. This attraction to cities has not been without consequences for public opinion in this country, most of it quite negative. However, urban communities in the United States possess what Bernstein (2000) calls hidden assets that help ensure sustainable communities.

Bernstein (2000) identified 10 assets that are often overlooked in any discussion of urban-focused social and economic intervention strategies and initiatives. The 10 urban assets identified by Bernstein (2000), ironically, have generally been viewed as deficits by society:

Purchasing Power

Concentration of residents equates positively with concentration of capital and market needs, even in the poorest communities. One study of Chicago's poorest 17 zip codes found a retail gap against consumer demand of approximately $1.8 billion. Further, the total purchasing power within a two-mile radius of one transit stop in West Garfield Park, a low-income community, is $2 billion per year (Bernstein, 2000). The concentration of capital and demand for products and services is an asset for indigenous-led businesses. Ironically the general public's view of low-income communities generally is one focused on needs and problems rather than on purchasing power and contributions to society.

Concentrated Workforce

Availability of a workforce is generally a consideration for the location of a new enterprise. Having access to a significant workforce facilitates the meeting of workforce demands, particularly in situations where the market speaks a primary language other than English and possesses very distinctive cultural values and traditions. This workforce, however, will require investments on developing the requisite infrastructure to prepare workers for entry-level positions and to create career ladders so that jobs are not minimum wage with limited benefits, or what Newman (1995) calls dead-end jobs.

Mass Transit Systems

There are few communities in this country where mass transportation is not important. The availability of public transportation is an asset for all sectors of a community—residents, employees, retailers, government, and schools. These systems do not have to be created, and they significantly decrease the need for automobiles as a principal means of transportation. Having ready access to public transportation increases the likelihood that anyone can live within the community, not just those who have an automobile. In fact, most real estate brokers will rate access to public transportation as one of the key factors in creating a strong real estate market.

Accessibility

General accessibility is a critical factor in helping to ensure development, social or economic. The combination of geography, mass transit, highways, and streets serves to increase accessibility inside and outside urban areas. Having easy geographical access to airports and bus and train terminals, for example, brings an important dimension to urban communities. Costs related to transportation of goods and services are reduced by having a market that is highly concentrated and increasingly subject to competition.

Abandoned and Underused Land

The availability of open land and buildings that have been abandoned makes land, a precious and highly costly resource, readily available at a reasonable cost. Ready provision of parking and access to streets and highways facilitates conversion of empty land and buildings to enterprises. Land cannot be fabricated. Land is a form of capital that can be translated into a form of commodity for a community, one that, unfortunately, is often overlooked when discussing distressed areas of urban America. When large parcels of land are available for development, cities benefit by using the resource as a bargaining chip with businesses or housing developments.

Underutilized Infrastructure

Long periods of active or benign neglect of communities can be interpreted in a variety of ways. Negatively, it can mean that limited maintenance can translate into high costs of upgrading or repair. A decrease in population has resulted in infrastructures that can effectively serve a wider population base and industry being rendered less efficient from a cost-benefit perspective. This underutilization, as a result, makes infrastructure development in urban areas unnecessary and as a result, more cost effective. Underutilization, unlike overutilization, lends itself to the creation of initiatives that encourage activity and use of existing infrastructural resources.

In-Place Infrastructure and Underutilized Carrying Capacity

The availability of electricity, gas, sewer system, water, telecommunications, roads, and mass transits effectively renders urban communities cost effective. These systems do not have to be created from scratch and result in considerable savings and minimal disruptions to community life than if they had to be created. Further, they lend themselves to upgrading more cost-effectively than building an infrastructure from scratch. Such efforts are also less disruptive to community life.

Already Assembled Rights-of-Way

Having already assembled rights-of-way pertaining to mass transit, utilities, roads, and so forth, offers tremendous incentive to establishing new institutions and businesses. The time and effort that is inherent in obtaining political consensus and rights is dramatically shortened in urban areas. These existing rights-of-way facilitate access and development where necessary.

Efficient Resource Use

The concentrated nature of urban living facilitates the creation of systems that allow for easier provision and consumption of goods and the recycling of wastes to occur. The potential for development of multistory housing and multiuse buildings, for example, decreases costs and increases efficiency. Having public transportation available within close geographical proximity of roads and airports increases efficiency of space.

Surprising Biodiversity and Natural Capital

It is not often that we think of urban areas as playing an important role in fostering biodiversity. It seems that this concept is usually associated with rural areas, and the word *diversity* is usually code for large numbers of different racial and ethnic groups. However, unlike agricultural areas, which tend to be monocultural and have reduced more complex habitats, urban areas have uncultivated land, which can be home to a large variety of species.

I would venture to add one more asset usually associated with urban living in this country—namely, the diversity and history of survival of the residents. Urban areas are home to this nation's majority of people of color and newcomers. Each group has brought its cultural heritage, and these traditions have survived numerous trials and tribulations over the years, sometimes, as in the case of African Americans, for centuries. An ability to survive under the most trying of circumstances is an asset that cannot and should never be overlooked when discussing urban policy in this country.

Elements and Boundaries of Sustainable Community Development

The paradigm of sustainable community development can be sufficiently broad to encompass multiple dimensions and considerations based upon local circumstances. Dimensions related to time, space, marginalized groups, dynamic economies, history, and local events might facilitate the adoption of this paradigm. Community as an arena for practice, too, is very broad and can encompass multiple perspectives on what constitutes community within this paradigm. Community can be defined narrowly in scope to a geographically defined entity, or it can be broad enough to include other measures, such as psychological makeup, ethnic-racial-cultural groups, and concentration of facilities.

Nevertheless, with flexibility in boundaries comes confusion and ambiguity. Muschett (1997, p. 1), in defining sustainable development, also touches upon the ambiguity of the paradigm: "As a paradigm and important environmental theme, 'sustainable development' is puzzling. On the one hand, the term means what it says; sustainable development means economic development and a standard of living which do not impair the future ability of the environment to provide sustenance and life support for the population. On the other hand, it is more difficult to envision all of the forms and implications of 'sustainable development' that relate to one's professional career or personal lifestyle."

A broad perspective on sustainable community development can be both its strength, by being so inclusive, and its weakness, by not being exclusive enough. The operationalization of the paradigm is influenced by the practitioner, his or her organization, and the community's perceptions of its needs and goals. The relationship between these three arenas is dynamic and requires practitioners to pay close attention to subtle and not so subtle shifts. Introduction of new population groups, for example, can wield a tremendous amount of influence in reshaping community perceptions of itself and its needs.

Muschett (1997b) identified 11 key elements of sustainable development: (1) population stabilization; (2) new technologies/technology transfer; (3) efficient use of natural resources; (4) waste reduction and population prevention; (5) win-win situations; (6) integrated environmental systems management; (7) determination of environmental limits; (8) refinement of market economy; (9) education; (10) perceptions and attitude changes (paradigm shift); and (11) social and cultural changes. These elements stress the close interrelationship between environment and people, and the importance of strategic and comprehensive initiatives. Not surprisingly, investment in the environment, community, and people is a central feature of these elements (Campbell & Heck, 1997).

Any paradigm that places special emphasis on environment and community, for example, increases the likelihood that learning will be relevant by providing youth and other participants with an understanding of who they are and their place within the community and society (Theobald & Nachtigal, 1995). Such grounding serves multiple purposes that are broadly social and individual in nature and makes a paradigm very appealing for practice across disciplines and arenas.

The paradigm of sustainable community development is applicable to both rural and urban settings. Ruben (1995), for example, describes a program (From the Ground Up) that combines environmental change and access to nutritious food in an inner-city community. Ruben, in turn, introduces the term *community food security* to capture the importance of nutrition and community development. Gaum and Van-Rooyan (1997), too, stress the feasibility and importance of urban agricultural projects based upon sustainable ecological-agricultural principles, interdisciplinary approaches, and competency through the development of practical problem-solving skills.

Gamble and Weil (1997) identified a series of facilitating and hindering forces that operate while using a sustainable development framework. Lawrence and Singh (1996) apply the paradigm to full employment and propose the concept of sustainable livelihood to all forms of making a living. The authors go on to establish a set of conditions that must be in place in order for employment to meet the criteria of sustainable livelihood: (1) be pursuable independently without compromising personal security; (2) have stability over an extended period of time; (3) be mutually beneficial to individuals and their immediate social groupings; and (4) be compatible with the physical environment.

Robinson (1992) stresses the point that successful sustainable community development requires the fusion of traditional economic criteria with community and corporate culture. In essence, the quest for well-being requires that economic goals be grounded within the community and organizations' value structures. This fusion, so to speak, is challenging because it necessitates the creation of a working language that transcends very different worlds. Without a common understanding of goals, principles, strategies, activities, and measurable outcomes, collaborative partnerships are not possible. Dawson (1996), in turn, brings an often-overlooked dimension to sustainable community development—the role of gender. Women can and should play an instrumental part in sustainable development planning. Harmsworth and Sethna (1994) outline the use of such strategies as training, provision of tailored technical assistance, facilitation of funding for smaller business activity, and the importance of exchange visits and study tours as means of strengthening the role of women's organizations in sustainable development.

Sustainable Community Development, Education, and Career

The paradigm of sustainable development can be far reaching in influence and does not have to be restricted to the arena of community development. It can, for example, find a home within the educational arena (Bradley, 1999; Dowdeswell, 1998). Unlike its community capacity enhancement counterpart, sustainable community development has a history and a wide number of advocates, nationally and internationally. This history also provides advocates with an opportunity to build upon the past and use it as a foundation for future advances. Further, it also serves as a valuable source of lessons learned for shaping sustainable community development initiatives.

The popularity of this paradigm has resulted in colleges and universities offering undergraduate and graduate degrees in this area of practice. International organizations, in turn, hire staff with this particular expertise to work in developing nations. The increased number of persons formally educated in this paradigm bodes well for the future of the paradigm to find its way into practice and draw requisite funding for programs and research. Achievement of the goals promoted by sustainable community development will encounter numerous obstacles. These obstacles, however, are not insurmountable (McKenzie-Mohr & Smith, 1999). Changing human perceptions and behaviors, even at the most elementary level, requires programs and activities that are effective in changing people's behavior.

Some would argue quite persuasively that the future of sustainable development can only be realized if it is introduced into elementary and secondary education. Sustainable development, like social youth entrepreneurship, can lend itself for inclusion in various academic subjects within a secondary curriculum—math, science, language arts, social studies, history, visual arts, family studies, technology educational, business education, and vocational education (Hren & Hren, 1996). This flexibility is very attractive for curriculum development because it allows the introduction of content throughout a curriculum or selective sectors of a curriculum depending upon the goals and abilities of instructors. Thus, it is never an all or nothing curriculum proposition. For example, schools with particular strengths in one area of a curriculum can incorporate sustainable community development content.

Maser (1997, p. 207) quite eloquently ties in education and community sustainability:

Education, both as formal academic training and as the experiences one has in the journey of life, is absolutely necessary for sustainable community development. Formal academic training and the experiences of life come together to make one literate, which means to be a well informed, educated person. Literate also means having the ability to read and write. Literacy is thus the sum of one's ability to use language to share one's knowledge, intuition, experiences, values, and talents (communication), without which democracy, and thus sustainable community development, is impossible. There are many facets to literacy, of which five are particularly important to sustainable community development: academic, environmental, economic, democratic, and community.

Dippo (1998), in one of the few examples of tying in sustainable development specifically to vocational education, argues for the utility of sustainability as a conceptual framework for locating career development within equality, social justice, and economic/environmental issues. The grounding of sustainable community development within social and economic justice praxis, for example, makes this paradigm highly attractive and viable for use within marginalized communities across the United States.

Education for sustainable development is predicated upon a multidisciplinary and multisectoral foundation (Hopkins, Damlamian, & Lopez Ospina, 1996). Vocational education can incorporate the concept of sustainability by providing a broad vision that includes ethical as well as economic imperatives (Dippo, 1998). These two elements are generally not a part of most secondary curriculum let alone vocational education curriculum. Vocational educators, as a result, are challenged to ground their lesson plans within the broader societal context—social, political, economic, environmental, and social judicial.

Haddow (1998), for example, provides an excellent case example of how sustainable development and marine education can be complementary for youth. Classroom activities based on sustainable development principles can highlight the importance of cooperative behavior between people and natural resources such as fishery. Sustainable development, in this instance, involves both people and natural environment in a manner that is complementary and can serve as a model for other forms of collaboration between practice fields and vocational education.

The lack of precision regarding what is sustainable community development can be both a strength and a weakness. Jickling (1994a) touches upon this very point in discussing the challenge of introducing the concept into the broader arena of education. Jickling (1994b) identifies two important impediments to introducing sustainable development into a curriculum—a lack of attention to educational philosophy and the difficulty of using a concept to teach that is a contra indicator of day-to-day practice. These two challenges are not insurmountable yet can be quite formidable. Any effort to place social youth entrepreneurship within a sustainable community development paradigm will have its share of obstacles to overcome in putting forth this orientation toward youth, enterprise, and social responsibility. However, there really is no reason to excuse secondary schools, including vocational education programs, from embracing and acting upon the principles of sustainable community in developing lesson plans.

CONCLUSION

The reader has no doubt come to the realization of the importance of paradigms in shaping how practice is conceptualized and carried out on a daily basis in the real world. Paradigms, in effect, are the guiding lights that help us navigate through the fog. This guidance is never so detailed and precise that it doesn't allow for deviation or creative impulses. However, flexibility is still essential in marshaling resources and the efforts of organizations. Further, a paradigm can help us communicate within and between professional and other interested groups and across national boundaries. This ability helps us better learn and understand from the experiences of others.

There certainly is no dearth of paradigms that can be used to ground youth career and social entrepreneurship. Pittman, Irby, and Ferber (2000, p. 20) comment that shifting paradigms are quite appropriate when addressing youth: *"Paradigm shift* has become one of the many overused phrases of the 1990s. In this case, however, it is the appropriate term. The decade spawned the development of a number of frameworks put forth as either descriptive or predictive youth development models. Behind them all are an unflinching commitment to broaden the goals to promote not only problem reduction but preparation for adulthood; increase the options for instruction and involvement by improving the quality and availability of supports, services and opportunities offered; and redefine the strategies in order to ensure a broad scale of supports and opportunities for young people that reach beyond the existing status quo."

The two paradigms presented in this chapter lend themselves well to shaping youth social entrepreneurship projects and initiatives. However, neither paradigm has the potential of youth development, which is the most popular paradigm within the United States. Community capacity enhancement is too new to assess its potential contribution. There is no denying, however, that sustainable community development has much more global appeal. Community capacity enhancement is the newest of the three and will no doubt increase in popularity within the next decade as more leaders and scholars use it to transform communities. Nevertheless, I believe that tying school-to-career transition to a youth development paradigm greatly increases the currency of the topic in this country.

This society's tendency to view narrowly social issues and problems seriously undermines any comprehensive and strategic initiative addressing youth. Youth-related needs and problems too often are treated as if they were not related to each other. School dropouts, for example, are usually closely tied to youth unemployment and underemployment. Lack of employment, in turn, increases the likelihood of drug use, criminal activity, early parenthood, and other social problems usually associated with youth. A holistic perspective not only serves to tie together youth-related issues and problems, but also does so in a manner that highlights the magnitude of the challenge and the importance of this country's having the political will to find comprehensive solutions.

CHAPTER 4

The Challenges for Marginalized Youth

INTRODUCTION

It is impossible to be a youth in this society without facing a host of challenges in day-to-day living and having to wrestle with the uncertainty the future holds (Delgado, 2000b; Mitcheal, 2001; Walker, 2001). These challenges and uncertainties, however, materialize in a variety of ways depending upon the profile of youth being discussed. Youth, contrary to popular opinion, are not a monolithic group that lends itself to be described in very general terms. Youth have numerous subsets depending upon age, documented status, level of acculturation, gender, family composition, sexual orientation, race, ethnicity, socioeconomic class, physical and cognitive abilities, religious affiliation, rural-urban backgrounds, to list but a few of the most prominent factors.

The interactions of this subset of characteristics, in turn, increase or decrease the likelihood of success or failure in making a successful transition from school-to-career (Moss & Tilly, 2001; Nesdale & Pinter, 2000; O'Connor, Tilly, & Bobo, 2000; Santiago, 2000). Each of these factors wields a tremendous amount of influence in dictating society's view of young people and in turn, their view of society, hopes for their futures, and likelihood of achieving their dreams. When a set of factors converges, as in the case of youth of color residing in economically distressed urban communities, effects can be profoundly negative (Bernhardt, Morris, Handcock, & Scott, 2001; Camino, 1995; Carnegie Council on Adolescent Development, 1989; Nesdale et al., 2000).

These effects defy simple answers and solutions because the lives of youth are intractably intertwined with the communities they live within. This level of complexity often results in the general public not wanting to hear the entire stories youth bring with them. These stories can incidentally be uplifting or depressing as the cases may be (Kay, Estepa, & Desetta, 1998; Way, 1998). Instead, government-sponsored initiatives often turn out to be short-term, limited in scope, and focused on achieving unrealistic goals.

Newman's (1995) conclusions pertaining to the challenges facing workers in the nation's poor inner cities dispel stereotypes and uplift the incredible challenges facing this society. Workers in these communities work hard, relish their independence, are reliable, and have the requisite skills to move up the organizational ladder. However, they are caught in dead-end jobs that offer minimum wages and no possible escape from poverty. They lack access or bridges to the kind of work that offers challenges, livable wages, and a future. This lack of access, unfortunately, is reframed to blame the victim.

Social youth enterprises can effectively help marginalized youth earn money in a positive fashion, provide a service to their community, and benefit the community in the process. Street Souljahwear, based in Arlington, Virginia, does a wonderful job of illustrating this goal (*Youth Venture*, 2002, pp. 26–27):

Street Souljahwear is a clothing line created by 17-year-old Samir of Arlington, Virginia. Samir's specialty is designing t-shirts that display his poetry and artwork and the work of other teen artists. The mission of Street Souljahwear is to provide opportunities for youth to express themselves through their artistic talents and promote the message of social awareness, activism, and self-determination. Samir has committed to donating 10 percent of his profits to the Uhuru Organization and as Street Souljahwear's business expands, will increase the amount of donations to this organization.

Samir is excited about becoming a Youth Venturer and is excited to have the opportunity to express the artistic talents of his generation. As a Youth Venturer, Samir aims to encourage more young people to get involved in his venture. At the Selection Panel, Samir stated, "Through Street Souljahwear, young people will be given a chance to show their talent to the world. Many youth have beautiful talents, but they do not apply themselves to their full potential. This company will give serious youth the opportunity to display their talents, make a profit, and will enable them to donate money to a cause they care about." Samir has already published a book on activist poetry and has already designed two different t-shirts displaying positive social messages, which he sells at local musical and cultural events and at a local restaurant.

Moss and Tilly's (2001, p. 16) observations of the challenges facing people of color in the labor market point to the need for a multifaceted strategy for bringing workers from marginalized backgrounds into productive and rewarding careers: "The barrier of employment for people of color with limited skill in urban America is not a monolithic box. . . . Rather, the 'stories employers tell' reveal that the obstacles grow out of dozens of small decisions by each employer: where to locate, how to define and design each job, how and where to recruit, what methods to use for evaluating candidates, what to look for in a preemployment interview, and so on. At each step, disadvantages for inner-city blacks and Latinos arise both from problems rooted outside the labor market—inadequate schooling, segregated residential patterns—and from employer discrimination. Overcoming this set of disadvantages will require efforts on many fronts." A focus on school-to-career transition for youth of color and, more specifically, social enterprise development, must be a part of any solution to their limited social and economic mobility (Bartik, 2001).

Success in transition from school-to-career is dependent upon the interplay of numerous complex factors that have unique ways of being operationalized depending upon the contextual setting (Horatio Alger Association, 1998; Matthews, 1995; Moss et al., 2001; O'Connor el al., 2000; Osterman, 1989; Werner, 1989). These factors, in turn, can be found within multiple social arenas and may wield disproportionate impact on differing subsets of youth depending upon their sociodemographic composition.

Although the subject of gainful employment/career in this country is not restricted to any one youth group, its applicability and relevance takes on added significance when addressing this nation's marginalized groups (Browne, 1999; Committee for Economic Development, 1997; Elliott & King, 1999; Lee, 1994; Reskin, 1999; Walker, 1997). The following case example shows how these youth can be quite creative in developing strategies for overcoming barriers and how a social youth enterprise can be an avenue for purpose (*Youth Venture*, 2002, p. 16):

Job Shop. Washington, D.C.-based Maritza, age eighteen, launched Job Shop to help girls secure employment opportunities and, in turn, to increase their self-confidence among young women. Designed to prepare young women for employment opportunities, Job Shop sells donated business clothes to girls, as well as offering workshops and direct assistance in resume development and job preparedness. Through her work, Maritza prepares young women for job opportunities by providing the professional guidance they need to be successful candidates. "Job Shop will help girls get jobs and feel good about themselves," explains Maritza. "It is hard to find nice clothes to wear to work, and now women in the community can give the clothes they no longer want to girls who really need them."

Youth of color living in certain sectors of cities face a host of challenges (social, political, and economic) and represent a central core of marginalized youth in this country (Stevens, 2000). Jobs, dead-end or otherwise, are not plentiful in low-income urban communities across the country, even in periods of so-called economic prosperity (Newman, 1999, p. 62): "From the vantage point of central Harlem . . . jobs, even lousy jobs, are in such short supply that inner-city teenagers are all but barred from the market, crowded out by adults who are desperate to find work." Their experiences in growing up differ dramatically from those of their white non-Latino counterparts living in more affluent areas of the city or in suburbia. Achieving normative tasks associated with adolescent development, for example, will vary between youth from different socioeconomic and racial/ethnic backgrounds (Lee, 1994).

Youth of color face a series of significant barriers to successfully making a transition from school-to-career. Public perceptions of youth of color, for example, tend to place them in a negative light and have low expectations of their potential. This negative view, in turn, gets manifested in the type of initiatives that target these youth. African American males, probably more than any other sociodemographic group, bear the brunt of this bias (Mincy, 1994a, b). Youth of color have historically not been the recipient of assistance in preparing for transition from school-to-career. The fact that these youth invariably have high rates of disengagement from formal schooling before completion severely limits the potential impact of high school and post high school-based programs. Thus, if society focuses almost exclusively upon youth attending high school, what happens to those youth who have disengaged from formal schooling? One strategy for reaching youth out of school may not be applicable for reaching youth that are on the verge of dropping out or for youth who will complete their education without a plan in place for life after school.

Skinner (1995), based upon a meta-analysis of the literature on urban labor markets and young black men, raises serious questions about the economic returns of high school or community college education for this group. Skinner goes on to argue that there is limited value in securing entry-level jobs for young men of color that can lead to fruitful career paths solely based upon educational attainment. The possibility of society emphasizing formal educational credentials for employment in many entry-level jobs is just another way for racial discrimination to occur since many of these jobs do not require a particular level of education.

To the uninitiated there may be the perception and belief that low-income youth of color have not got the slightest notion of entrepreneurship. This perception is totally erroneous. Unfortunately, some of this knowledge can revolve around illegal activities such as engaging in the drug trade (Feigelman, Stanton, & Ricrado, 1993; Li & Feigelman, 1994; New York Times, 1988, 1989; Stanton & Galbraith, 1994; Weisman, 1993). The enterprise Yea Café, Baltimore, illustrates how low-income youth of color can direct their energies and creativity in positive directions (Youth Venture, 2002, p. 34):

Yea Café. Baltimore, Maryland-based Nathaniel, Demetrius, Shamika, Cheyenne, Jamal, Allen, Lauren, Stacey, Ronnie, Jermal, Antione, Illeisha, Jan, Tavon, and Theodore launched the Yea Café. A youth-created, youth-led coffee and juice bar, Yea Café aims to teach young people basic business skills. Today, more than 20 teens ages eleven to fifteen manage the café. Yea Café provides a local eatery for the community, while simultaneously supporting the initiative of young people and "informing the public of how productive teens can be," the team explains. "We will benefit the community by keeping kids off the streets, giving teens the motivation to stay in school and apply themselves, and creating a warm atmosphere where the community can meet."

Any in-depth interview of youth involved in illegal businesses will uncover knowledge and competencies related to supply and demand dynamics, economic incentives, judgment of character, pricing principles, marketing, logistical relevance to obtaining raw products and transforming them into finished goods, customer service, capital generation, budget development and auditing, new product development, conflict resolution, team building, staff development, public relations, and performance incentives.

Padilla (1994, pp. 149–150) specifically touches upon one business talent in describing gang behavior in drug dealing: "Another major role of dealing that youngsters must learn is to work together as a team, or network. This entails conducting their business operations as a collective unit of three or more sellers at all times, sharing potential clients among themselves. Street-level dealers gather daily on the street corner or block and establish relations as business partners as well as friends. These youngsters become committed to one another, protecting each other, and sharing various clients. In short, the team approach to dealing allows sellers to have a fair share of the market."

Any entrepreneur possessing knowledge and competencies in these areas would be an attractive candidate for a senior-level management position in a firm. The fact that these business lessons were learned in pursuit of illegal activity does not diminish the potential of these youth learning and applying entrepreneurial knowledge and skills to legal activities. However, a change in lenses or perspectives is in order before the potential of youth for contributions can be fully appreciated and acted upon by society.

Ellis (1992), in turn, specifically addresses this potential for entrepreneurship in his critique of current employment policies targeting marginalized groups who are gang involved. The development of what Ellis (1992) calls "urban youth enterprise zones" as a strategy for youth and community revitalization emphasizes the need for small businesses with a community base. These initiatives, in turn, have very high visibility within the community, are youth intensive, and stress the importance of small businesses as a means of social and economic development.

Halpern (1999) coined the term *the Forgotten Half* (youth and young families) and used this construct to examine how they have faired during the recent boom economy. This term is quite graphic and captures a social condition that is endemic to life among certain groups within this society. Halpern (1999, p. 1) goes on to note that many youth have not benefited in this country: "The critical transition from school to the workplace has become more painful than a decade ago. Moving to permanent employment is taking longer. Young workers who do not go on to college or career training are experiencing longer periods of unemployment and are relying more than ever on part-time, dead-end jobs. Moreover, their tenure in jobs is shorter and less stable."

Who are those Halpern calls the Forgotten Half? Halpern (1998, p. 3) defines them in the following way: "In nonstatistical terms, they are the young people who build our homes, drive our buses, repair our automobiles, fix our televisions, maintain and serve our offices, schools and hospitals, and keep the production lines of our mills and factories moving. To a great extent, they determine how well the American family, economy, and democracy function. They are also the thousands of young men and women who aspire to work productively but never quite 'make it' to that kind of employment. For these members of the Forgotten Half, their lives as adults start in the economic limbo of unemployment, part-time jobs, and poverty wages. Many of them never break free." From a racial and ethnic perspective, those who comprise the Forgotten Half tend to be disproportionately of color, primarily African American and Latinos (Santiago, 2000). Halpern's report played an instrumental role in bringing national attention to those individuals who did not attend college and pushed attention and support for age groups who were not in college but were not in trouble (Pittman, Irby, & Ferber, 2000).

Even in a booming economy, full- and part-time employment rates among the Forgotten Half were actually lower in 1997 than in 1989. And for minority youth, full-time employment is 20 to 30 percent lower than among their white counterparts. Overall, inflation-adjusted earnings for 20- to 24-year-old male workers fell by one-third, while young women were earning 16.5 percent less. In March 1997, more than one-fourth of out-of-school young adults who were working full time were earning less than the poverty line income standard of just over $16,000 annually for a family of four.

The goal of creating more employment within low-income urban communities has a tremendous impact on all sectors of the community, outside and inside the labor market. However, job availability is but one dimension of economic potential (Newman, 1999, p. 274): "Merely being able to put more workers in each household into the labor market increases the resources available for families as a whole. But without the jobs to absorb them and tighter labor markets to drive their wages up, they are likely to labor in poverty for much of their lives." Clearly, work alone cannot materially change the socioeconomic landscape in many of the nation's inner cities. To do so will require a much broader and significant agenda that not only addresses employment but also brings into the discussion creation of wealth.

Wentling and Waight's (1999) review of the literature on barriers typically encountered by youth of color in transition from school-to-career found four major types—school-related, work-related, societal-related, and individual-related. I will go on to add family-related barriers to their list. Wentling and Waight's (1999) four barriers to success are not necessarily distinct and mutually exclusive of each other; there is, not surprisingly, a high degree of overlap between them. Nevertheless, for the purposes of this chapter they will be treated as distinct in an effort to arrive at a better understanding of their considerable influence on outcomes.

SCHOOL-RELATED BARRIERS

A cultural-ecological perspective toward schools is necessary in order to better understand the nature of the forces involved in educating youth and how these forces operate differently depending upon the racial/ethnic and socioeconomic backgrounds of students (Borman & Rachuba, 2001; Ogbu, 1989). More specifically, school-related barriers to success can only be understood and appreciated through the use of a cultural-ecological perspective. These institutions are far too important in this society to relegate them to a one-dimensional picture. Their importance, however, is matched by their complexity.

The importance of formal education as a means of facilitating successful youth transition from school-to-career has historically been well recognized and regarded in this society. The primary source of knowledge was relegated to schools, although libraries did play an important role, too. Much has changed since the early part of the twentieth century.

The acquisition of knowledge and competencies, however, are no longer restricted to school settings. Knowledge acquisition, as a result of technological changes, can be obtained in many different settings. The Internet, for example, can be conceptualized as a global classroom that is accessible at any time of day and any day of the week for those who have access to this information technology. However, this information does not provide users with a multicultural perspective, and some critics argue that the same can be said for formal education. Formal educational achievement, nevertheless, is still a criterion for entrance into the most prestigious and economically rewarding careers.

Schools located within economically marginalized communities with high concentrations of students of color, face incredible challenges in preparing these youth for productive and highly paid employment (Stone, Doherty, & Jones, 1999, p. 340): "Enlisting schools in a broad agenda of community development activities is ideal. What about the reality? Particularly in the nation's cities, where communities of concentrated poverty are beset with social problems, schools on their own often lack a constructive relationship with the surrounding community. Isolated, and with limited financial and social capital, educators in poor communities may see themselves as facing an unwinnable struggle. They may simply accommodate to what they see as a harsh and unrelenting reality by lowering expectations, adopting a defensive posture, and minimizing their contact with the community." The conditions described by Stone, Doherty, and Jones (1999) highlight the enormity of the task of creating partnerships between schools and other community institutions, business and social. These partnerships are without little question prerequisites for comprehensive and meaningful initiatives.

Critics of schooling systems are quick to note that marginalized youth would go so far as to say that these institutions are primarily set up to prepare youth for life as a surplus population, and for those who actively resist, prisons are the institution of higher learning that awaits them (Anderson, 1999; Breggin & Breggin, 1998; Chinyelu, 1999; Males, 1996, 1999; Newman, 1999; Sum et al., 1997). This perspective is gaining currency within communities across the United States and raises serious questions about the types of initiatives that are needed involving, or as the case may be, not involving schools (Delgado, 2001).

The role and function of schools in this society can arguably be categorized into two types: (1) providing youth with a sense of purpose, direction, and competencies for entering the labor market—training, if you wish; and (2) providing a socially acceptable outlet for youthful energy and keeping them out of trouble—warehousing, if you wish (Grub, 1989; Stern and Eichorn, 1989). A society's desire and ability to provide all youth with competencies, hope, and a vehicle to direct their energy will play a significant role in how this population group views their place in society and the world. In addition, it will directly, positively or negatively, influence their perceptions of themselves and those around them.

Unemployment increases dramatically for youth that either did not complete high school or obtain a GED certificate (Sum, Fogg, & Fogg, 1997). It is estimated that 23 percent of 18 to 24 year olds in the United States have dropped out of high school and do not have a diploma or GED. In 1999 the country had an estimated total of 5.4 million unemployed young adults who had not completed their high school education. These statistics can be considered a national disgrace and an omen for future developments within the country, particularly involving urban communities of color.

In 1997, 15.3 percent of out-of-school youth were unemployed, more than 50 percent higher than high school graduates (9.6 percent) and almost 500 percent higher than college graduates (National Collaboration for Youth, 1999). Only 35.3 percent of non-high school graduates were employed full-time, compared to a significantly higher percentage for high school graduates (60 percent) and college graduates (82 percent). Taking race and ethnicity into account presents an even more dismal picture for youth of color. In 1999, 75 percent of all-white non-Latino youth were employed compared to 66 percent for Latinos and 59 percent for African American youth (National Collaboration for Youth, 1999).

The lifetime wages gap between school dropouts and graduates is widening at a steady and significant pace. This nation's demand for an increasingly skilled workforce is largely responsible for this trend. It is estimated that a school dropout in 1993 earns $212,000 less in his or her lifetime than a high school graduate and $812,000 less than a college graduate. Another perspective has the earnings of a school dropout doubling in the past 20 years while tripling for college graduates. School dropouts, not surprisingly, constitute almost 50 percent of the households on public assistance and who have a member in prison (Schwartz, 1995). The financial and social costs to society are quite staggering when considering the life costs of maintaining individuals in prison, for example, and the lost wages of these individuals. Taxpayers are effectively turned into tax consumers.

It has been estimated that 50 percent of our high school graduates do not go on to obtain a college education, and 50 percent of those who go on to college leave before obtaining their degree. In essence, 75 percent of this nation's youth do not receive a college degree (Charner, 1996). These statistics are even more dismal when looking at African American and Latino youth, particularly those who are children of migrant workers, for example (Lopez, Nerenberg, & Valdez, 2000). School-to-career transitions are applicable to the vast majority of youth in this country, but they take on greater significance when addressing poor and urban youth of color. The concentration of these youth within urban areas has a detrimental effect, unlike that of the concentration of poverty in rural America.

Latino presence in the nation's public schools, particularly those that are urban based, is significant and projected to increase in the next three decades. By 2030 Latinos are expected to be 23 percent of the 9 to 12th grade school population, up from 13 percent in 2001 (ERIC Clearinghouse on Urban Education Digest, 2001). High graduate rates from secondary schools have remained the same over the past several years at 63 percent. This compares with 81 percent for African Americans and 90 percent for white non-Latinos. The Latino dropout rate is more than double for those who are non-United States born (44 percent versus 21 percent). Martinez (1999) notes that in California, where more than 7.5 million Latinos live, of which more than one-third are under the age of 18, they have the highest dropout rates (45 percent) of any ethnic or racial group. Over one million Latino students are classified as having limited English proficiency.

Latino enrollment in colleges and universities has increased dramatically (202 percent) between 1976 and 1996. However, the majority (53 percent) of Latino college students are enrolled in community colleges whereas the majority of African Americans (51 percent) and white non-Latinos (56 percent) are in four-year institutions (ERIC Clearinghouse on Urban Education Digest, 2001). Latinos in four-year programs tend to major in business, social sciences, and education. Those in two-year programs major in liberal arts, business, and the health professions (ERIC Clearinghouse on Urban Education Digest, 2001). Latinos overall, however, are less likely to complete a four-year degree, which is widely recognized as one of the most significant keys to career entrance and advancement (Schemo, 2002).

WORK-RELATED BARRIERS

Career success, not surprisingly, is complex and dynamic and very much determined by the interplay between environmental circumstances and sociodemographic characteristics. Changing technological needs have resulted in the need for a changing workforce, and one that must be proficient in information technology of various kinds. Thus, any attempt to understand the role of work-related barriers for youth cannot be complete without an understanding of how technological changes have transformed the workforce in the United States.

Shaklee (2000, p. 13), in reviewing employment trends over the last 50 years notes the following: "Educational trends changed substantially over the century; the nature of work has also changed dramatically. . . . In the 1950s only 35% of the labor force were involved in the production of services (medical, business, personal), but 65% of today's employees work in the service sector. Only about 25% of today's workers hold traditional blue-collar jobs, while 58% do white collar work as managers, clerks, technicians, etc. Jobs are increasingly computer dependent, with over half of workers today using computers on the job. . . . These jobs require at least a high school diploma, and many require post-secondary training as well." Why are these trends classified as work barriers for some youth? Simply, these trends effectively leave out of the workforce a countless number of youth of color who have left formal schooling before receiving their high school diploma.

Zeldin, Kimball, and Price (1995), in their review of the literature on work and youth, concluded that work can be beneficial to youth in a variety of ways. However, for it to be beneficial, it must provide youth with the following four opportunities: (1) learn new competencies; (2) relate to current educational and occupational aspirations and pursuits; (3) develop skills that are perceived to be useful in adulthood; and (4) allow for completion of complex tasks. The interplay of these four types of opportunities increases the likelihood of youth entering a career that has a meaningful future.

There is a general public consensus on the benefits of work for youth. Work experience not only keeps youth out of trouble, but it also prepares them for their eventual adult roles as contributing members of society. However, workplace-related hazards bring an often-overlooked perspective on the value of work in the lives of youth (Greenhouse, 2001). The National Research Council (1998, p. 1) notes: "Yet working can be dangerous. Each year, tens of thousands of young people are seen in hospital emergency departments for work-related injuries; hundreds of them require hospitalization; and more than 70 die of work-related injuries."

Work-related deaths among youth, for example, vary according to type of employment, with agriculture having the highest number, followed by retail and construction work. Deaths as a result of motor vehicle accidents, electrocution, and homicides are the most common causes. One 1998 North Carolina study of teenaged workers found that 31 percent of them used forklifts, tractors, or mowers; a 1997 Massachusetts study found that 19 percent used food slicers, and 13 percent used box crushers as part of their work responsibilities even though federal law prohibits the use of this equipment by anyone under the age of 18 (Greenhouse, 2002).

Not surprisingly, characteristics of youth injured on the job highlight important differences among this age group. Older adolescents compared to younger adolescents are more likely to have workplace-related injuries. This may reflect the willingness of older adolescents to engage in more hazardous work and the willingness of employers to hire them into these jobs; males are twice as likely as females to be injured on the job (National Research Council, 1998).

Youth from low-income families, when compared to youth from affluent families, are more likely to be working in jobs that are hazardous, such as agriculture, manufacturing, and construction (Lopez et al., 2000; National Research Council, 1998). Unfortunately, very little data have been collected on newcomer youth. When data are available, no distinction, for example, is made between those who are citizens or documented and those who are undocumented (Jasso, 1997). One study covering the 1998 to 2000 period found that 20 percent of all adolescents who died as a result of work-related duties were Latino, yet they represented fewer than 10 percent of all adolescent workers (Greenhouse, 2002). Newcomer youth, particularly those who are undocumented, are more likely to work and to do so in unsafe types of jobs than their citizen counterparts. When a Latino youth is injured, it is unlikely that this occurrence will be reported to authorities, not dissimilar to the way an adult incident would be treated. Thus, youth, regardless of their backgrounds, require special protection in the workplace, and some are in particular need of protection.

SOCIETAL-RELATED BARRIERS

Society is an enormous construct used to fully grasp and do justice to the understanding of school-to-career transition. Nevertheless, failure to bring this construct into an equation, so to speak, is to ignore an important source of influence on any form of outcome, youth-centered or otherwise. The enormity of the task cannot be ignored or short-shrifted in any analysis and discussion of school-to-career transition success or failure. There are numerous factors, such as demographic composition of a community or market, for example, that wield a prodigious degree of influence on any initiative, social or market driven.

The importance of demographics is well understood by policy makers, academics, practitioners, and even the average person in the street. Demographic profiles and trends serve to provide a critical foundation from which society can arrive at strategic decisions and initiatives about this nation's economy. Utilization of demographic data, although not for the faint of heart, is nevertheless not without its limitations based upon methodological decisions. However, demographic data is still an important and very often used source of information.

Recent 2000 U.S. Census Bureau statistics highlight how youth of color have been and are projected to increase numerically in the next 50 years, making a focus on this population very relevant. California's youth, for example, is even more diverse than its adult population. It is estimated that 53 percent of the state's population is of color. However, youth of color make up 65.2 percent of the state's children. White non-Latino adults make up 46.7 percent of California's population but only 34.8 percent of the state's youth (Heredia & Haddock, 2001). Youth of color will continue to represent an increasingly larger portion of this nation's potential workforce. Opportunities for these youth to enter the workforce and establish careers must be enhanced in order to maximize this nation's position in the global economy.

Racial and ethnic distinctions pertaining to rates and types of employment patterns for youth are largely influenced by group differences in family socioeconomic characteristics. Youth of color from economically poorer families and communities are less likely to have paid jobs while attending high school than those in families with higher economic resources who also live in communities with higher per capita income (National Research Council Institute of Medicine, 1998). Youth of color who do work generally do so in service-industries, where upward mobility is severely limited and wages and fringe benefits are totally inadequate to support a family.

Any effort to develop a solid understanding of youth employment and unemployment will necessitate an interdisciplinary perspective on the subject. No one discipline can do justice to the topic because of the multifaceted causes of employment/career or lack thereof. Out of school youth, for example, have historically not been the beneficiaries of targeted initiatives. Concerns about their lack of motivation to continue their studies combined with a range of personal issues and problems, have often impeded these youth from getting a second chance to further their education (National School-to-Work Learning and Information Center, 1996a). Lack of attention, in turn, resulted in many of these youth not registering as unemployed. The development of special initiatives seeking to enhance workforce and economic development, as a result, often overlooked them.

The 1990s witnessed an incredible upsurge in economic opportunities in this country that resulted in significant employment and earnings potential for all age groups. Not surprisingly, youth unemployment decreased. This decade created a tremendous amount of consumption of goods and the belief that the future would not be anything but bright and prosperous. Among 16 to 19 year olds, unemployment rates fell considerably from over 20 percent in 1991 to approximately 14 percent in 1999 (Lerman, 2000). This trend had great significance for schools and the organizations that serve youth. Youth unemployment, like their adult counterparts, is quite complex and necessitates paying greater attention to specific subgroups.

Perez and Salazar (1997) point out that dramatic demographic gains achieved by Latinos in the 1990s did not translate into corresponding increases in educational attainment and economic stability and mobility. Latinos, in turn, have a higher likelihood of contracting certain diseases, receiving less prevention care, and having less access to health education. All of these social and economic forces have prodigious implications for the status of Latino youth and their active and meaningful participation in this nation's labor force.

Guzman (1997) sounds a similar note to that of Perez and Salazar (1997) and other scholars. Namely, youth of color unmistakably face different sets of resources and socially constructed circumstances from those faced by white non-Latino youth. These circumstances are significant influences on their under- and unemployment status (Freeman & Holzer, 1986, p. 114): "A variety of social and economic factors have contributed to the crisis. On the demand side of the market, we find evidence of several determinants, including local labor market conditions and demographics, discriminatory employer behavior, and the unattractive characteristics of the job held. On the supply side of the market, we find aspirations and churchgoing, opportunities for crime, the family's employment and welfare status, education, and the willingness to accept low wage jobs all to be important."

As noted earlier in this chapter, joblessness among youth of color has historically been and currently remains troubling (Lerman, 1999, p. 4): "In October 1998, out-of-school black 16 to 24 year olds experienced a 17 percent unemployment rate. Only about one in three black high school dropouts in this age group was working. While black young women have achieved record levels of employment in the tight U.S. economy, black young men in their early 20s actually saw their employment go down, as the proportion holding down jobs declined from 61 percent to 59 percent. Unemployment rates of black 20 to 24 year old men did climb sharply from the 24 percent levels in 1991 and 31 percent levels of 1982 and 1983 but remained above 15 percent in the content of a national unemployment rate of 4 percent." Lerman's summation of unemployment statistics speaks well to the embeddedness of unemployment in urban communities of color for both youth and adults and to the importance of breaking down statistics to look at how unemployment is experienced by subgroups of youth.

Dorfman and Schraldi (2001) report in their study on youth, race, crime, and news coverage that youth of color, particularly African Americans, are overrepresented as perpetrators of crime and underrepresented as victims, casting them into criminal roles. These negative perceptions, or stereotypes, seriously influence the employment outcomes for youth of color by not encouraging potential employers to take chances on hiring youth of color for jobs that have a potential for acquisition of skills that will enhance lifetime upward mobility. Latino youth, too, are viewed quite stereotypically in this society (Montero-Sieburth, 2000; Rodriguez, 1997). Perceptions, some would argue, are even more powerful than reality. Thus, any serious interventions focused on transitioning urban youth of color from school to the world of career must address stereotypical perceptions and racist barriers in order for success to be achieved (Abe, 2001; Williams, 2001).

Economic inactivity among youth not in school and young adults not in the workforce is particularly acute for those of color (Haveman & Wolfe, 1994, p. 216): "The problem of declining work effort—or joblessness—has become an increasingly important social policy issue, especially as it concerns particular race and ethnic groups and particular age groups." Elliott and King (1999) identified three cultural factors that work against the effectiveness of even the most promising strategies: (1) economic forces are reducing income and job security of low-skill workers; (2) change is increasingly quite complex and the pace is extremely rapid, making it arduous to intervene in labor markets; and (3) public policy is not embracing long-term and flexible support, which is essential for implementing initiatives. Each of these forces is quite formidable. When combined, they overwhelmingly, significantly, and seriously undermine any concerted and comprehensive efforts at addressing youth transition from school-to-career.

The importance of successful transition from school-to-career cannot be overstressed with any youth, but particularly with marginalized youth. The literature on substance abuse, for example, reflects this important transition. Youth of color, particularly those who are African American/black, increase their drug use and abuse later on in adolescence and young adulthood, compared to their white non-Latino counterparts. There is much speculation pertaining to this late onset of drug use and abuse. White non-Latino youth tend to experiment and use drugs earlier in their adolescence. However, they grow out of this drug-using behavior by late adolescence and early adulthood. Youth of color, in turn, start in late adolescence and early adulthood and continue well into adulthood.

One possible reason for this difference falls on their perceptions of what postsecondary school life holds for them. Unlike white non-Latino youth, who can be expected to go on to college or to jobs with a good chance of a future, or at least the hopes of one, youth of color do not share the same prospects. College education, although increasing as a possibility within this society, does not offer a viable path for most youth of color. Employment in a job or a sector with a future, is not a viable path either. Thus, increasing the success of school-to-career provides hope for a better future and will result in less risk-taking behaviors. Economic inequality among youth of color cannot be fully understood or appreciated out of context of the opportunities offered within their communities.

The social construction of substance abuse within marginalized urban communities of color has almost exclusively focused on drug abuse as an act of escapism (Pattillo, 1998). However, the possible explanation of drug use and sales being a means of attaining self-worth and, in the case of drug sales, a viable means of economic self-support, is not new and can be traced back to the 1950s and 1960s (Covington, 1997). This perspective, particularly the economic means of support, is not widely discussed (Centers & Weist, 1998; Ricardo, 1994; Whitehead, Peterson, & Kaljee, 1994). Unfortunately, very little research on middle-class youth of color has been undertaken to help provide a more ecological perspective on this phenomenon (Pattillo, 1998).

Community plays an incredibly important role in helping practitioners and researchers better contextualize behavior. It is only through the contextualization of behavior that we can derive any meaning of substance when examining the state of youth, of color or otherwise. Communities of color in the United States invariably are urban-based and share a variety of sociodemographic profiles that are all indicative of limited opportunities for social and economic advancement for their residents. Their concentration within urban areas further serves to isolate them from the mainstream of social and economic activities within cities.

A number of authors have attempted to lodge the role of economic self-sufficiency within marginalized communities and their youth as a way of highlighting the importance of individuals and communities being self-supporting and the close interrelationship between the two (Heath & McLaughlin, 1993; McLaughlin, 1993; Virgil, 1993). McLaughlin (1993), for example, notes that by the end of the twentieth century in most inner-city urban communities, youth had virtually no hope of deriving their worth from the local labor market. One of a community's worst features from a young person's perspective was that it does not provide for them images of success or highly viable opportunities to engage in productive work within the confines of their own community.

William Julius Wilson (1996, p. xiii) probably better than any other scholar elucidated on the importance of having a grasp of context when examining the world of work in marginalized urban communities in this country: "For the first time in the twentieth century most adults in many inner-city ghetto neighborhoods are not working in a typical week. The disappearance of work has adversely affected not only individuals, families, and neighborhoods, but the social life of the city at large as well. Inner-city joblessness is a severe problem that is often overlooked or obscured when the focus is placed mainly on poverty and its consequences. . . . The consequences of high neighborhood joblessness are more devastating than those of high neighborhood poverty. A neighborhood in which people are poor but employed is different from a neighborhood in which people are poor and jobless. Many of today's problems in the inner-city ghetto neighborhoods—crime, family dissolution, welfare, low levels of social organization, and so on—are fundamentally a consequence of the disappearance of work."

Simply stated, there are no simple problems or simple solutions. The workforce participation of youth of color cannot be disconnected from the experience of their elders or from their surrounding circumstances. Interrelatedness and interdependence are critical to any initiatives focused on marginalized youth (Dippo, 1998). Contextualization of youth of color workforce participation, as a result, requires placing this phenomenon within a community's historical context and taking into account major global forces that are operating in this country (Bartik, 2001; Bernhardt et al., 2001; Ellwood et al., 2000).

Bygrave and Minniti (2000, p. 30) speak to the importance of community history with enterprise creation, for example, as a key consideration in using entrepreneurship as an economic strategy: "If entrepreneurship is self-reinforcing, then it is also path-dependent, randomly, a particular sequence of choices causes the dynamics of the process to push the community toward a specific outcome among all the possible ones. A different sequence, however, would have bent it toward an alternative outcome. This means that each person's choice contributes to the determination of the aggregate result though not with equal weight: earlier choices have more steering power. This implies that the entrepreneurial history of the community is important."

Communities of color in urban areas of the country, with notable exceptions, tend to have limited exposure to self-initiated or indigenous economic enterprises. In fact, it is not unusual to have most mid- to large-scale businesses being external to the community—namely, owned and managed by people outside of the community. This lack of history, control, and experience, unfortunately, severely limits who can and should venture into this uncharted territory. External control over businesses has historically been a sore spot for many urban communities of color in the United States, and conflict resulting from this disparity has led to urban unrest.

INDIVIDUAL AND FAMILY-RELATED BARRIERS

It would be irresponsible to seriously outline key barriers to successful transition from school-to-career and not examine individual and family-related barriers. Interestingly, the literature has generally touched upon most, if not all, of these factors and has done so in a manner that isolates these factors from each other. The synergistic effects of multiple individual and family factors interacting with each other may well make the whole greater than the sum of the parts (Pierret, 2001). This observation takes on greater significance when socioeconomic status and racial/ethnic factors are added into the equation.

There is little question that ultimate success in achieving transition to adulthood is very dependent upon the interplay of school, career, society, family, and individual factors. The youth development field has outlined at least five key individual factors that must be considered in any form of youth development programming: (1) cognitive, (2) emotional, (3) physical, (4) moral, and (5) spiritual. Each of these factors wields a considerable amount of influence on youth outcomes with family playing enhancing or detrimental roles. The interplay of some or all of these factors, however, wields influence far beyond that of any one factor.

Cognitive-Related Factors

Although cognitive abilities are vastly overrated in a society obsessed with level of intelligence, they are still a key factor that must be considered in transitioning youth to adulthood. Probably one significant reason for this overemphasis has to do with the number of years youth spend in school during this developmental period. It is not unheard of for a youth to spend 13 to 14 years of his or her first 18 years in a school setting. Although formal education has multiple goals in preparing youth for adulthood, knowledge acquisition is arguably the most prominent.

Much progress has been made to provide youth with cognitive impairments with formal education that can maximize their potential; however, much progress still needs to be made in the future. The importance of work is just as great for these individuals as it is for their typical counterparts. Special efforts must be undertaken to increase knowledge acquisition and competencies through use of new methods of instruction and necessary supports once a young person is placed in a job.

Circumstances related to families, however, cannot be ignored. Newman, Smith, and Murphy (2000, p. 87) rightly state that families are the primary venue for youth development and cannot be overlooked in any form of programming: "However, the ability of families to support the positive development of their youth varies greatly, based on a host of factors, including financial resources, available time, number of parents and youth in a family, physical and health circumstances, and special needs of a youth. The list goes on and on. Families contribute to youth development in ways that may never be calculated but are easily recognizable, extremely valuable, and vital to support." Failure of families to support youth in development of their cognitive skills, health (physical and emotional), spiritual, and moral dimensions can be quite detrimental to the life of youth.

Emotion-Related Factors

Emotional maturity is a concept that is often found in any discussion concerning youth and the world of career. In fact, it is not unusual to find it in any discussion of workforce readiness regardless of the age of the worker. Youth who are not emotionally capable of holding employment bring an important element to any discussion of individual barriers. Youth who have severe emotional disturbances, for example, not only experience great difficulty in working in highly stressed environments, they are also subject to much closer supervision, or monitoring. Concerns about their emotional-readiness for employment very often find these youth under high scrutiny; there is low tolerance for outbursts of any kind.

Teachers, practitioners, and employers sometimes label emotion-related factors as a lack of maturity. However, labeling emotional factors in this manner does not do justice to the importance of emotional readiness for the world of career. Lack of empathy, for example, is considered a serious character flaw and will increase the likelihood of termination from employment.

Physical Health–Related Factors

The physical health of young people plays an influential role in determining their abilities to carry out a host of roles in their family, community, and society. The poor health status of urban youth of color and their families is well documented in the professional literature. Youth of color living in certain areas of the nation's cities are often confronted with a disproportionate number of health issues when compared with counterparts in the suburbs. They are much more likely to be hospitalized with asthma, for example. They are also more likely to have inadequate diets, calcium deficiencies, and sexually transmitted diseases and to be injured as a result of violence and crimes (LaGreca, 2000).

Poor physical health becomes a significant barrier to full employment. Employers with jobs open to youth of color are often the least forgiving of health conditions and absences because of health factors. Many of these jobs, in addition, have limited or no health insurance coverage as part of the employment, further limiting youth access to quality health care. Many youth of color may have had limited access to health care during their lives, further exacerbating their health status.

The subject of disability and how it impacts transition from school-to-career has not gotten the attention it deserves in the professional literature, particularly in the case of youth of color from low-income communities (Quiones-Mayo, Wilson, & McGuire, 2000). There is a strong relationship between race/ethnicity and negative early adulthood outcomes, particularly for African Americans/blacks and Latino youth. Youth of color with disabilities, when compared to white non-Latino youth counterparts, have a decreased likelihood of a career and a lack of meaningful participation in social and recreational activities. It is estimated that 85.5 percent of African Americans with disabilities and 75.4 percent of Latinos with disabilities are not in the labor force (Hasnain, 2001). This compares quite poorly with white non-Latino counterparts with 47 percent in the labor force. The combination of limited access to employment with social isolation seriously limits their potential contributions to their family, community, and society.

Moral-Related Factors

The increased number of ethics courses in the nation's business schools attests to the needs in the field. Ethical transgressions in business practices raise the importance of ethical standards and behaviors. The subject of morality, not surprisingly, has also found its way into the youth development literature (Delgado, 2002). This content can be operationalized along a multitude of ways. However, the literature has focused on the role of organized religion in the lives of youth. Cook (2000), for example, examined the role of the church as an institution in the lives of youth of color and found this institution to play an important mediating role in their lives. In addition, these youth were more likely than youth not in churches to make a successful transition to the world of career and work.

Spiritual-Related Factors

The reader may well wonder why spiritual-related factors are included in this section. The subject of spirituality can take a variety of forms. It is not unusual to interchange the ideas of spirituality and morality. However, for our purposes, they are separate. Spirituality refers to the fundamental belief in the existence of a greater and all-loving presence in life (Cervantes and Ramirez, 1992). The presence of spirituality, or the embrace of the belief in the greater good, has been identified as an important element of youth development (Delgado, 2002).

Operationally, spirituality can translate into a belief that one is unique and part of a broader network, social and metaphysical. One's purpose in life is closely tied to the good one achieves in relationship to others, physical and metaphysical. Subscribing to a set of guiding principles is one way that this good can be achieved during a lifetime. The lack of connectedness and, more specifically, a belief that one's purpose on earth and one's measurement of success is not related to materialism can be detrimental consequences for youth. Thus, a narrow focus on self, without regard for others, is a serious breach of spiritual meaning. A lack of conscience is considered a direct manifestation of this breach.

CONCLUSION

The world of career and work is complex, and this applies to both adults and youth. Career and work cannot possibly be understood or addressed outside of a community context and without a grasp of the major forces that shape it. In addition, the importance of drawing conclusions regarding career and work for youth necessitates an approach that examines within and between youth groups and subgroups, with family income, ethnicity/race, documented status, and gender, standing out as prominent factors in determining who is privileged and who is marginalized in this society. The benefits associated with career and work, as a result, follow significantly different paths for youth in these two groupings.

There certainly is no lack of challenge for marginalized youth of color in this country. Some would argue that challenges can be converted into opportunities, with social youth entrepreneurship being but one example. Nevertheless, any serious initiative such as social youth entrepreneurship must recognize and surmount significant barriers, or they will doom any intervention to failure. Society's ability to have clarity about what barriers constitute these challenges is very often the first and most important step in the development of any initiative. Having the political will to do something constructive about it is the second crucial step in developing a brighter and more productive future for these youth.

Marginalized youth face the realities of society having low expectations of them, fear from the general population, and lack of adequate resources as experienced in many of this nation's urban schools. Nevertheless, these youth possess unlimited potential if provided with the chance and requisite support. Transitions from school-to-career provide an important frame or perspective for guiding interventions, particularly when using a youth development paradigm. However, we cannot view marginalized youth in isolation from their communities. This society values individualism. Yet, a broader view is in order so that we do not lose sight of the individual while appreciating the context in which they live and function.

It is important to emphasize that any serious efforts at successfully addressing the needs of marginalized youth cannot ignore those who have left school before graduation. Unfortunately, as Zuckerman (2000, p. 317) has noted, youth development and youth employment programs have historically not mixed: "It is not surprising that youth development is missing from out-of-school youth programs. The employment and training system has only included youth development in exceptional experiments or programs operated by organizations that were primarily youth-serving agencies for whom youth development was included in all services to young people. It is not surprising that youth development is not a priority because employment and training is generally a short-term intervention and has focused almost exclusively on basic education and vocational training, with jobs and returning to school considered acceptable outcomes." Bringing youth development and social youth entrepreneurship together may well represent a merger that will enhance the goals of these two types of initiatives and open the door for other possible mergers that have not yet been thought of.

PART II

The World of Career, Work, and Social Entrepreneurship

CHAPTER 5

Transition from School to Career: Challenges, Obstacles, and Possibilities

INTRODUCTION

The twenty-first century will present this nation's youth with rewarding opportunities or significant setbacks depending upon their competencies and ability to be flexible to take advantage of emerging fields of career. However, if opportunities and rewards are to dominate the future landscape, school and community must come together in an unprecedented manner (Abbott, 1995, p. 10): "If the school and the community can link together to create, through their separate strengths and resources, a genuine learning community that is friendly to children, then the progression of young people into world of work will be smooth, logical, and effective." Institutions that have youth as a focus of their mission will be severely tested and measured on their ability to meet the needs of youth and society at the same time. Although this linkage of goals seems logical in the minds of most practitioners and academics, it is still very elusive in this society and makes serving the educational and social needs of youth arduous to achieve. The consequences of failure to do so can be quite profound for the future of the nation.

Future society will either reap rewards or suffer dire consequences depending upon decisions made in the early twenty-first century. Transitions of any kind are invariably saddled with great anxiety and challenges. The transition from youth to adulthood is no exception and is probably the most challenging of any age-role transition, complicating the search for initiatives that effectively minimize barriers and challenges in facilitating entry into a career force. Age-sensitive interventions, like their ethnic, racial, and gender counterparts, require a keen understanding of how the developmental age of youth influences their perceptions and abilities to alter their circumstances.

The National Employer Leadership Council (1994) found that most youth undergo a two-year hiatus in their transition from high school to full-time employment, during which no formal assistance of any kind is provided to them. This period of transition represents a critical period, during which youth can benefit tremendously from some form of structured intervention. Any form of intervention, however, will necessitate an active outreach component and an attractive message for engaging youth. Transition from school-to-career, as a result, is either enhanced prior to graduation from high school or, for some youth, much later in life, if at all, as in the case of countless numbers of low-income youth of color. This window of opportunity necessitates the creation of interventions that can engage youth early in this period to maximize return on investment of funds and the early identification and intervention with youth who are at-risk for disconnecting from productive roles in society (Besharov, 1999).

According to the U.S. Department of Labor, between 1997 and 2005, there will be a 22 percent growth in employment in this country, which will provide youth with opportunities to pursue many attractive careers. Unfortunately, this increase in employment will not occur across the board. Some sectors offer greater potential than others—technicians, paralegals, and health technicians, for example, are the fastest growing occupations and will increase by 32 percent during this period; professional specialty will increase by 37 percent; service workers will expand by 33 percent (San Diego County Office of Education, 1997). The trends cited by the U.S. Department of Labor have important implications for education and labor market policy development by directing the education and training that will increase the likelihood of youth making informed choices pertaining to career-force entry.

Strategic initiatives need to be engendered to prepare youth for careers in profitable (livable wages and benefits) emerging fields. Failure to do so will ultimately relegate millions of youth to low-paying jobs or no employment at all, let alone careers of any kind. An important window of opportunity can be effectively closed for youth who are ill informed, or not informed at all, by appropriate school personnel. Emerson and Twersky (1996, p. 4) address this very point in their argument for greater emphasis on development of youth entrepreneurial skills and interests: "Many of those involved in the field of employment and economic development have concluded that the central issue for the American workforce is not simply one of accessing marginal jobs for folks and then hoping they will move up the ranks. Increasingly, the focus is upon the creation of workforce development strategies, which provide opportunities for retraining and development, which in turn will enable workers to constantly upgrade their skills and abilities in response to the changing needs of the labor market." Although engagement in entrepreneurial pursuits may not be intended for all youth or may not be feasible for that matter, it is still an option for some if they are provided with guidance and support for doing so.

There is no disputing that national legislation has played an influential role in getting attention to focus on youth-to-career issues. The School-to-Work Opportunities Act of 1994 is such an example (Hamilton & Hamilton, 1994). This legislation, in turn, provided an impetus for various educational reform efforts to better address the needs of youth. However, in spite of this legislation and requisite funding, many challenges lay ahead for youth, particularly those that are marginalized in this society and face incredible hurdles to becoming productive citizens within their communities. Major national legislation can play an instrumental role in placing an issue on the national landscape, but it is also necessary for the private sector to play a significant role. This partnership will increase the likelihood of any initiative having the sustaining power for the long term.

Being a productive member of a community and society is widely acknowledged to be a key element in a youth development paradigm. Gainful employment is a central component of being a healthy and contributing adult member of this society. This chapter, as a result, will identify the key challenges, obstacles, and possibilities in youth transitioning from school to career and adulthood (de Jesus, 1997; Gruber, 1997; Linn, 1998). Every effort will be made to draw upon a multidisciplinary perspective to highlight the complexity of the challenges facing youth, particularly those who are marginal in the workforce and society.

SCHOOL-TO-WORK OPPORTUNITIES ACT

Funding for school-to-career has come from a variety of sources. However, the federal government has spent over $1.6 billion since passage of the 1994 School-to-Work Opportunities Act in 1994. This act was specifically intended to provide all youth, in and out of school, with access to programs that integrated academic and occupational goals and better prepared them for the world of work. This federal initiative represented a systems-building strategy approach and was designed to reinforce reform efforts, workforce development, and economic development. In addition, it provided states with tremendous latitude in carrying out this mandate.

The 1994 act also represented a dramatic departure for a federal educational initiative because it did not treat schools as insular identities disengaged from the community and surrounding institutions (Hamilton et al., 1994). Such an approach naturally encourages bold activities (Goldberger, Keough, & Almedia, 2000, p. 8): "School-to-career promotes high academic standards by engaging all students in a rigorous college-preparatory curriculum that stresses the application of concepts and knowledge to real-world problems. The real-life context breaks down barriers between academic disciplines and encourages thematic instruction and practical problem-solving. Through field-based projects and internships, students come in contact with supportive adults. . . . Engagement with the world outside schools adds authenticity to academic endeavors and enlists the resources of employers and community agencies in the task of educating youngsters."

The expansion of the learning arena to include the world outside of schools and a wide variety of unconventional hands-on activities brings excitement and relevance to the educational experience of youth, but it also challenges conventional wisdom on how best to prepare youth for adulthood. Achieving a consensus on best practices, as a result, is an essential but time-consuming process.

The act represented a dramatic shift from the usual programmatic efforts (American Youth Policy Forum, 2000, p. 1): "The School-to-Work Opportunities Act of 1994 (STWOA) represented a bold, strategic effort to help states and locales put in place the necessary resources, where few had existed, through schooling and career preparation into further education and careers. It acknowledged the seminal role of education in preparing young people for careers and the vital importance of community partnerships required for the development of a skilled workforce." The 1994 act, for example, had school-based enterprises listed prominently as one method of providing youth with work experience. This prominence, not surprisingly, resulted in numerous school-based enterprises being created across the nation.

The School-to-Work Opportunities Act, as a result, has played a significant role in attracting the attention of states and nonprofit organizations. This attention has resulted in creation of numerous models and principles for guiding local-based initiatives, one of which is the educational strategy predicated on schools developing collaborative partnerships with community organizations, particularly the business community (Pines & Spring, 1997). Doing so has opened up previously unavailable opportunities for launching new initiatives, particularly those that are enterprise driven.

There should be at least four key elements or features of any model of school-to-career initiative (Goldberger et al., 2000): (1) small learning communities and personalized support; (2) availability of a college preparatory curriculum that stresses real-world applications; (3) learning in the workplace and community; and (4) supported transition to postsecondary education and employment. These elements are not restricted to school settings, however. Community-based organizations can also incorporate these elements. When community-based organizations enter into educational collaborative partnerships with schools using these principles, the potential for learning goes up dramatically, and so does the potential for community transformation. All parties benefit from these collaborative ventures, but most of all youth are the ultimate beneficiaries.

School-based learning, work-based learning, and connecting activities represent the key provisions of the 1994 act (Benz, Yovanoff, & Doren, 1997).

In the late 1990s the act focused on career preparation of all youth and on the futures of the disadvantaged, with a reemphasis on youth unemployment as a distinct problem (Lerman, 2000). This is not to say, however, that the construct of school-to-work or career is fully grasped by key stakeholders in the public and private sectors (American Youth Policy Forum, 2000). Knowledge acquisition and competencies can be accomplished through a variety of methods that are based in schools or in other settings.

School-to-career transition has drawn increased academic attention on the part of scholars, too. Krumboltz and Worthington (1999) have approached the subject from a learning perspective. Career development counselors, among other professionals, can find value is using learning theory to assist them in their assessments, develop new learning environments, and measure student progress. Worthington and Juntenen (1997) and others, for example, have pushed a human capital theory for guiding school-to-career transition. This theoretical perspective is founded on two influential processes—labor market forces will reward the better educated and skilled worker, and nations with better prepared workforces will exert considerable global influence. Investments in education translate into enhancement of the human capital characteristics of youth. Everyone benefits from this investment—youth, their families and neighborhoods, and society (Krumboltz & Worthington, 1999).

Zeldin, Kimball, and Price (1995) stress the use of active learning as a mechanism to help all youth achieve in school and ultimately succeed in transitioning to adulthood. Active learning, according to the authors, necessitates the following activities to occur: discussion of information and ideas with others; use of these ideas to make decisions, goal setting, creation of rules; reflection on knowledge and experiences; making choices and being responsible for their own learning; and, being challenged to use and practice higher-order thinking skills. Active learning, however, is not restricted to in-school learning and can be found in out-of-school settings and within families.

Kazis and Pennington (1999, p. 1), like myself, view the beginning of the twenty-first century as representing a critical juncture in the school-to-career movement and an opportune time to make significant progress in this area: "The school-to-career movement is at a critical juncture after a decade of enthusiasm, experimentation, and progress, and after five years of moderate federal support. . . . On one hand, the school-to-career movement and the federal funding that has fueled it during the past five years has sparked much activity and progress in localities across the country. . . . Yet, short-term dilemmas face school-to-career advocates and practitioners."

The nation is entering the next phase in efforts to tackle the persistent challenges of raising student achievement, promoting positive youth development, and preparing all youth for careers and further learning. This phase, if not properly conceptualized and strategically addressed, can set back the movement and progress in this arena and waste valuable time, energy, and resources, not to mention a generation's potential contributions to this country's economic and social well-being.

School-to-career has received national attention as the result of a series of concerns that have been voiced in a wide variety of sectors in this country over the past decade or so (Benz et al., 1997; Hamilton & Hamilton, 1997; Kazis & Pennington, 1999): (1) concern about global competition and its impact on this country's economic well-being; (2) rediscovery of the forgotten half; (3) dissatisfaction with the quality of high school education; and (4) crisis in vocational education—the need to modernize vocational education to train less narrowly and raise academic expectations in the process. A number of broad tenets helped guide the movement to address the above concerns. However, a recognition that youth, schools, and communities need help in providing successful transitions for youth and the importance of both academic/ educational achievement and employment/career prospects stand out.

Not surprisingly, school-to-career transition has an international following. Countries such as Germany, Japan, Scotland, Australia, England, Spain, the Netherlands, Korea, France, and Sweden, to list but a few of the most prominent ones, also vigorously address school-to-career policies and initiatives (Stern, 2000). All of these countries have acknowledged that the traditional role of vocational education has been too narrow in scope to prepare students for the challenges inherent in learning-intensive economies. Dramatic changes in workforce needs cannot successfully be addressed with curriculum that is narrowly defined and based upon past situations and goals. Further, there was a consensus for a closer connection between vocational and academic education as a means of better preparing the future workforce.

The American Youth Policy Forum (2000, p. v) identified 10 essential principles in helping youth succeed in transitioning from school-to-work (STW), which fall into three arenas. The following principles incorporate a holistic perspective on youth and career and stress the importance and need for major changes in how we currently address these issues:

1. *Improving the school experience:*
   a. STW promotes high standards of academic learning and performance for all young people
   b. STW incorporates industry-valued standards that help inform curricula and lead to respected and portable credentials
   c. STW provides opportunities for contextual learning
   d. STW helps create smaller, more effective learning communities
   e. STW expands opportunities for all young people and exposes them to a broad array of career opportunities
   f. STW provides program continuity between K–12 and postsecondary education and training

2. *Expanding and improving work-based learning opportunities:*

a. STW provides work-based learning that is directly tied to classroom learning

b. STW assists employers in providing high-quality work-based learning opportunities

3. *Building and sustaining public/private partnerships*

a. STW connects young people with supportive adults, mentors, and other role models

b. STW promotes the role of brokering/intermediary organizations

SPECIAL CHALLENGES FOR YOUTH OF COLOR SUBGROUPS

Challenges in making school-to-career transition do not fall equally on all youth. Even within groupings of youth of color some segments face greater challenges than others (Dominitz, Manski, & Fischhoff, 2001). This reality, as a result, needs to be taken into account in any understanding of why some youth of color succeed while others fail in making a smooth transition to adulthood (Newman, 1999). Youth of color, and particularly those who are newcomers to this country, for example, are not new to the world of work (Taylor, 2000). However, their experiences in this realm are quite different from their white, middle-class counterparts.

Taylor's description (2000, p. 1E) of the typical day of Gilberto Diaz (Minneapolis) captures both the work ethic of youth and the challenges they face in making a life for themselves in this country: "In the deep blue of dawn, Gilberto Diaz leaves a Chanhassen warehouse where he has packed boxes of books all night. Now he must rush to prepare for school, the second chapter of his 14-hour day. He looks tired, but he hurries into the bathroom, tosses water on his face. Within 15 minutes, he has transformed himself from a weary graveyard shift worker to a trendy student wearing spicy cologne, black Nikes, a suede jacket, jeans, and baseball cap. On the way to Abraham Lincoln High School in Minneapolis, where the day begins at 8 A.M., he grabs a bottle of juice . . . before hopping on a bus."

Gilberto Diaz obviously is not alone in this quest for an education and employment across the United States. Working is not necessarily an activity that gets accomplished to buy life's luxury items. Many youth work out of necessity to obtain food, basic clothing, and housing. Many, in addition, are required to send money to family left behind in their country of origin. In the case of Gilberto Diaz, he wires at least $200 to Mexico to help his family. Fredy Zhaqui (Ecuadorian), age 19, of Minneapolis, has a very similar regime to that of Diaz—he works in a nightclub five days per week from 1:30 A.M. to 7 A.M. and from 2 A.M. to 8 A.M. on weekends. He, too, sends a significant portion of his pay to family back in Ecuador (Taylor, 2000).

These two case examples are not atypical and serve to highlight the tension immigrant youth face in trying to be both breadwinners and students at the same time. Both jobs noted above do not offer advancement, opportunities for meaningful interaction with adults, or teach new and exciting cognitive skills that will translate into future employment at livable wages. Youth representing groups that are newcomers to this country present a unique set of challenges. Memories of what caused their families to leave their countries of origin for the United States are fairly recent and vivid. Their work ethic, in turn, is reinforced by a desire to send money to family members left behind and also requires working extra hours under less than beneficial conditions.

Youth working in dead-end jobs can develop a determined outlook to obtain a college education and effectively escape this trap as noted by the following youngster (Newman, 1999, p. 133): "If you don't get an education you can't be what you wanna be. I wanna be a corporate lawyer, so I have to get my education, all my degrees that I need to get. All the tests that I need to pass, I'm gonna pass them to be a corporate lawyer. Yeah. If you don't have a degree, you don't have an education, you don't have nothin'. You can't do nothin'. You don't have a job. Well, you may have a job at Burger Barn. But I mean you can't get a good job, good-paying money. You can work in Burger Barn all your life. What I want is a job that's gonna bring me six or seven hundred dollars, maybe even a thousand [a week]."

AN ECOLOGICAL PERSPECTIVE ON TRANSITION

Any effort to understand how successful transition from school-to-career occurs necessitates drawing upon a multidisciplinary social ecological perspective to better appreciate the world youth live in on a daily basis (Dickens, 1999; Rosenbaum, 1997; Stone et al., 1999). Social arenas such as family, peers, schools, and communities all interplay to either facilitate or hinder transition. The social ecology of high school must be keenly understood if school-to-career transition is to be achievable (Ogbu, 1997).

Newman's (1999, p. 218) description of the challenges facing African American and Latino youth who work illustrates the complexity of successful transition and why an ecological perspective is in order to better understand these challenges: "Black and Latino youth who work have already made key decisions about who they must avoid at school and in the neighborhood. They know who the major troublemakers are and make sure to give a wide berth to anyone known to be a problem case." Urban schools, in essence, cannot afford to define their educational mission along narrow dimensions and totally ignore the operative reality marginalized urban youth of color face in the daily struggle to learn and enhance their self-worth.

The mention of urban schools in any discussion pertaining to youth will, as will any other urban terms, elicit negative images in the public's mind (Boyd & Shouse, 1997). Schools should serve as the primary settings to prepare urban youth for either higher education or careers offering a livable salary and the potential for advancement. The National Collaboration for Youth (1999), for example, strongly advocates for youth exploring career paths that are considered nontraditional for a youth's gender, race, ethnicity, and social-economic class. Why must marginalized youth of color restrict their aspirations to just a handful of professions when they can make significant contributions to all professions?

Seidman and French (1997) identify key transition points, such as elementary to junior high school and high school, as providing excessive stressors for urban youth of color. These same junctures also provide opportunities for interventions to prevent the onset of risky behaviors and for enhancing youth social and academic competencies. The fostering of educational resilience in inner-city schools is not only possible but also a reality. Wang, Haertel, and Walberg (1997) identify several key factors that facilitate resilience—social climate, effective instructional methods and curriculum, teacher actions and expectations, and schoolwide policies; all serve to raise student learning, motivation, and perceptions/attitudes toward school.

The perspective of having youth and, more specifically, adolescents as workers is certainly not alien in this or any other society. Youth often work throughout the calendar year, not just during summers. Family circumstances very often necessitate that youth from economically marginalized families work outside of the home throughout the calendar year and very often can result in these youth leaving school before graduation in order to financially support their families. When youth are employed, however, they invariably do so in jobs that are either manual or do not systematically tap and develop analytical or interactional competencies that can serve as springboards for future employment and careers. Consequently, both employers and schools do not capitalize upon a valuable opportunity.

Very often the virtues of career and work are extolled in society. Nevertheless, there are negative consequences that can occur when youth work. Lack of proper sleep, poor eating habits, such as missing meals, lack of physical exercise, decreased leisure time, decreased performance and grades, and increased conflicts with parents have been identified in the professional literature (Bachman & Schulenberg, 1993; High & Collins, 1991; Lindner & Cox, 1998; Manning, 1990; Sampson, 2000; Steinberg, Fegley, & Dornbusch, 1993). These consequences take on added significance because of the physical and emotional development phase adolescents are going through at that stage in their lives.

The National Research Council's (1998) meta-analysis of research found that most adolescents are employed in jobs that do not reinforce content covered in school, do not involve skills necessary for future advancement, and offer little meaningful interactions with adults. Haimson, Hersey, and Silverberg (1999) found that although youth obtain valuable work experience, the majority of the cohort (almost 60 percent) does not obtain any meaningful qualification beyond a general high school diploma as a result of employment.

Nevertheless, there can be positive consequences from youth working. More specifically, the benefits of employment can also entail acquisition of social skills, higher self-esteem, improved school performance, increased participation in school-related activities, increased autonomous function, greater self-efficacy, not to mention generation of money (Hardesty & Hirsch, 1992; Kablaoui & Paulter, 1991; Lindner et al., 1998; Shanahan, Finch, Mortimer, & Ryu, 1991). Chaplin and Hannaway (1996) and Ruhm (1998) found that youth employment significantly improved career outcomes.

Needless to say, there are a variety of mediating factors operative in determining whether the work experience is primarily beneficial or detrimental to youth (Lindner et al., 1998). Barling, Rogers, and Kelloway (1995) found that youth could offset the detrimental consequences of long hours at work by the quality of the work being performed. Worley (1995), in turn, found that adolescent youth increased their school grades when they worked in nonstructured work settings as compared to those who worked in highly structured settings. One national study found that most adolescents hope to find meaningful employment that offers them job security and time to be with their families (Magruder, 2000). The balance between work and family is very important because they have witnessed the stressors within their own families.

The paradigm of youth development, particularly when viewed from the importance of a successful transition from youth to adulthood, needs to be defined in a broad and multifaceted manner. Failure to do so will seriously limit the potential of this paradigm. Nevertheless, a comprehensive perspective challenges policy makers, practitioners, academics, and youth themselves (Pauly, Hilary, & Haimson, 1995). Youth development has been conceptualized to identify and address the key elements necessary to help youth make the transition from youth to adults.

Wentling and Waight (1999) identify a series of barriers (school, work, society, and individual) that youth of color confront in successfully making a transition from school to the workforce. These barriers, the reader must be reminded, are not mutually exclusive; youth most likely encounter multiple types. Some of these barriers, however, wield a disproportionate amount of influence on youth of color. These barriers, in turn, are dynamic and can increase or decrease in importance and influence depending on the development stage of youth and the effectiveness of interventions.

Haveman and Wolfe (1994) have developed the concept of economic inactivity as a means of capturing the multifaceted nature of economic self-sufficiency, and it will be used in this chapter. Their concept is neither labor force nor full-time schooling biased. According to the authors, economic inactivity can be defined as not in any of the following groupings: (1) attending school full-time; (2) working at least one-half time; (3) attending school and working at least part-time; (4) having primary responsibility for an infant or two or more children under the ages of six years; or (5) combination of child care time and either part-time schooling and/or part-time work.

Besharov's (1999) construct of disconnectedness complements economic inactivity but with a focus on youth and brings a more expansive social dimension to the discussion. Disconnectedness, as a result, does not blame the victim and instead requires an understanding of the multiple roles adults play in creating a situation that is not conducive to youth growth and development. Youth as the result of major social problems are disconnected from the broader society during periods in their lives. Prolonged disconnectedness, in turn, can result in withdrawal, with little hope of belonging to community and society (Brown & Emig, 1999; Committee for Economic Development, 1997; Hill, 1999).

Disconnectedness from the workforce can take a variety of perspectives in addition to unemployment. Underemployment and mismatched employment, that is, working in a job that does not maximize the potential of youth, can be equally damaging to a youth's development. Lerman (1999) highlights the complexity of linking high schools and careers for marginalized youth. On paper, it may seem to be a natural for partnerships and collaborations of various kinds. However, this natural relationship may not ultimately result in benefit for youth. Nevertheless, high schools can do much more in facilitating transitions to the world of career for all youth, but particularly those who may not aspire to continue their education at a college or university.

The increased importance of community for youth employment and youth development initiatives holds much promise for creative and significant partnerships and collaborations. Community-based resources, in turn, can be mobilized to implement these initiatives. Community-based organizations (CBOs), for example, can be enlisted as partners in all facets of school-to-work programs (National School-to-Work Learning and Information Center, 1997, p. 1): "CBOs are often overlooked as partners in school-to-work systems, yet they are frequently able to expand the scope of school-to-work by providing opportunities for young people to address community issues and by incorporating a unique youth perspective into the development of school-to-work opportunities. CBOs can sometimes provide educational opportunities that formal schools cannot. Some CBOs also enhance school-to-work partnerships by assuming a variety of important functions and services that other partners may be unable or unwilling to fulfill."

SCHOOL-TO-CAREER TRANSITION—HOW TO PREPARE FOR THE TWENTY-FIRST CENTURY

Although it is impossible to predict the future, much progress can still be made to increase the likelihood of eventual success for youth through careful study and an openness to consider a wide range of possibilities, even if they are totally new (O'Connor, 1999; Stone, Doherty, Jones, & Ross, 1999). This progress, however, cannot rely solely on schools to prepare youth for transition to careers. Numerous other entities, such as community development corporations, businesses, and other community based organizations, may also play influential roles, sometimes in collaboration with schools, sometimes parallel to schools (Stoutland, 1999). The importance of community in these endeavors, however, cannot be overlooked (Sampson, 1999).

School-to-career transition is greatly facilitated when work-based learning sites are expanded to include community-based organizations. Expansion of sites also has the benefit of creating relationships between schools and community, which can then lead to more ambitious partnerships and coalitions (Academy for Educational Development, 1995). In addition, youth are provided with an opportunity to engage in community service. The Secretary of Labor's Commission on Achieving Necessary Skills (SCANS) specifically focused on how to prepare youth for employment in the twenty-first century. SCANS identified a set of foundation skills and competencies that are required for successful school-to-career transition (San Diego County Office of Education, 1997, p. 1):

Foundation Skills

A. Basic Skills: Reading, writing, arithmetic and mathematics, speaking, and listening;
B. Thinking Skills: Thinking creatively, making decisions, solving problems, seeing things in the mind's eye, knowing how to learn, and reasoning;
C. Personal Qualities: Developing individual responsibility, self-esteem, sociability, self-management, and integrity.

Competencies

A. Resources: allocating time, money, materials, space, and staff;
B. Interpersonal Skills: working in teams, teaching others, serving customers, leading, negotiating, and working well with people;
C. Information: acquiring and evaluating data, organizing and maintaining files, interpreting and communicating, and using computers to process information.
D. Systems: understanding social, organizational, and technological systems, monitoring and correcting performance, and designing or improving systems;
E. Technology: selecting equipment and tools, applying technology to specific tasks, and maintaining and troubleshooting technologies.

The foundation skills and competencies identified by the U.S. Department of Labor should not come as any great surprise to the reader. How we can effectively enhance youth assets in these areas, however, still remains a challenge in the United States. Formal education systems cannot develop these skills and competencies by themselves. Other sources of support are needed to accomplish the goals associated with transition-to-career for youth of all socioeconomic and racial/ethnic backgrounds (Johnson, Schweke, & Hull, 1999). These sources of support will come from the family and community through formal and informal efforts.

Schools, in turn, will need to reexamine how education is conceptualized and carried out on a day-to-day basis and be prepared to address the following: (1) begin career exploration and preparation early; (2) integrate workplace know-how with an academic curriculum; (3) teach skills in context; (4) require students to become active in their own learning; and (5) utilize performance assessment practices that relate to those used in business (San Diego County Office of Education, 1997).

Contextual learning, otherwise known as service-learning, is well accepted as the core of any school-to-career transition program and is based upon the fundamental premise that education, when relevant to the life of youth, has a higher likelihood of influencing their receptivity to education. This form of learning is broad in definition and actively seeks to build upon life experiences and existing knowledge. Further, this form of learning is based upon cooperation, sharing, exploration, invention, and discovery (American Youth Policy Forum, 2000).

Goldberger, Keough, and Almeida (2000), in turn, emphasize four key elements or factors of any successful school-to-career learning model: (1) small learning communities and personalized support; (2) availability of a college preparatory curriculum that stresses real-world applications; (3) learning in the workplace and community; and (4) supported transition to postsecondary education and employment. These elements broaden the role of education beyond the traditional school classroom into the broader community and provide policy makers and practitioners with a mandate to develop collaborative relationships and partnerships across boundaries and institutions, including schools.

POTENTIAL OF SMALL BUSINESSES

It is a rare experience to witness any major public discussion on the health of the nation's economy with a focus on the role of small- and medium-sized businesses. These discussions invariably focus on the Fortune 500 companies, reflecting a clear national bias against small businesses. The importance of small businesses in this society is often overlooked and as a result underappreciated and -valued. For example, Fortune 500 companies have, over the past 40 years, slowly moved away from being major employers in this country. In 1960 they employed 15 percent of the American workforce. In 1970 this number increased to 21 percent. However, starting in the 1980s there was a steady and significant decline to 9 percent in 1995. Between 1985 and 1995, a total of five million workers were laid off (Smilor, 1996). In 1992, 53 percent of all private sector workers were employed in small businesses, and an additional 10 percent were self-employed (Starr, 1997).

Small businesses are widely considered to be the prime employers of the United States workforce. In fact, small businesses hire a majority of younger and older employees, including people of color (Starr, 1997). Since demographic patterns highlight the increased number of people of color, particularly youth, in the youth end of the labor force, small businesses increase in importance in any future of economic and community development initiatives. Thus, it is not hard to see why some advocates of small business view these institutions as this country's prime conduit between school and career.

Ellis (1992), although specifically addressing urban youth gangs, advocates the use of economic development approaches such as community-based business enterprises to help youth avoid gang membership and to revitalize communities in the process. The ability of society to effectively channel the energies of youth who are involved in criminal activities of various kinds not only saves the country enormous funds currently directed towards social programs and law enforcement, it also effectively takes what is widely considered a negative force and transforms it into a positive, and tax paying, force.

Any shortage of workers, particularly those well qualified, impacts most greatly on small and mid-sized businesses since they will have to compete with larger business for workers. These large businesses can pay higher wages, provide better fringe benefits, and offer greater opportunities for upward mobility within the company. Small businesses have accounted for two-thirds of the net new jobs (created jobs minus terminated jobs) in the United States since 1970. Small businesses have been defined by the Small Business Administration as firms employing 500 employees or fewer.

However, 90 percent of all small businesses employ fewer than 20 employees (Slaughter, 1996). Slaughter (1996, p. 4) comments on the forces at work in changing patterns of U.S. employment: "The pressures of global competition combined with the long-awaited realization of productivity improvements from computer, telecommunications, and organization development technologies have resulted in a fundamental restructuring of corporate America during the last 20 years. An entirely new jargon of terms such as *downsizing*, *re-engineering*, *right-sizing*, *flat organizations*, *self-directed work teams*, *telecommuting*, and *videoconferencing* describe a major shift in employment patterns in America."

One of these new terms is *lifestyle entrepreneurs*. Smilor (1996) coined the term *lifestyle entrepreneurs* to describe ventures that are essential to a community's well-being. Smilor (1996) does not like the term *small business* because it does not capture the "fight for survival, the innovation, or dynamism" that is part of any enterprise. Lifestyle entrepreneurs need to customize their ventures to the communities within which they are located. Finding their niche requires in-depth understanding of the customer's needs and the most efficient and culturally based methods for reaching them. The term *lifestyle entrepreneur*, as a result, does much to capture the excitement and spirit of adventure associated with enterprise development. According to Smilor (1996), it does so much more effectively than the term *small business owner.*

COMMUNITIES OF COLOR AND SMALL BUSINESS DEVELOPMENT

There has been an expanding body of literature and research focusing on ethnic/racial groups and the opportunities for upward mobility through small business development (Fawcett & Gardner, 1994; Sarason & Koberg, 1994). This literature has been both positive and critical of the potential of entrepreneurship for helping to transform socially and economically marginalized urban communities in this country. The importance of small businesses to urban communities is borne out by the creation of business incubators providing assistance to population groups that have historically not been business owners. Incubators not only provide space for new enterprises, they also provide a supportive environment to increase the likelihood of these businesses succeeding.

The concept of business incubation in the United States has its roots in the 1980s, when government agencies, most notably the federal government's Small Business Administration, funded incubators (Brown, 1998). Incubators serve vital roles within marginalized urban communities by creating jobs, providing technical assistance and funding, creating products and services that meet local needs, and just as importantly, serving as a catalyst for strengthening local economies. The case example of Food from the 'Hood, which will be addressed in chapter 8, illustrates the attractiveness of incubators. This social youth enterprise moved from the school (Crenshaw High School, Los Angeles) to an incubator because of the technical and financial support it would be eligible for by moving into the community.

Advocates of small business stress that inner cities can support well thought out indigenous-based enterprises and in the process employ residents in these initiatives. Unfortunately, the absence of potential role models for youth of color to imitate or have to access to for advice is a major barrier to having more businesses started by youth (Matthews, 1995; Walstad & Kourilsky, 1998). Gender may also play a significant role, with males coming from family backgrounds in small businesses being more likely than female counterparts to start or work in small businesses (Matthews, 1995). Youth who have parents or other close relatives who own small businesses are at an obvious advantage over those who do not. For example, they have the vantage point of seeing up close the trials and tribulations associated with enterprise creation and maintenance and have ready access to advice. Further, learning about enterprises occurs in a very natural state of everyday conversation with people they both know and respect.

Having more small businesses owned by adults of color will serve as a natural impetus for youth to follow. According to the U.S. Census Bureau, there were slightly over three million small business firms owned by people of color in the United States in 1997, or 14.6 percent of all small businesses. Latinos, among groups of color, accounted for 39.5 percent of the small businesses followed by Asian and Pacific Islanders (30 percent), African American (27.1 percent), and Native Americans and Alaska Natives (6.5 percent). Although the period from 1987 to 1992 witnessed a significant increase in the number of African/Black American owned businesses (424,165 to 620,912), an increase of 46 percent, or almost double that of white, non-Latino businesses, these businesses were still small in size. These businesses accounted for approximately 1 percent of all sales and receipts (Walstad et al., 1998). The vast majority of African/Black American businesses did not have employees (90 percent), further highlighting the need for these businesses to expand in size to employ workers, preferably from the community they serve.

Gittell and Thompson (1999) argue that thriving small businesses within marginalized communities are a prerequisite for normal life within these areas. Resident access to merchant establishment is a vital part of any community life, and failure to have a wide range of small businesses impacts the quality of life within the community and effectively shuts out a valuable source of employment for local residents. Marginalized communities are often isolated from major retail and entertainment centers in a city and have limited access to public transportation. This geographical isolation reinforces the need for these communities to have businesses within their borders. Small businesses are often in a strategic position within the community to launch innovative products and services, not to mention innovative employment for residents, and to do so in the primary language of the residents in cases where it is not English.

Small businesses within urban communities, for example, are in a propitious position to better understand the need for services and products and, as a result, can successfully develop marketing plans that are culture-specific to the community (Phillip, 1995). Useem's (1996) description of how the Amish people have succeeded in small businesses while concomitantly rejecting technology and self-advancement is an excellent example of how culture can play an important role within a community. This emphasis on better understanding the cultural context has been extensively addressed in the human service field and literature. However, this concept is relatively new to the business and entrepreneurial fields.

Small businesses owned by people of color, for example, are more likely to hire employees of color than small businesses within the same locale owned by white, non-Latinos (Bates, 1997). These businesses effectively serve multiple roles within their respective communities. The money they generate serves to pay local residents, purchase supplies from local businesses, and rent local space, and ultimately bank locally. It is estimated that inner cities across the United States possess more than $85 billion in annual retail spending power, or almost 7 percent of total retail spending in the United States.

Urban communities possess the basic ingredients for launching successful business ventures—availability of workers, concentration of consumers, knowledge of consumer profiles and needs, access to highways, and proximity to downtown businesses (Goff, 1996; Lehrer, 1999). The challenge becomes to direct this economic power toward serving the needs of residents by residents and maximizing the circulation of money within the community whenever possible (Mayo & Ramsden, 2001). This economic power does not rest solely with one or two age groups within a community. It is necessary to consider the needs and purchasing power of all age groups to increase the likelihood of a venture succeeding.

Development of enterprises and, more specifically, those that are social may be one way of creating wealth in marginalized urban communities of color. In 1999, for example, almost two-thirds of African American households in this country held zero assets or were in debt (Malveaux, 1999). Creation of wealth is impossible when making minimum wage. Consequently, strategies that can both create employment and wealth are very much needed within urban communities of color in the United States.

Butler (1995) has quite astutely noted that from an historical perspective, measurement of economic success in the United States has generally been based on white Europeans standards. European immigrants historically started at the bottom of the economic ladder and eventually, over a period of time and several generations, moved up this ladder. African Americans, and for that matter, Native Americans and other groups of color, do not follow this pattern. The introduction of skin pigmentation as a critical factor requires the development of a different career path for groups of color in this country. This social history necessitates creating economic self-help initiatives as means to overcome a hostile social environment and gaining an understanding that what worked for one ethnic or racial group may not necessarily apply to others.

Light and Rosenstein (1995) note that there is great potential for entrepreneurship in urban communities of color and argue that, although difficult and requiring long hours, self-employment efforts must play an influential role in any urban development strategy in this country. Bonacich and Modell (1980) analyzed the economic success of Japanese people on the West Coast and concluded that they were successful by concentrating on small business enterprises. Zhou and Bankston (1998) concluded that Chinese and Korean immigrants emphasized the importance of small enterprises and, as a result, achieved at a far higher rate than Vietnamese people who immigrated during the same time period.

Bates (1997), in turn, argues that self-employment is limited to only a select group within marginalized communities and, as a result, will be of limited importance in dramatically changing the socioeconomic character of communities, even if these businesses are a prime source of employment for local residents. Finally, Waldinger, Aldrich, and Ward (1990) argue that the highly concentrated nature of communities of color in the United States lends itself to the creation of businesses to support them. These businesses, in turn, not only meet expressive and instrumental needs of residents but also provide them with an avenue for self-sufficiency even though English language skills may be limited.

I (Delgado, 1999) bring a different perspective to the role of small businesses within urban communities of color. These small businesses do provide access to goods and services for groups of individuals who either do not feel comfortable or are not able to leave their communities to conduct business. Language and cultural barriers, particularly in the case of newcomers to this country, may be quite significant. Indigenous-owned businesses, however, can provide a wide range of services that typically are not provided in businesses owned by outsiders. The concept of nontraditional setting brings in a social service dimension to these businesses.

Nontraditional settings are places within a community where residents either shop for services or goods, or simply congregate. However, in the process of conducting business, for example, they also receive assistance with a wide range of social service needs such as translation of materials and letters, advocacy, credit, and information/referrals for local social services. Small businesses, as a result, become very important within these communities because of the social role they perform to help residents. The lack of these businesses further isolates residents within this society and has dramatic, long-term consequences for social and economic mobility.

THE PROMISE AND PITFALLS OF VOCATIONAL EDUCATION

Vocational education has a long history in this county. Major federal shaping of vocational education can be traced to passage of the Smith-Hughes Act of 1917, and its purpose was to prepare youth for jobs resulting from the Industrial Revolution. Vocational education served to provide an alternative to the general education found in public schools of the day (Lynch, 2000). Eventually, vocational education evolved to include a wide variety of subjects such as agriculture, trades and industry, and home economics.

Vocational education has seen periods in U.S. history when it was in vogue and had wide public support and when it was out of fashion. In 1990 Congress decreed that federal funds for vocational education must be spent on programs that specifically integrated academic and vocational education. Stern, Stone, Hopkins, McMillion, and Crain (1994, p. 53) attribute this goal to the hope "that such integration will improve vocational instruction by raising the level of academic skill and knowledge involved and at the same time improve academic instruction by demonstrating more practical application."

The 1990s not unexpectedly witnessed a resurgence of interest in this form of education, and this has resulted in states looking at vocational education as a viable alternative for non- college-bound students. Seventy percent of 39 states surveyed reported an increase in vocational education funding (Husain, 1999). This renewed interest has brought with it a need to reexamine how vocational education must better prepare youth for careers in the twenty-first century.

There is concern, however, about the role of vocational education in this country. These educational programs have historically been viewed as dumping grounds for academically weak students (Lerman, 2000). Other concerns focus on how school-based vocational education programs teach skills that can become outdated, seriously limiting the opportunities these students have for entry into highly competitive fields. Lerman (2000, p. 9) notes: "Too often, the offerings in school-based vocational education programs depend less on market demands than on available teachers, materials, and frequently outdated equipment." Failing to effectively prepare students for future careers brings unprecedented challenges for society to undo the wrong and the social and economic costs associated with missed opportunities.

The diverting of students from academic preparation to the almost total focus on vocational preparation, or tracking, is widely considered to be discrimination toward youth of color from low economic backgrounds. The strategy of integrating vocational and academic tracts or pathways has gained in popularity. Use of internships, school-based enterprises, volunteering, job shadowing, service learning, summer youth component programs, and career magnet programs have been found to increase the self-confidence of youth of color in acquiring skills that lead to college enrollment (Lerman, 2000).

Lakes's (1996b, p. 67) vision for vocational education is quite innovative and places this form of education within a community economic development perspective. Using an entrepreneurial approach provides school systems with a vehicle for accomplishing this goal: "What chances do urban youths have for meaningful job prospects in their local communities of color? I offer an alternative perspective: Enhance the transition management for low-income youths through entrepreneurial ventures. In other words, entrepreneurship education is a vehicle by which to stimulate job creation as well as promote community building in urban areas."

Unfortunately, few educational reformers have taken this perspective to school-to-career programs and, in not doing so, have missed an excellent opportunity to influence the lives of countless youth, their families, and ultimately their communities (Smith & Rojewski, 1993). The absence of discussions in this area may well be the result of institutional bias toward youth of color. They may not be seen as entrepreneurial material. Instead, they may well be thought of as low-level workers who are not capable of starting and sustaining businesses that are legal in nature.

CONCLUSION

Predicting the future is often best left for those who are psychic, fearless, or foolish. No one can predict the future, although one would not guess this based upon the countless numbers of individuals seeking to do so. However, it is possible to increase the likelihood of accuracy in predicting the future. Transition from school-to-career is fraught with challenges and obstacles for all youth (National Employer Leadership Council, 1994). Nevertheless, these same challenges and obstacles can be turned into possibilities and rewards for youth if the right paradigm is used to reach them and the activities developed are faithful to the goals of the paradigm. True, one paradigm may not fit all. However, a carefully selected paradigm and attention to details in developing accompanying strategies, activities, and tactics can reach many youth.

It would be a grave mistake to put the onus of successful youth transition from school-to-career solely on the nation's education system, however (Hamilton et al., 1997, p. 690): "The growing disparity between the well-educated affluent and the inadequately educated who struggle to maintain a decent standard must be reduced if the United States is to remain a prosperous and secure democracy. Education cannot reduce that disparity without complementary changes in the economy, particularly the labor market. But education—in the form of the school-to-work initiative, and especially work-based learning—is a powerful means of improving knowledge and skills of the American workforce, which is, after all, most of our citizens."

This chapter has provided the reader with a broad overview and understanding of what it takes for youth to make a successful transition to adulthood and the world of career. Ensuring a high degree of success will require a comprehensive and concerted effort that will result in solidifying existing partnerships and creating new partnerships. Transition from school-to-career on the part of marginalized youth is not a local or state issue; it is national in scope, requiring national responses similar in nature to national defense. This country's defense or economy is not local in character nor should the future of youth be localized. There is national attention focused on youth transition on the part of government, corporations, and foundations. Nothing short of this will succeed in our efforts to reach youth.

The importance of small businesses within marginalized urban communities across the United States has generally been overlooked by government and community-based organizations. Small businesses fulfill a variety of critical functions within the community that are economic, social, and political in character; their absence seriously undermines the basic fabric of the community. In addition, small businesses provide residents with opportunities to become self-employed and employ local residents who may not be considered an attractive workforce to the external community. Small businesses, however, are generally not capital intensive but are labor intensive, and this can be both an advantage and disadvantage for start-up enterprises. Walstad, a researcher in the entrepreneurial field, stated quite eloquently why youth must be a part of enterprises (Phillps, 1999, p. 2): "We find America's youth to be optimistic about the prospects of starting a business. If we lose the opportunity for them to succeed, we could lose ideas that would benefit consumers and philanthropic contributions to communities. Entrepreneurial dreams are continually challenged or lost because of a failure to recognize the most powerful future entrepreneurial reservoir—our youth."

CHAPTER 6

Entrepreneurship: The Foundation for Social Youth Entrepreneurship

INTRODUCTION

The subject of entrepreneurship has certainly received its share of attention in the nation's media, business, and higher education sectors in the 1990s and early 2000s. It is not unusual to see the prefix of *promise, future of, spirit of,* and *potential of* in front of *entrepreneurship* to describe this nation's fascination with this perspective toward business creation (Frumkin & Kim, 2000). Further, increasingly, terms such as *venture philanthropy, investment,* and *social return on investment,* or *SROI,* are finding their way into the human service literature and foundation funding initiatives. The emergence of these terms signifies a dramatic shift in thinking about how services that have social goals are conceptualized, staffed, and funded in the field.

Recent demographic statistics show how this country is both graying and browning at the same time with profound implications for the country as a whole (Blank, 2001; Camarillo & Bonilla, 2001; Nakanishi, 2001; Sandefur, Martin, Eggerling-Boeck, Mannon & Meier, 2001; Thorton, 2001; Zhou, 2001). Much attention has been paid to the subject of aging with its implications for the social security system and for a workforce that will be relatively young supporting a population age group that will live longer. An increasingly aging population will need increasing numbers of younger workers supporting the social security system and willing to invest in a system that by many accounts will be bankrupted by the time these workers get to retirement age.

The browning of the United States, in turn, highlights how the racial and ethnic composition of the country will transform communities and the career force across the nation. This demographic trend further reinforces the importance of youth of color as entrepreneurs and their meaningful participation in this country's workforce of the future (Bouvier & Grant, 1994; Murdock, 1995; LaGreca, 2000; Sum et al., 1997). Increased joblessness, or limited access to careers, for people of color increases the attractiveness of entrepreneurship initiatives (Phillip, 1995). These trends highlight the importance of concerted strategic efforts at preparing youth for the world of career and the potential return of investment for the nation.

Initiatives that actively reach out to create partnerships and coalitions where youth act as central players offer the greatest potential for dramatic individual and social transformation in communities across the country and internationally (Bornstein, 1999; Canadian Centre for Social Entrepreneurship, 2001; Mariani, 1994). Social youth entrepreneurship, I believe, has this potential. However, before the reader can fully appreciate this perspective, it is necessary to understand the roots of social youth entrepreneurship. These roots have origins in both economic and social spheres, with the latter more specifically focused on entrepreneurship, a field that is receiving a tremendous amount of attention in the nation's academic institutions. The introduction of a social purpose to enterprise requires a working knowledge of the language, concepts, and values that these two different worlds subscribe to in order to merge them into a coherent and cogent initiative.

ENTREPRENEURSHIP

Smilor (1996) rightfully argues that it would be very foolish to think of entrepreneurship simply as an economic phenomenon with a narrow focus on job creation. Entrepreneurship, like any other social construct, can be defined and operationalized along a wide variety of dimensions depending upon the discipline and goals used to guide this endeavor. It can be very narrow in scope or very broad, encompassing multiple arenas not normally considered a part of entrepreneurship. This flexibility in conceptualization can be exciting or overwhelming depending upon the practitioner and his or her organization.

Its potential for transformation goes far beyond that narrow arena. Its reach can easily be conceptualized as a catalyst for community health and well-being by creating a group of social change agents that use the economic power of entrepreneurship as a vehicle for achieving social goals. The emergence of entrepreneurial initiatives is very broad in appeal and goes far beyond this nation's borders. In 1993 the General Assembly of the United Nations passed a unanimous resolution supporting the use of entrepreneurship as a significant social and economic vehicle for increasing living standards throughout the world (Slaughter, 1996). Reynolds, Hay, and Camp (1999) report that entrepreneurship as an economic strategy is now center stage in most countries around the world. However, the United States provides the greatest and most widespread examples of entrepreneurship.

Needless to say, there is no established or widely accepted definition of entrepreneurship, and there may never be one (Bornstein, 1999; Caird, 1992; Canadian Centre for Social Entrepreneurship, 2001; National Center for Social Entrepreneurs, 2001). Entrepreneurship, as already noted earlier in this book, is the act or process of creating a new venture by taking advantage of previously unrecognized profit opportunities (Bygrave & Minniti, 2000; Dees, 1998; Gartner, 1988; Kouriloff, 2000; Drueger & Brazeal, 1994). Active engagement in pursuit of an enterprise can be an effective vehicle for providing hope for a future for many youth, particularly those who are marginalized (Smilor, 1996 p. 8): "Entrepreneurship holds a secret weapon against apathy and anger. It presents an ace in the hole for anyone who wants to build community. Entrepreneurs are inveterate optimists! They usually don't know what they can't do. This optimism, this belief in the possible, is a remarkably potent resource for building community."

Chigunta (2002, p. v), in turn, defines youth entrepreneurship as the "practical application of enterprising qualities, such as initiative, innovation, creativity, and risk-taking into the work environment (either in self-employment or employment in small start-up firms), using the appropriate skills necessary for success in that environment and culture." Chigunta's definition grounds entrepreneurship within a learning context for youth.

Entrepreneurship as a field of study draws upon a multidisciplinary group of scholars such as economists, psychologists, and sociologists (Amit, Glosten, & Muller, 1993; Kouriloff, 2000). Entrepreneurship, as a result, can be studied from a variety of perspectives and frameworks depending upon the lenses of the researcher (Aldrich & Baker, 1997; Terpstra & Olson, 1993). Its broad appeal maximizes its potential for being embraced by a variety of professions, funding sources, and levels of government. This broad appeal increases the likelihood of entrepreneurship receiving important attention from scholars and practitioners alike.

Kouriloff (2000), for example, relies upon a behavioral perspective to develop a classification of entrepreneurs that expands the different types from a developmental point of view: (1) potential (individuals who have thought about the virtues of starting an enterprise but have not acted upon these thoughts); (2) intending (individuals who have taken requisite steps in actualization of their goals but have not been able to actually start an enterprise as a result of a variety of factors such as inopportune timing, lack of adequate funding, etc.); (3) actual entrepreneurs (these individuals have realized their goals and are actually engaging in the carrying out of their business); and (4) no wish to start a business (these individuals either do not aspire to start an enterprise or believe that the obstacles are too great to overcome). Kouriloff's developmental classification helps the field ascertain the needs and supports each type of entrepreneur requires in order to develop a viable business.

Bygrave and Minniti (2000, p. 26), in turn, bring an ecological perspective to entrepreneurship and expand the reach and influence of entrepreneurial initiatives: "The entrepreneur is someone capable of enhancing the production possibility of the economy and, by doing so, of creating opportunities for other entrepreneurs. . . . In other words, we suggest that every time an entrepreneur sizes a new product or service, that creates the opportunity of complementary products or services and generates new entrepreneurial opportunities." The ecological perspective, as already noted in chapter 5 in examining school-to-career transition, places tremendous emphasis on a multidisciplinary approach to studying the factors that facilitate or hinder enterprise development.

Stern et al. (1994), for example, provide numerous case examples where a youth enterprise provided a service or product previously unavailable within the community, served as a catalyst for expanding a local market, or resulted in an established businesses entering into partnership with youth. These examples stress the point that an endless number of possibilities for enterprise creation exist within every community regardless of the socioeconomic composition of its residents. These opportunities are just waiting for the right entrepreneur to come along.

Finally, entrepreneurs who are successful at the community level also encourage others to try their hands at business development that may not necessarily be complementary. In essence, role modeling occurs. Entrepreneurs can be thought of as catalysts of economic activity for a nation's economic growth. When this activity transpires within marginalized communities, it can lead to economic growth within the community and serve as potential employment sources for residents who for a variety of reasons are out of the labor force.

Chigunta (2002, p. v) identified eight key benefits of promoting entrepreneurship for youth: "(1) Creating employment opportunities for both the self-employed youth and other young people. (2) Bringing back the alienated and marginalized youth into the economic mainstream. (3) Helping address some of the sociopsychological problems and delinquency that arise from joblessness. (4) Promoting innovation and resilience in youth. (5) Promoting the revitalization of the local community. (6). Young entrepreneurs may be particularly responsive to new economic opportunities and trends. (7) YREs give young people, especially marginalized youth, a sense of meaning and belonging. (8) Enterprise helps young women and men develop new skills and experiences that can be applied to many other challenges in life." Chigunta's assessment of the benefits of youth entrepreneurship goes beyond individuals to include their community and society.

A review of the literature on entrepreneurship will highlight the importance of social relationships for accessing resources (capital and human), information, and social support (Smilor, 1996). Reingold's (1999) research on the social networks and the employment problems of the urban poor found that residents encounter a labor market that is organized to a certain degree by their networks of social relations. Residents with higher levels of formal education do not have to rely solely on word of mouth and can access more formal sources for employment.

Social relationships in enterprise development and maintenance have only increased in importance in this age of information. These skills are sometimes referred to as soft, but their importance is not diminished in the world of customer service and satisfaction. In essence, the context in which an enterprise is launched is not just about timing or history; it is also about the right social network being in place to increase the likelihood of success occurring; the wider the social network the higher the likelihood of success.

Entrepreneurship can and must be closely tied to community development. However, it is essential to conceptualize community development, or to use the term I prefer, *enhancement of community capacity*, as encompassing both people and institutional capital. All too often the term *community development* is narrowly defined and applied to bricks and mortar. Smilor (undated) focuses on the social impact of successful enterprises. Entrepreneurship can create social value and be a key ingredient for achieving community development. There is a myth that low-income urban communities of color have no entrepreneurs or the potential to develop entrepreneurs. This is a myth rather than a reality!

Youth-driven entrepreneurial activities can fulfill a variety of educational goals by teaching youth academic subjects resulting in educational benefits (Carroll et al., 1991; Mariani, 1994; Paquin, 1991). These academic subjects, however, are very often disguised as concrete activities and tasks that require competencies in math, science, and language arts. Learning, in effect, can be meaningful and fun without being stigmatizing to the learner. Many marginalized youth have effectively turned their back on learning because of a history of negative experiences within formal educational settings. This does not mean, however, that they are unreachable. It does mean that reaching them will be challenging and that new methods of instruction will be needed.

Contrary to popular opinion, there is no ideal age group to start teaching entrepreneurial process. Maselow (1995) argues that it should start with elementary school children developing an understanding of economics. Lobsenz (1991), in turn, advocates for 1 to 21 year olds being the prime target for entrepreneurial education. Entrepreneurial education has been advocated for the gifted and talented (Mann, 1992), as well as for those with special needs (Ketcham, Taylor, & Hoffman, 1990). Entrepreneurial education can easily be modified to take into account the developmental stage of youth and their intellectual and physical challenges. It is also sufficiently flexible to take into account a wide range of goals and local circumstances. Stern et al. (1994) identifies such benefits as applying and extending knowledge from the classroom, problem solving, developing social competencies, and achieving economic rewards.

Entrepreneurial activities can also result in important social benefits for youth and their communities, such as reduced risk for dropping out of high school; a positive profile of youth within the community; identification of potential, current and future leaders; concern for the importance of a quality service or good; providing a community with an opportunity to be a part of a new business venture that is owned and operated by residents (Klein, 1998; *Los Angeles Times*, 1998). A community service dimension to a youth-driven enterprise makes distinct the transformation of a youth enterprise into a social youth enterprise.

Enterprise creation is never simple and invariably must surmount numerous obstacles and barriers before success can be achieved and sustained. Kouriloff's (2000) meta-analysis of the literature on what has been studied pertaining to barriers for enterprise creation identifies six characteristics or factors that can be present and seriously considered by anyone wishing to engage in enterprise development: (1) range of barriers (sociocultural, psychological, political, economic) concomitantly affect proclivities and competencies to engage in enterprise creation; (2) intensity of barriers can be conceptualized along a continuum with minimal to absolute influence; (3) domain-specific barriers such as culture, politics, and levels of economic development can significantly facilitate or hinder enterprise creation; (4) invisible barriers are conditions in the environment that impede development of certain types of enterprises or do not create a climate where potential entrepreneurs see themselves in this role; (5) combination of barriers are a reality since it is rare to find only one barrier active in preventing the start-up of an enterprise; and (6) sequential order of barriers determines the likelihood of a venture's success since formidable barriers encountered at the start-up phase will wield greater influence on outcome than when encountered at a latter stage of an enterprise's life.

The above listing of barriers is quite extensive in scope and highlights the multitude of challenges associated with enterprise development. Navigation around these barriers necessitates the development of strategic and comprehensive plans of action to complement the competencies of the entrepreneur. Ultimate success will ultimately be based upon the interplay of numerous individual and environmental factors. This success will need to be measured along a variety of dimensions, as in the case of social entrepreneurship, one of which is profit. Profit, nevertheless, is a very narrow but important and widely acknowledged measure of success.

Engaging in an entrepreneurial initiative can be thought of as egalitarian— entrepreneurs do not require diplomas, degrees, or special certification. Entrepreneurs, however, do require passion, optimism, and a willingness to work hard and long hours (Smilor, 1996). Tragedies, for example, can lead to creation of new enterprises as noted in the case of Roberto Alfaro of the Mission District, San Francisco (Smilor, undated, p. 4):

Latinismo uses its T-shirt business to create bridges of understanding among Hispanic gangs that terrorize their community. Alfaro said he started with T-shirts because, "T-shirts were kind of the closest thing, because we already knew how to make T-shirts;

we already had a few connections . . . so we just started with that." Their designs focus on peace in the gang communities, they've seen too much violence. "Everybody in here has friends who have died, someone who's been hurt in some way or another." The company is not only about selling T-shirts, it's about promoting understanding. "People won't take the time to listen to people, but if you only take the time and effort to understand somebody, you see a whole different picture."

There is a consensus that enterprises are more likely to succeed when highly qualified individuals who share a similar vision and mission staff them. Sharing similar values, however, is the foundation for all other aspects of entrepreneurship (Slaughter, undated). Success of enterprises can be arduous to measure at times (Smilor, 1996, p. 2): "The ultimate destiny of any start-up company is difficult if not impossible to predict. Apparent winners sometimes lose; and certain losers sometimes win. Consequently, the entrepreneurial process can appear to be chaotic, complicated, and disorderly and thus hard to understand, influence, nurture, and support. . . . The entrepreneurial process revolves around four key factors: talent, opportunity, capital, and know-how. By understanding the forces behind these factors and by seeing how they relate to one another, it is possible to identify ways to support and accelerate the entrepreneurial process and thus provide not only economic but also social values to communities."

YOUTH RECEPTIVITY TO ENTREPRENEURSHIP

The reader may well ask what are the thoughts of youth themselves about engaging in learning about youth-driven entrepreneurship? The answer to that question is critical if a youth development perspective is to be applied to youth enterprises. If youth are not interested in establishing enterprises or believe that they do not possess the competencies to do so, then this strategy for youth and community development is doomed to fail. In essence, enterprise development may well be an adult concept and activity that does not transfer well to youth.

Walstad and Kourilsky (1998), in a rare study of black youth entrepreneurial attitudes and knowledge, found a strong interest in entrepreneurship. Kourilsky and Esfandiari (1997) report on the findings of a Gallup Poll focused on African American high school students' attitudes and knowledge of entrepreneurship. Among other findings suggesting the promise of entrepreneurship education (84 percent believe that there should be more entrepreneurship education in high schools), 75 percent want to start a business of their own, and 80 percent believe it is very important for entrepreneurs to give something back to the community.

Another Gallup Poll conducted in 1994 that focused on high school students in general found results similar to those of the 1995 Gallup Poll on African American youth (Kourilsky, 1995). The majority of those youth (70 percent) wanted to start their own businesses, compared to 75 percent of African American youth, and 68 percent believed it was their obligation to give back to their community, compared to 80 percent of African American youth.

A 1999 survey of 14 to 19 year olds by the Kauffman Foundation found that 60 percent of females, 7 percent of Latinos, and 80 percent of African American youth were very interested in starting a business of their own (Phillips, 1999). However, only approximately 25 percent of these students had taken a course in business or entrepreneurship in high school. A large majority of the adolescents surveyed reported having minimal or no exposure in high school to how business or the economy functions. In a corresponding survey of teachers, only 20 percent indicated having taken a college-level (undergraduate or graduate) course in small business or entrepreneurship.

The results of the surveys reported above serve as important indicators of the potential of youth enterprises, particularly when grounded within a social context, for actively engaging youth in pursuit of an education. This education requires youth to play an active and meaningful role in shaping it and determining how to measure the ultimate success of their experiences. This student-focused approach holds great promise and ties well into many key youth development principles.

Panayiotopoulos and Gerry's (1997) international survey of government-sponsored small enterprises targeting youth highlights both the success of these ventures and the challenges that lie ahead in using youth entrepreneurship as an intervention in individual and community development. The importance of start-up capital in helping youth create their enterprises was one of the most frequently listed concerns from the field. However, in spite of numerous challenges and obstacles, there was no lack of desire or initiative to start enterprises. This positive attitude can wield a tremendous amount of influence in shaping schools and their views of their mission in society.

EDUCATIONAL PREPARATION

There is general acknowledgment that entrepreneurial education in the nation's schools is generally either missing or seriously deficient (Kourilisky & Walstad, 2000). This glaring barrier must be successfully addressed if youth enterprises are to constitute a significant activity in preparing youth for the world of career and for educators to use this perspective to help teach valuable content matter. Addressing these limitations, however, can be challenging at a variety of levels, ranging from curriculum revamping to teacher preparation.

Kourilsky and Esfandiari (1997) found that, if available, entrepreneurial education could effectively serve as an intervention for providing youth of color with the requisite intellectual and affective resources for achieving socioeconomic gains. The teaching of any form of entrepreneurship, including social, requires that new arenas and methods be created and utilized. Conventional methods and approaches to instruction, such as classroom focused, are widely acknowledged to be required in preparing entrepreneurs in this century. This form of business practice necessitates thinking out of the box and having the competencies to plan and implement innovative businesses and business strategies.

The Private/Public Ventures organization (2000) identified three trends that will influence social policy towards youth well into the twenty-first century, with particular relevance for those who are currently marginalized within this society: (1) the number of adolescents will increase dramatically in the United States in the not-too-distant future, and this country will have the most teens since the 1970s; (2) the growing number of high-profile crime events involving schools will continue; and (3) the emergence of a new global economy will necessitate more demanding competencies on the part of adolescents entering the workforce. The influences of the first and third trends stand out in shaping social youth entrepreneurship. These trends, incidentally, can be expected to continue well into the twenty-first century.

The importance of what has been referred to as contextualized education and informal education provides two conceptual approaches that are complementary in nature and from which to examine career- and workforce-related factors, such as the changing nature of the world of work. Contextualized education focuses on the development of curriculum content and pedagogical processes that increase the relevance of education for youth and facilitate transition from school to career (Charner, 1996). Informal education, in turn, refers to the learning that occurs as part of being involved in youth and community organizations. The ability of educators to ground education within the operative reality youth face increases the likelihood of educational outcomes with real meaning for the student.

Shannon (1992, p. 1), in critiquing public education, puts forth an agenda that emphasizes an active linkage between schools and the real world: "Most people today agree that deficient public education is a root cause of the nation's social and economic problems. Most also blame teachers and schools. I agree about education's deficiencies but do not blame teachers and schools. I'm convinced that the fundamental problem with public education is that *our schools are divorced from their communities; education is divorced from everyday life.* Americans are arguing over abstractions like restructuring, choice, and equity, but what I believe education needs most is a hands-on link to the 'real world.' "

The learning that goes on in daily life represents the sum of all forms of learning and increases the relevance of the lessons learned—classroom based as well as life experiences. Learning related to academic subjects, for example, can transpire in a classroom within a school setting and as part of a community activity such as mural painting (math, chemistry, etc.) or planting a community garden (botany). This form of learning is just as valuable, and some would argue that it is even more so, than formal learning within a school. Internships, apprenticeships, and field trips bring informal learning into a school, for example.

Slaughter (1996) advocates the position that current pedagogy emphasizes the existence of a right answer, which is counter to what is found in successful entrepreneurial settings—there are multiple right answers. This state of affairs gives preference to using a process that encourages multiple perspectives or voices to be heard in finding solutions to presenting problems and challenges. Experimentation, as a result, is encouraged and fostered for team members. Not being tied to one answer gives students liberty to problem solve the best answer. The overemphasis on one answer is counter to what is typically found in real life (Prestegard, 1997).

CONCLUSION

The reader no doubt recognizes how a series of factors or forces have converged to create a situation that lends itself to youth becoming social entrepreneurs. Demographics and social conditions, such as poor schooling and limited career opportunities for those with limited competencies, can lead to an explosive condition in this country, as witnessed by the history of urban unrest and riots. These events are rarely the result of one incident and can only be fully understood when examined within an historical perspective. This perspective, in turn, necessitates a series of multifaceted viewpoints to appreciate how social, economic, political, and cultural factors interacted to cause an event.

The importance of economic well-being is well understood by all in this society. Economic well-being invariably means having access to careers that hold promise for advancement and that pay a livable salary. These careers translate into families and communities being transformed as a result of the stability of employment, a willingness to invest in the future and postpone immediate gratification, improved schools, and creation of a sense of community. The so-called disintegration of inner-city families and communities can never be traced to just one force or element. However, lack of access to viable employment stands out as a key factor in any form of social analysis and development of social-based interventions.

The future is here and now, and there is no way of going back to the good old days. Those days were never good for marginalized people and communities. The very idea of a nonprofit social agency engaging in for-profit activities is widely accepted in today's world (Brinckeroff, 2000, p. 18): "In 2000, the idea of a not-for-profit making money is quite widely accepted. The idea of a 501 (c) (3) as a not-for-profit business no longer draws gasps of dismay, but rather almost universal nods of agreement, if not yawns of boredom, it's old news."

CHAPTER 7

Social Youth Entrepreneurship: Definition, Values, Goals, Elements, and Approaches/ Considerations

INTRODUCTION

The emergence of the term *social entrepreneurship* has helped to bring together what appeared to be very disparate parts or fields into a cohesive whole. The concept of social entrepreneurship has been around for approximately a decade. Dees (1998, p. 1), however, would argue that social entrepreneurs have been around for hundreds of years: "The language of social entrepreneurship may be new, but the phenomenon is not. We have always had social entrepreneurs, even if we did not call them that. They originally built many of the institutions we now take for granted. However, the new name is important in that it implies a blurring of sector boundaries."

Social enterprises, as this chapter will address, are businesses that trade in the market to achieve social aims and do so by brokering people and communities for social and economic gain (Social Enterprise London, 2001). Some advocates would call these enterprises *market capitalism with a social conscience*. The arrival of the twenty-first century, in combination with a continued and distinctive shift to a global economy, has provided a context for the emergence of innovative practice that transcends sectors. Social entrepreneurship, including social youth entrepreneurship, has developed in response to the opportunities available in this changing context.

Social entrepreneurship, unlike its entrepreneurial counterpart, does not seek to generate earnings for the entrepreneur and his or her family as a central goal. Social entrepreneurship is not focused on creating an income; it is focused on generating wealth with a social goal in mind. One youth stated this combination of goals quite well (Shaw, 2001, p. B1): "We want to create things that serve a social need, and also pay for themselves." These types of enterprises also seek to create employment and bring about change for the social good of the community (Shaw, 2001).

The *social* in *social entrepreneurship* effectively measures success far beyond what the typical entrepreneur would consider a goal—generation of capital, an income, or wealth. The lofty goals of social enterprises make this form of entrepreneurship far more significant than its counterparts that are focused solely on profits and the generation of wealth. The social enterprise Sugar and Spice brings these goals to life (Youth Venture, 2002, p. 28):

Ranya and Dominique of New York City launched Sugar and Spice, a chocolate lollipop catering business. The chocolates are sold for many types of occasions. The Venture also offers activities for young children and free social and educational events at local schools & youth organizations. The girls have planned workshops, for children 6–10 years old, which will provide an opportunity that offers an interactive demonstration of how to make the lollipops while practicing math and reading skills involved in the process.

Social entrepreneurship as an intervention strategy lends itself to working with marginalized populations, the homeless being but one type, as evidenced in initiatives funded by the Roberts Foundation in their Homeless Economic Development Fund (Emerson, 1996). The Delancy Street Foundation, a drug rehabilitation program based in San Francisco, with a high percentage of staff members with criminal justice backgrounds, is another example of social enterprise. Delancy Street operates a wide range of programs that are profit-centered; the cash generated in turn provides employment and training for program participants. Funding for these programs primarily comes from the generation of income from the businesses (Delgado, 2002).

The reader may initially respond to the concept of social youth entrepreneurs as junior capitalists in training. Although profit may play an important role in successful business development, it can coexist within a social and economic context that stresses community benefits, or what is referred to as social entrepreneurship. The centering of activities within social and economic goals effectively identifies these initiatives as social enterprises.

There is no denying that those of us in human services and education probably have a long distrust of the business sector and have countless numbers of horror stories to share pertaining to economic exploitation of marginalized groups by business enterprises in this and other countries. This bias, so to speak, can effectively serve as a significant barrier to many of us seriously considering social youth entrepreneurship as a vehicle for youth and community transformation. A failure to systematically examine and include the world of career within a youth development paradigm means that we have effectively narrowed the potential of this perspective to successfully transform youth, their communities, and this society.

The interconnectedness that results from social youth enterprises brings youth centrally into their own communities and does so in a manner that lends itself to creation of youth-adult partnerships and interactions that historically have not been present in this society. Boyd et al. (1997, p. 8) are quick to promote community revitalization through enterprise: "Outreach to children and families through, for example, assisting in the growth of social capital, bringing together the forces necessary to improve learning, bridging the gap between parents and educators is by no means incompatible with notions of community revitalization through enterprise and education." Collaboration between school, community, and youth themselves as prominent partners has a great deal of potential for achieving community revitalization and for investing in future leaders.

Indigenous-driven social enterprises initially are rarely started or sustained by one individual, at least generally not the ones that are successful. It is important to address the misconception that entrepreneurs do not require the assistance of a team to help them in carrying out their vision or dream. Invariably, countless numbers of other individuals are part of any given venture from the beginning. Entrepreneurs, however, have the ability to share their vision with others and convince them of the potential of these enterprises for profit as well as for social change. Nonprofit social agencies are facing an ever-increasing challenge to find new funding sources, and this need has served as an impetus for entering the commercial arena; the ventures must successfully leverage or replace old funding sources (Dees, 1998).

DEFINITION AND BOUNDARIES

As already noted, definitions are critically important when directed at social needs or problems. Not surprisingly, like the term *youth development*, there is considerable confusion surrounding the definition of the term *social entrepreneurship*, and although the concept is gaining popularity, it means different things to different people. Julian Dobson (1993, p. 1) compares defining social entrepreneurship to "a bit like nailing jelly, but however you describe it, it thrives on making unusual and inspired connections."

Social enterprise is one of a countless number of terms that have emerged over the past decade to describe business with a social conscience, or business with a heart. Some of the more common terms are *community business, social firms, social economy, social entrepreneurs, mission-based venture development*, and *community enterprises* (Brierton, 2001). Social entrepreneurship has also been labeled as the Third Way, not-for-profit and not the usual for-profit enterprise, with an emphasis on both social and economic rates of return (Canadian Centre for Social Entrepreneurship, 2001). The blurring of traditional boundaries and definitions of private, public, and voluntary sectors has led to the need for the creation of initiatives that can successfully transcend these historically distinct spheres of practice. Social entrepreneurship, in essence, is a blanket trend that seeks to capture a movement towards integrating business and social ethics and goals (Organisation for Economic Co-operation and Development, 2001).

Dees (1998, p. 4) defines social entrepreneurs as change agents in the social sector who engage in actions guided by a strong sense of public duty: "Adopting a mission to create and sustain social value (not just private value), recognizing and relentlessly pursuing new opportunities to serve that mission, engaging in a process of continuous innovation, adaptation, and learning, acting boldly without being limited by resources currently in hand, and exhibiting a heightened sense of accountability to the constituencies served for the outcomes created." Dees (1998, p. 3) goes on to note that: "Social entrepreneurs are one species in the genus entrepreneur. They are entrepreneurs with a social mission. However, because of this mission, they face some distinctive challenges and any definition ought to reflect this. For social entrepreneurs, the social mission is explicit and central. This obviously reflects how social entrepreneurs perceive and assess opportunities. Mission-related impact becomes the central criterion, not wealth creation. Wealth is just a means to an end for social entrepreneurs." Those social entrepreneurs that best exemplify the above actions best fit the model of social entrepreneurs. Some entrepreneurs may embrace only some of the above actions; consequently, it is best to think of these innovators on a continuum rather than in a dichotomy.

It would be selling youth short to strictly view them as a market or labor pool. Entrepreneurship is the dream of many and the reality of a few, youth as well as adults (Black, 2000). Youth have the potential to develop businesses, too. Lindner et al. (1998, p. 2) define youth entrepreneurship as "adolescents identifying opportunities, gathering resources, and exploiting these opportunities through action this process by working in nonstructured (for example, babysitting, yard work) and semistructured (such as paper courier, contract workers) work environments."

The Lindner and Cox definition encompasses a problem-solving perspective within a social and economic context. This context entails the creation of a service or product that is age-sensitive—namely, adolescence—and places youth in a position to dictate the enterprise being created and the market it targets. Youth, in essence, are empowered to create and shape the nature of their business. Dees (1998) and Lindner et al. (1998), in turn, broaden the nature of enterprise to include noncapital intensive businesses and place the community itself as the prime setting for the enterprise.

The entrepreneurial process is neither clear nor predictable (Smilor, 1997, p. 2): "The ultimate destiny of any start-up company is difficult if not impossible to predict. Apparent winners sometimes lose; and certain losers sometimes win! Consequently, the entrepreneurial process can appear to be chaotic, complicated, and disorderly, and thus hard to understand, influence, nurture, and support. But we actually know a lot about what causes companies to succeed and fail. There are recognizable patterns to how a company starts and grows. And there are factors that can be identified and developed to enhance the success of new and emerging ventures." Smilor (1997) identified four critical factors that encourage entrepreneurial efforts that provide economic and social values to communities—talents, opportunity, capital, and know-how.

Social Enterprise London (2001) also identified three key characteristics that must be present to make an enterprise social in nature: (1) enterprise oriented—it produces goods or services within a distinct market; (2) social aims—it has a commitment to community capacity building and is accountable to membership and the wider community; and (3) social ownership—it represents an autonomous organizational structure based upon democratic principles and distributes profits for the greater good of the community. The interplay of these characteristics is quite powerful from a community transformation perspective, particularly those urban communities that are socially and economically marginalized in this society.

AVENUES FOR STARTING AND SUSTAINING SOCIAL ENTERPRISES

There are a variety of institutional and noninstitutional (indigenous) avenues that can be pursued in order to start a social enterprise; some communities have had experiences with multiple approaches, yet other communities have had no experience with any type. For the purposes of clarity, this section will address each of these avenues as if there were no overlaps between them. However, in real life there may be a tremendous amount of overlap as evident in the following example (Klein, 1998, p. D2):

Pablo Cisneros, 17, is the first recipient of a loan from the Youth Enterprise Development Institute, a program that teaches young people from low-income communities how to start and operate their own businesses. . . . Pablo, the second-youngest of nine children, lives with his mother in the Pico Gardens housing project in Boyle Heights and serves as president of the Los Angeles Housing Authority's citywide youth council. He used his loan to open a sports-apparel business and says the mentors who have inspired him have been invaluable in getting his business off the ground. "The class was three hours every Saturday for 12 weeks. They had different instructors come in and talk to us in real-life terms. The part I liked best was on how to market ourselves. They told us not to just introduce ourselves but tell people how we could help them and how they could help us. Getting some older guys to give me advice and help me has really done a lot for me. These are guys who started their businesses out at the swap meet, and now they have real stores. . . . They promise to introduce me to some distributors who will give me good prices on merchandise, and they will go in with me on some deals so we can purchase merchandise in bulk and get lower prices. "

The case example of Pablo Cisneros illustrates the dynamic nature of enterprise development within low-income communities. Pablo had the benefit of a formalized training and loan program in addition to consultation with community residents. All these elements came together to direct his dream of owning a business within his community.

Institutional-Driven Social Enterprises

With little question, institutional-driven enterprise creation is probably the most common avenue used for social enterprise development. This finding in many ways should not come as any great surprise to the reader. The ready availability of expertise and resources to help start an enterprise can do wonders for creating them. Boschee (1995) divides institution-driven enterprise creation into two categories—affirmative businesses and direct-service businesses. Affirmative businesses provide jobs at competitive wages and offer career opportunities and ownership possibilities for people who are marginalized by this society. Affirmative businesses provide a product or service and actively seek to make their organizations economically self-sufficient.

Direct-service businesses, in turn, are created to serve a particular market, one that has historically been served by human services organizations, such as individuals with developmental disabilities, emotionally troubled youth, those recovering from substance abuse, and so forth. Both of these types of social enterprises bring a distinct advantage over their traditional counterparts. Namely, they are usually started with programs already in place and a market niche already developed (Boschee, 1995).

Another excellent example is that of the Fairfax County Public Library in Fairfax, Virginia. Clay and Bangs (2000) present a case study of how a public service organization reinvented itself as a public service corporation that embodied the principles of social entrepreneurship covered in this book. The Fairfax County Public Library, in response to severe budget cuts, developed a management committee (Enterprise Group) that initiated a fund-development program and partnerships that resulted in a substantial increase in operating funds.

Stern, Stone, Hopkins, McMillion, and Crain's (1994) book entitled *School-Based Enterprises* (SBEs) provides an excellent definition of an organization-driven enterprise (in this case a school). School-based enterprises are "any school-sponsored activity that engages a group of students in providing goods or services for sale to or use by people other than the students involved" (Stern et al., 1994, p. xi). The Stern et al. (1994) definition shows how enterprises can take on many different types and shapes, so to speak, and lend themselves to incorporate and respond to local circumstances within a school.

Banks, through their lending policies and practices, can develop special initiatives to spawn social enterprises (Johnson & Smith, 1998). Over the last two to three decades, major banks effectively left many of the nation's inner cities and in the process left a void of potential start-up capital for enterprise development. Microenterprise funding is one type of banking initiative for financing small businesses and entrepreneurs in urban communities of color. These types of initiatives function best when funding is combined with comprehensive support for the loan recipient (Rossman, 2000).

The example of Middleton Middle School in Tampa, Florida, reflects the potential of school-based enterprises (Scherzer, 2000, p. 1):

Heart-shaped helium balloons took off as the first product sold by Middleton Middle School student entrepreneurs. As they came to understand supply and demand, profit and loss, sales and service, the Middleton students at the 21st Century Learning Center branched into T-shirts sales, Mother's Day flowers and Thanksgiving pies. . . . Since February, federally funded after-school programs at Middleton and five other middle schools have offered firsthand experience of business plans; product development; manufacturing and marketing. Called 21st Century Learning Centers, each borrowed curriculum from Junior Achievement and other programs to form a school-based enterprise to teach real-world skills.

Five Elements Greeting Cards, based in Ossining, New York, shows a community-based business approach (Youth Ventures, 2002, p. 12):

Diana . . . developed her venture based on her passion—the elements of Hip Hop. Through expressive art and lyrics, her greeting cards help young people find the right card for all occasions, while simultaneously educating young people about the positive aspects of Hip Hop. 5 Elements will establish the Make It Happen Fund once they have made a profit and will devote ten percent of net profits to Make It Happen Fund, which serves to encourage the careers of aspiring artists through classes, studio rentals and internships.

Self-efficacy, a critical component in the creation of business enterprises, benefits from institutional support. Kruger (2000, p. 18), commenting on how best to create and reinforce self-efficacy, touches upon this perspective: "Increasing self-efficacy requires more than just teaching competencies; students and trainees must fully internalize the competencies by experiencing mastery of the skills in question. Also, psychological and emotional support from management and peers reinforces perceptions of increased self-efficacy." A common mechanism is to provide credible models of key behaviors through effective mentors and champions. Consequently, formalized efforts to encourage and support would-be entrepreneurs are best and more efficiently provided by institutional entities with a mission of creating and supporting businesses. However, it is important not to forget that institutions do not create innovations, but individuals within them do (Krueger, 2000).

How can youth engage in social entrepreneurship? There are two basic approaches to achieving this goal of participation (institutional and indigenous), which in turn can be divided into four ways for youth to engage in social enterprises. Three of these approaches are institutional-affiliated (schools, community-based organizations, banks, businesses, universities, and foundations), and one is noninstitutional affiliated (indigenous-driven).

Institutional-driven social youth enterprises entail having the sponsorship of organizations, such as schools (school-based-enterprises), or offering programs with the specific intent of teaching youth (self-efficacy, knowledge, and competencies) how to initiate and sustain businesses (Carroll et al., 1991; Lobsenz, 1991; Masselow, 1995; Paquin, 1991; Stern et al., 1994). A 1992 survey of school-based enterprises (SBEs) found that 18.6 percent of public secondary schools sponsored at least one SBE (Stern et al., 1994). Institutions sponsoring youth enterprises invariably have applied for and received targeted funding for these types of initiatives. Major foundations have funded such initiatives, and, not surprisingly, this has drawn greater attention to youth enterprises, social and nonsocial.

Funding may be a part of a foundation, business, or bank initiative targeting youth-created social enterprises. Universities and colleges with degree programs in business may also sponsor internships or other supports such as workshops, start-up funds, space, and/or technical assistance as part of their community service. Businesses such as information technologies may also offer internship programs to expose youth to enterprise principles and techniques (Delgado, 2002).

Indigenous-Driven Social Enterprises

The final route towards enterprise development, and the only one that is not institution-affiliated, is the indigenous-driven enterprise. This form of enterprise, not surprisingly, is very heavily dependent upon an individual's perception of self-efficacy. This belief in oneself is an essential antecedent of perceived opportunity (Kruger, 2000). The reader may well argue that self-efficacy is essential in all avenues of enterprise development, institution or noninstitution affiliated. However, it takes prominence in indigenous-driven enterprises because of the absence of any formalized efforts to assist through such activities as technical assistance and mentoring.

Contrary to common myths pertaining to indigenous-driven social enterprises, these types of enterprises are not started or sustained by one individual; at least not the ones that are successful in the long run. These entrepreneurs also are able to identify an important need that can be successfully addressed through the creation of an enterprise (Useem, 1996).

Indigenous-driven social youth enterprises, in turn, have youth initiating and sustaining enterprises with minimal or no support from institutions. These types of enterprises invariably have the support of a youth's social network, such as family, neighbors, or friends. Starting and maintaining self-initiated enterprises are impossible without expressive and instrumental assistance from a supportive social network. However, there is no direct or formal institution sponsoring this type of enterprise. It is important to note that self-initiated social youth enterprises, although not large in numbers, rarely have the sustainability to maximize their potential for youth and community transformation.

Social youth entrepreneurship is predicated on the belief that youth are capable and have the right characteristics (attitudes, knowledge and skills) to start their own businesses. In addition, these businesses contribute to the well-being of a community beyond the creation of jobs, and this is clearly one of the most important goals of any initiative. The following two social enterprises highlight the importance of community well-being.

Mack Knick Knack shows how a social youth enterprise can involve a wide circle of youth. This enterprise was based in an after-school setting (Youth Venture, 2002, p. 19):

Launched in April 2002 by Danielle, Mack Knick Knack Boxes (MK2) creates decorative boxes that hold small materials, such as paper clips, candy, buttons and coins. The boxes help make people's lives more organized in a beautiful way. In addition, MK2 benefits the school community by involving youth in creating the boxes. Danielle offers an after school opportunity to celebrate creativity and develop pride in producing craft work.

The case example of Kibibi Stationaires, on the other hand, brings an environmental and an illness-specific focus to the enterprise (Youth Venture, 2002, p. 17):

Kibibi Stationery, launched by Lydia K. Smith, will offer high quality individualized stationary to individuals and small business owners. As one of her [goals] Lydia is seeking to promote environmental awareness with her products by using recycled paper and soy ink. In addition, Lydia would like to regularly offer a variety of events that will benefit her community. Eventually she will design the Give It All Back programs of her venture to focus on youth who may be developmentally delayed or have Attention Deficit Disorder.

Services and profits can be invested back into the community as a central feature of any business enterprise that is social entrepreneurship based. Smilor (1997, p. 1) notes: "But I don't want to talk about the economic impact of entrepreneurship, as significant as it is. I want to focus instead on the social impact of entrepreneurship. Entrepreneurship is not just an economic phenomenon. It is a force that creates social value and a resource for community development." Smilor does a commendable job of lifting up the potential of enterprises when placed within a social context, one that explicitly embraces individual and social transformation as a central goal.

Formal instruction in social entrepreneurship principles, strategies, and techniques is essential to increasing the likelihood of eventual success. Kourilsky (1995), however, notes that all segments of youth would benefit from this form of education, with lower socioeconomic status youth standing to gain the most from a formalized curriculum. Access to this content generally occurs in the home in situations where schools do not address this curriculum. Youth coming out of at-risk circumstances, however, have a low likelihood of getting this information at home or as a result of observing role models in the community. Lack of access to entrepreneurial education, as a result, is most prevalent in communities where it can have the greatest impact.

The concept of social youth entrepreneurship is multifaceted and highly adaptable to various social and economic circumstances. Like any concept involving human beings, with youth not being an exception, it has a specific defining nature and is founded on a set of values that can be identified and examined in depth. Value-driven youth entrepreneurship necessitates value-driven education (formal or informal).

ASSUMPTIONS, VALUES, AND GOALS

The grounding of social entrepreneurship and how it becomes operationalized is very much based upon a set of assumptions, values, and goals that guide it on a daily basis. In essence, it needs to be contextualized. Social entrepreneurship in one community may look dramatically different from that in another community; this can be exciting as well as frustrating for the entrepreneur seeking to benefit from the experiences of others.

A small business plan must be sufficiently flexible in design to take into account a wide range of factors including the cultural background of the participants and the community they are targeting. Essenberg (2000), for example, emphasizes the importance of the parish church, long-term relationships, the relocation of leaders to the community, interethnic and class relations as key variables in promoting urban community development. The interplay of these sociocultural factors and considerations may look dramatically different within urban communities and between communities that are not urban.

Community development corporations, as a result, can play an organizing role in bringing together different factions to achieve economic change. Atfort Solutions is an example of a social youth enterprise influenced by a community development corporation (Youth Venture, 2002, p. 4):

Atfort Solutions is a web development corporation. The company will design websites for businesses and community organizations. It started operations after Richie, who studies with the Community Development Corporation at Benjamin Banneker HS, created a successful web design. He quickly had requests to complete more projects and saw that These [sic] were potential customers. In addition, Atfort Solutions will host a variety of workshops to help people become Internet literate and to teach basic computer skills.

The emergence of the constructs of social capital and social value brings an important if often overlooked dimension to any discussion pertaining to social entrepreneurship. Purdue (2001) defines social capital as the sum of trust relationships between a community and its leaders. Social capital, in turn, has been shown to be important to the effectiveness of social entrepreneurs. The regeneration of a community requires leaders with requisite qualities pertaining to vision and vocation. Trusting relationships, or social capital, can be considered the glue that holds the work of social entrepreneurs together.

Quarter and Richmond (2001), in turn, use the concept of social value or social mission to advance a closer collaborative relationship between non-profits and for-profit sectors. It is possible for a for-profit organization to embrace a social mission to help guide and foster a for-profit service or product (Brierton, 2001; Crowe, 2001; Pike, 2001). This does not happen by accident, of course. Relatively few for-profit enterprises would even consider embracing a social value perspective to guide these businesses. Nevertheless, there are a growing and significant number of enterprises, some starting as nonprofits and others as for-profits, that use a social value foundation to guide their ventures.

Rick (1999), although specifically addressing the assumptions underlying school-based enterprises, identified three assumptions that can also be applied to social youth enterprises: (1) entrepreneurship is important for learning and for success in life and work; (2) experience is critical, but it is not enough by itself; and (3) enterprises can, and should, model socially responsible entrepreneurship. These assumptions are predicated or founded on certain values. Social economic enterprises must carefully consider the social and financial benefits of their initiatives without losing sight of their mission, a mission that incidentally must carefully take into account funding (profits) because without it there is no lasting social or community change. The marketplace, as a result, is the target for services, products, and social benefits.

The National Center for Social Entrepreneurs (2001) identified what it called three bedrock principles guiding the development of social enterprises: (1) attention must ultimately be paid to two bottom lines—financial returns on investment and social returns on investment; (2) focus must be on earned income that offers unlimited potential for degree of control versus dependence on grants; and (3) a social enterprise is a business—find a niche, be a major player, price aggressively, and build the right team.

The circulation of the capital generated by social youth enterprises will take various forms, for example: (1) wages for community residents; (2) purchases of materials, equipment, and services from community-owned and -operated businesses; (3) investment in social capital such as college tuition for workers; (4) local banking; and (5) purchasing advertisements in local newspapers and other forms of communication. Each of these purchases and investments help to ensure that capital does not leave the community quickly without passing through the hands of local merchants and community residents.

Youth, according to Mariani (1994), must adhere to four simple, yet important, rules when considering starting a business enterprise: (1) never allow an enterprise to interfere with school performance; (2) have an understanding of the legal and tax requirements; (3) starting an enterprise is a zero-sum equation—the opportunity costs of running a business means curtailing or eliminating social activities usually associated with being a youth; and (4) making a profit is not guaranteed. One additional rule of thumb needs to be added when youth are considering starting a social enterprise—profit without community good should not be the primary outcome of a business venture.

Emerson (1996, p. 2) traces the origins of new social entrepreneurs to the beginning of the nexus of community services and development: "This history of commitment to social justice and economic empowerment is what feeds their passion for the creation of social purpose business ventures." Needless to say, historically, entrepreneurial initiatives have rarely had social and economic justice underpinnings. Nevertheless, the 1990s and the early part of the twenty-first century have shown how this concept has evolved. Social entrepreneurship as noted by Morino (1998) has benefited from commercial applications of information technology such as the Internet. Information technology can play an important role in advancing initiatives with social benefits for community and society.

The following case illustration does a wonderful job of bringing together the influence of several fields of practice (Nixon, 1996, p. 1):

It has only been a few months since Fernando Martinez graduated from high school, but he's already hard at work getting a new business off the ground. Two days a week, the 18-year-old reports for work in a small room behind a Central Avenue beauty salon. For the next four hours, Martinez pours warm beeswax into molds shaped like Santa Claus. The candles are then tucked into gift packages with jars of barbecue sauce. The label on the gift packages bears the flashy logo of the new company: Santa Clara River Valley Hometown Creations. Products in the development stage include pistachios, honey, vinegar and T-shirts. This business is more than just an upstart outfit exporting family concoctions to big-city gourmets. This is in fact an innovative social service program employing 36 youngsters from low-income families. In return for a minimum wage salary, the kids ages 13–18 learn business—everything from inventory to marketing. "It's an educational thing," Martinez said. "I'm learning how to make candles and a little about business."

Any in-depth review of the professional literature on the subject of youth enterprises will reveal a set of very specific goals that inform these ventures. Social youth entrepreneurship initiatives use five guiding principles in shaping community service in their enterprises:

Inclusiveness

Traditional business enterprises have generally not paid very much attention to how to be inclusive. Social youth enterprises must actively seek to be inclusive of all who wish to be a part of the experience and thus bring a dimension to business creation that is rare. The goal of achieving inclusiveness fulfills multiple purposes within an enterprise. Learning from and contributing to an enterprise must provide all participants with an opportunity based upon their competencies. An enterprise that is social in nature cannot discriminate to systematically keep certain groups out. This does not mean that everyone, regardless of interests and competencies, can do and should do all jobs within the enterprise. Some youth may have excellent people skills and are best in functioning within public relations or customer service activities, for example. Yet others may prefer the financial side of the business and are more able to focus their talents in financial management. Still others may prefer product development, and so on. However, each youth should have an awareness of all of the different aspects of an enterprise.

Successful social youth enterprises value inclusivity rather than exclusivity, and this attitude ultimately benefits the community at large, particularly if it has youth who have effectively been limited in their search for meaningful employment because of some social condition (Ellis, 1992; In Focus, 2001; Ketcham et al., 1990; Paquin, 1991). Even within highly marginalized communities there are individuals and groups that have experienced even a greater degree of separation from the community at large as well as within their own respective communities. Social youth enterprises are not about further excluding groups from participation in social-economic enterprises.

Service to Community

Service to community is a central feature of a social youth entrepreneurship approach towards business enterprises. The emergence of community service as an instrumental activity for engaging urban youth is not new and can be traced back to the 1980s. However, community services have increased in popularity as an attractive vehicle for learning, meeting a community need, and engaging in capacity enhancement (Lewis, 1992; Delgado, 2002). In short, it is an activity that lends itself to incorporating numerous goals for an initiative. The social enterprise Twin Angel Designs is such an example (Youth Venture, 2002, p. 33):

Founders Nicole and Diana created this jewelry design business to help girls fulfill their community service hours, promote social awareness, and raise money for Ophelia's House (a non-profit organization located in Washington, DC). Girls make a bracelet, then make a matching one to sell. With each bracelet sold, Twin Angel Designs also includes a message about issues relevant to teenage women—all based on personal experiences of the Twin Angels Team.

A community service theme is sufficiently flexible in scope to take into account goals, interests, and competencies of youth, types of services, time periods, and community settings. A wide variety of settings have used youth community service as an active element of programming. Schools, community-based organizations, museums, zoos, aquariums, libraries, and for-profit businesses, have developed programs of instruction that use service to community as the central vehicle for imparting knowledge and the development of competencies (Delgado, 2002). In fact, there are no community-based institutions that cannot accommodate a youth in service to community. Special projects or internships can easily be developed that cover a wide range of goals, time periods, and levels of intensity.

Bringing a community service focus to social youth entrepreneurship reinforces the goal of social benefits for the community and minimizes the likelihood of goals focusing almost exclusively on profits and learning for youth. Both of these goals are important. However, they take on added significance when community benefits must be a part of the eventual outcome of any undertaking. Including community within youth entrepreneurship, in addition, brings this form of intervention well within the youth development field. This field has slowly moved away from individual youth benefits to community benefits as manifested through community service activities.

Pride in Quality of Service or Product

Having pride in quality of service or product is very much grounded in current business thinking. Similarly, the importance of consumer satisfaction is very much tied in to product or service recognition. Thus, it should not come as any great surprise to see this value playing an influential role in social youth entrepreneurship programs. Further, when the market is one's immediate community, then the service or product being sold must be of high quality. One's neighbors, friends, family, and acquaintances are the prime beneficiaries of the business. This social network, at least in the initial stages of the creation of a business creation, is extremely important from an experiential and instrumental perspective.

Latino youth, for example, are in a propitious position to develop a product or service that capitalizes upon language and cultural competencies and awareness. Any assessment of Latino purchasing power will be quick to note their economic influence in this nation's marketplace. The annual Latino market in the United States increased from $75 billion in 1984 to $300 billion in 1996 to $440 billion in 1999 (Valdes & Seoane, 1999; Zuniga, 2001). The effective use of positive cultural symbols and language can serve as an advantage in reaching this market particularly when compared to those who are external to this culture and community.

The same can be said for Asian and Pacific Islander youth in reaching a market that wields a tremendous amount of influence in this nation (Brumback, 2000). The Asian and Pacific Islander market is demographically much smaller than the African American market yet is considered to be the fastest growing and most affluent market of color in the United States. It has a purchasing power of over $100 billion per year (Brumback, 2000). This community is projected to number 15 million by the year 2010, up from 3 million in 1990 and 10 million in 2000 (Konig, 2000). Unlike the African American community, which does not require specific language competencies, the Latino and Asian and Pacific Islander communities present innumerable challenges to outsiders. These challenges effectively place those who share these cultural backgrounds at a tremendous advantage in all aspects of enterprise development with the possible exception of obtaining start-up capital.

Innova Apparel is a social youth enterprise that effectively capitalizes upon the youth's knowledge of their community (Youth Venture, 2002, p. 15):

Deana and Dawn founded their venture to solve a common problem they saw people had when wearing knit hats. With inspiration from personal experience, Innova designs and sells winter hats that protect hairstyles. A portion of their proceeds is contributed to a scholarship fund for students in their school who wish to design and who will pursue a career in design.

Process Is as Important as Profit and Service to Community

The coprioritizing of profits with process and service to community may seem unusual from a typical business standpoint. Social youth entrepreneurship, needless to say, is not a typical enterprise. Further, social youth entrepreneurship is also a mechanism for teaching and learning. Profit and service to community, as a result, will have minimal lasting potential if youth cannot learn from their experiences. These multiple goals can only be achieved if process is emphasized.

What do I mean by process? Simply stated, it refers to the provision of ample opportunities to have youth participate in as many aspects of the undertaking as possible. This effectively translates into creation of mechanisms that seek their input in pursuit of the goals set by the enterprise. The ownership of the enterprise goes far beyond holding stock in the company; it also refers to feeling a part of the daily activities. This type of ownership can only be achieved by youth's time, energy, and commitment. Youth ownership of the process requires that adults actively embrace roles that support youth participation. Adult feedback, in turn, seeks to enhance youth actions without compromising the goals of an enterprise.

Reinvestment in Community Capacity

The importance of economic reinvestment within marginalized urban communities is critical for the future of this country and can take a wide variety of forms (Armistead & Wexler, 1997; Cahill, 1997; Mayo et al., 2001). Actively seeking to create enterprises, youth- or adult-driven, that reinvest in the community is a very attractive element of social enterprises—offering scholarships, transforming space from negative to positive use, providing a service or product that enhances the health and well-being of the community, and so forth.

Reinvestment through social enterprises can take on a variety of manifestations: (1) providing training and support for staff; (2) renting space within the community and contracting out for resources; (3) investing in other start-up enterprises that can supplement or enhance the original social enterprise; (4) providing scholarships for community residents; (5) brokering external resources to aid other community businesses; and (6) purchasing community land and buildings and transforming them into resources for future businesses.

Empowerment

Little dispute exists that social youth entrepreneurship seeks to empower participants in the process of creating enterprises. This empowerment, in turn, transfers to other aspects of a participant's life. Empowerment is a philosophy, principle, process, activity, and goal, all at the same time. Empowerment is a critical element in all facets of youth programming founded upon youth development principles. However, for youth social entrepreneurs to be empowered, they must believe in themselves, have requisite knowledge about how to transform their lives, and possess the prerequisite skills to do so within the context of their lives in a community. They must also possess hope for a better future. Street Sport Fashions is an example of an enterprise with an important message for other youth (Youth Venture, 2002, p. 27):

George and Stacey are reaching out to the community by designing a full line of clothing. Through their designs and artwork, which express real life issues, they are reaching out to every young person nationwide. Their message: "Keep on dreaming on." They want to be an inspiration to young people as well as adults: though there may be many obstacles in one's way, one has to believe in themselves and keep striving hard to make their dream come true.

Empowerment is a flexible construct that can be modified to take into account local circumstances and cultural factors. Youth from cultural backgrounds that have parents playing very influential roles in their lives, for example, must modify how empowerment plays out in the home, school, and community. Empowerment as a goal, even under the most difficult of situations, must continue to be a goal with social youth enterprises.

ELEMENTS

The conceptualization of youth entrepreneurship elements is closely tied to the stages of entrepreneurship, or a framework guiding program devel-

opment. The Working Group on Youth Entrepreneurship, a Canadian organization, developed a four-stage framework: (1) formative; (2) development;
(3) start-up; and (4) growth. Each of these elements encompasses a set of
specific goals and activities.

A framework serves important functions in helping youth better understand
all of the phases of social enterprise development; it also helps teachers/men-
tors better prepare youth for the rewards and challenges associated with each
stage of a framework. A framework, as a result, serves to provide boundaries
and directions in an enterprise that may initially be surrounded by ambiguity.

APPROACHES/CONSIDERATIONS

Is youth entrepreneurship a relatively recent concept? Few initiatives or
constructs can be considered new, and youth entrepreneurship is no exception
according to Faris (1999, pp. 2–3): "In truth, youth entrepreneurship is as old
an idea as working itself. Many youth get their first taste of personal responsibility and earning money through entrepreneurial initiatives such as mowing
lawns, walking pets, and even operating lemonade stands. However, organizations and curriculum approaches . . . designed to have entrepreneurial skills
may not only help to facilitate the would-be youth entrepreneur, but may also
awaken the spirit in children and young adults who would otherwise not consider entrepreneurship as an option." Faris's (1999) observation concerning
the etiology of entrepreneurship within youth is quite striking. There are
probably very few readers who can't recall a time in their youth when they
sold a toy and made a profit or when they made a small investment in some
venture with the hopes of making a significant profit (Bodnar, 2001).

Faris's (1999) and Bodnar's (2001) reviews of how youth participate in en-
trepreneurial-related initiatives note that some simply do so on their own
without any formalized assistance, yet others are participants in formal programs and projects specifically targeted at demographic subgroups. Some
youth, however, regardless of their current status in the field of entrepreneurship, have invariably started on their own and at a relatively early age.
The enterprise Bookey was started by such an individual (Youth Venture,
2002, p. 7):

Alex, a junior at SUNY Albany in New York, plans to launch his business enterprise
this fall [2002]. From The Students, For The Students will buy, buy back, and resell
textbooks to university students at reasonable prices. Currently, students can only
purchase textbooks from one supplier at high prices. Additionally, students can only
sell back their textbooks to the one supplier at low prices. From The Students, For
The Students will allow students to also buy and sell each other's textbooks at more
reasonable prices and the profit the business makes will be reinvested in the education
that benefits the community, school, and especially the students.

The National Foundation for Teaching Entrepreneurship and the Entrepreneurial Development Institute target at-risk youth of color. An Income of Her Own, in turn, targets young women. Dabson and Kauffman (1998) conceptualize formal entrepreneur education as falling into four categories: (1) school-based entrepreneurial education; (2) training of trainers; (3) business placement (internships); and (5) local initiatives. Entrepreneurial education can transpire in a variety of settings and does not have to rely upon one setting to put forth this perspective for youth.

Buttenheim (1998) in an article titled "Social Enterprise Meets Venture Philanthropy: A Powerful Combination," identified two key trends regarding enterprise creation in undervalued communities that have direct applicability to youth: (1) Nonprofits are increasingly running businesses that provide participants with real-world job training and competency development that will result in permanent employment with a living wage. These nonprofits incidentally have social enterprise as a central part of their organization's mission. (2) These organizations are engaging in pursuit of creative approaches to the generation of operational funding. These exciting developments have resulted in organizations paying closer attention to the needs of youth as well as looking at youth assets in the creation of community-centered enterprises.

Like youth development, youth entrepreneurship is sufficiently flexible to take into consideration local circumstances and priorities in determining how it gets operationalized on a daily basis within a program and community. Certain values and goals, for example, can take center stage in one community and backstage in other communities. This flexibility can be both a blessing and a curse. Consequently, two youth entrepreneurship programs may coexist side by side and look dramatically different from each other, yet both use the label *youth enterprise* in their program title.

Although youth entrepreneurship is usually associated with adolescence, the concept is not restricted to that or any other age group. The case example of Los Perales Elementary School in Moraga, California, expands the age-group possibilities for this approach towards developing youth competencies and facilitating their transition within youth age categories rather than being restricted to school-to-work transition (Guynn, 2001, p. 1):

Chris Kolner pauses to reflect before he answers the question. Why did he and his pals band together to launch a startup? "Well," he says, "it has been my dream for a long time to invent things. I figured it was a good idea to start a company early on in life." Kolner and his friends, all fourth-graders . . . are too young to drive, let alone vote or drink. But they're apparently old enough to make their mark in the New Economy. Kolner [9 1/3 years old] and 10-year-old pal Jonathan "JD" Digali started Rainbow Technologies last fall. . . . Their first big hire was chief engineer David Levonian, a 10-year-old electronics whiz who collects circuit boards and devours books about electronics. The trio recruited a handful of classmates to help run the business.

At first sight, the above case illustration may seem out of the norm. However, the literature is replete with examples of entrepreneurial ventures started and sustained by youth of many different ages, some of whom are as young as six or seven years old. The nature of the business and the sophistication of the marketing plan will vary considerably and will depend upon the developmental level of the entrepreneur. Nevertheless, the desire and hope behind the enterprise venture does not differ significantly between different age groups. Although studies have not been done on the developmental path of very young entrepreneurs, it would not be surprising to find that those who are actively and successfully engaged in enterprise creation as adolescents had their start relatively young in life.

ENTREPRENEURIAL EDUCATION

A central goal of any youth-centered entrepreneurship initiative is to encourage business ownership as a viable alternative for all youth and, in the case of this book, marginalized youth of color (Harris, 1994). One teacher stated this goal well (Harris, 1994, p. 29): "If you can't find a job, you can make your own. . . . And even if you don't start your own business, entrepreneurship training can help you develop the kinds of skills employers need— the ability to think on your feet, make plans, and service customers."

An absence of entrepreneurial education is a glaring gap in any effort to advance social youth entrepreneurship. It is not possible for social youth entrepreneurship to exist within settings such as schools without instruction on entrepreneurship and a climate that values this form of practice. Some advocates would go so far as to say that it would be ideal for schools to teach social youth entrepreneurship. However, the social piece of this intervention can just as easily be taught outside of a school setting. The entrepreneurial piece, however, is more arduous to address outside of schools, although it is possible, as noted in the social youth enterprise Mannatex Corporation (Youth Venture, 2002, p. 19):

John plans to launch his own business, Mannatex Corp., in New York City. John's business, which sells natural shampoo bars, is committed to marketing 100% natural products, as well as paving the way for a more socially responsible, humane business environment. John plans to donate a portion of his profits to the National Foundation for Teaching Entrepreneurship.

The absence of entrepreneurial education within the United States is glaring and a major barrier to having youth engage in this form of business and seriously limits the launching of social enterprises (Starr, 1997, p. 2): "While ownership of a small business is a valid and popular career choice, this fact is not reflected in the course offerings at most American schools. Most business education is directed to vocational and career paths that result in people becoming employees. In contrast, entrepreneurial education presents self-employment as a legitimate career choice and provides students with classroom and life experiences relevant to becoming small business owners." If most education in this country is preparing youth to become employees, what is the likelihood of school systems reaching marginal youth of color offering them enterprise creation as an option? I would venture to say that it is quite slim in probability.

Kourilsky et al. (1997) report on the effectiveness of an entrepreneurship education curriculum intervention for lower socioeconomic African American youth. The authors advocate for the use of entrepreneurship as a driving force in opening access to economic success for marginalized youth. The New Youth Entrepreneur (NYE) curriculum stressed the identification of market opportunities, generation of a business idea, acquisition and commitment of resources, and creation of an operating business organization to implant the opportunity-motivated business idea.

The curriculum consisted of twelve modules: (1) Getting Ready for Entrepreneurship: The Entrepreneur; (2) Getting Ready for Entrepreneurship: Opportunities; (3) Getting Ready for Entrepreneurship: Business Ideas; (4) How to Sell Your Idea; (5) Money to Get Started; (6) Where to Do Business; (7) Types of Business Ownership; (8) Where to Get Help; (9) Records and Books); (10) The Rules of the Game; (11) How to Mind Your Own Business; and (12) You Can Make It Happen. Like most curricula, this curriculum necessitates that educators use the modules sequentially since each module sets the stage for the next.

Effective Teachers: Qualities and Competencies

Teachers, be they part of a school system or mentors in communities and community-based programs, represent the cornerstone of youth entrepreneurship initiatives, social or strictly business-focused. However, their role within these enterprises is generally not highlighted in the professional literature nor are the qualities that are essential to be successful in this role (Harris, 1994). It is almost as if the individuals who seek to perform this role need only the same qualities and competencies that any teacher needs to be effective. The content area, so the thinking goes, is not important. Nothing could be further from the truth on this matter. A sincere belief in the philosophy behind school-to-career and social youth entrepreneurship is the essential element from which to create youth-focused and -driven initiatives (Cutshall, 2001).

Essentially, there are at least seven qualities that a teacher must have to be effective in this realm: (1) a personality that encourages youth to take chances and not fear failure; (2) experience in owning and operating a business of his or her own; (3) ability to bring curriculum to life in a way that youth can relate to; (4) residence in the community or a solid understanding of the community; (5) the ability to establish and work with a supporting advisory board to tap for expertise; (6) excellent broker skills to help youth navigate political waters and obtain necessary funding for enterprise start-up; and (7) flexibility in designing and carrying out an enterprise. Needless to say, such a teacher/mentor is not your typical person in or out of a school system.

Personality

The qualities that make for a successful entrepreneur, however, can also bring negative consequences to enterprise development (Kets de Vries, 1985). An ability or willingness to be in control over all aspects of an enterprise can be both positive and negative. Attention to detail can be an excellent quality to possess during the initial start-up phase of an enterprise but disastrous in later phases. Consequently, having the ability to understand when personal qualities can be enhancing and when they can be detrimental cannot be overly estimated in entrepreneurial initiatives.

Failure is such a stigmatizing outcome in this society that youth, not surprisingly, shy away from adventures that can result in failure. However, I am very fond of saying that I can learn more about an individual and their resolve, so to speak, by how they handle failure rather than by how they handle success. There is no adult who can stand up and say that they have never experienced failure of some form in his or her life. Growth does not exclusively come from success. Growth can also come from failure. Thus, it is crucial for a teacher seeking to prepare youth for social enterprises to be able to encourage youth to take chances. Developing an ability to learn from their mistakes and the mistakes of their colleagues will provide youth with lessons that will stay with them for a lifetime.

Previous or Current Experience with Business Ownership

Expertise can be derived from both formal education and experience. The former is usually associated with university degrees of various kinds and established curriculum content. Research and scholarship, in turn, influence this content.. The latter, however, can be obtained only through a variety of activities that result in experience, positive as well as negative. Being able to combine both is the ideal situation in putting forth social youth enterprises that are institution-driven (Meyer & Nauta, 1994). It is like having a driving teacher with no driving experience instructing the novice driver. Ideally you would want someone who is an excellent driver and who can communicate effectively with the student driver.

Needless to say, any form of instruction that stresses practice necessitates having someone teaching who has had practical experience with the subject matter. This position is not restricted to the world of business. Human service professional schools have historically sought professors who teach content on practice to have a minimum number of years of actual practice or field experience. Why? The answer is quite simple; students need assistance in applying theoretical concepts to real-life situations. The wisdom the professor brings to a classroom situation translates into practical advice that will probably be used in the field.

Excellent Teaching Skills

An ability to motivate students to learn and experiment with new ways of thinking and doing can only achieve so much in creating a successful enterprise. True, excellent teachers can and must motivate. However, they also have to impart knowledge and wisdom in order for their students to achieve. A teacher with excellent teaching skills is astute enough to identify potential learning opportunities that are not too easy as well as tasks that are not so arduous as to be considered impossible. Such a teacher is also able to identify the process and outcomes that will signify success for students. Social youth entrepreneurship necessitates development of criteria for success that goes far beyond profit, and this is a challenge. Students should be able to evaluate their experience in terms that can be easily quantified and in terms that are not quantifiable, too.

Last, but not insignificant, an excellent teacher can help students problem solve the nature of the product and service they wish to market to a community. This requires teachers to develop activities that will help the students reach this goal. These activities, however, need to be grounded within a keen understanding of the community they seek to involve. Thus, excellent teaching skills must be multifaceted and encompass more than an ability to convey information to a student. Some would argue that preparing students for real life requires teachers who understand the challenges and rewards that students will face in carrying out these types of ventures.

Live in or Have In-Depth Knowledge of Community

A keen understanding of a community, or market if you wish, is an essential aspect of any successful social youth entrepreneur program or initiative. Teachers who possess this awareness and knowledge are in excellent positions to anticipate potential barriers to a successful enterprise and be able to help guide youth in their selection of products, services, and marketing strategies. Their knowledge of a community and its history, for example, can help contextualize the development of a product or service and identify potential resources that can be mobilized to help youth launch their endeavor.

Needless to say, very few teachers actually live in marginalized urban communities, a fact that makes this recommendation arduous to achieve. Nevertheless, it is still possible for teachers to develop a more in-depth understanding of communities through active efforts to visit local business establishments and community-based organizations. Venturing out of the classroom and into the community with students in order to research the market for a product or service is another way of increasing awareness. Finally, the development of an advisory board or committee, as addressed in the following recommendation, brings community into the school.

Supporting Advisory Board

Very few teachers in this country have extensive experience in working with advisory groups of any kind, let alone one that actively seeks to support youth enterprise initiatives. Rick (1999) coined the term *intrapreneur* to capture the significance of an effective teacher being able to work within their organization, school, or setting to create youth entrepreneurship programs. An educator, in essence, is acting as an entrepreneur within their system and thus can be considered an intrapreneur.

Finding allies inside and outside of an organization is essential in putting forth a successful youth enterprise. Successful ventures of any kind, but particularly businesses, owe their success to the work of a team. The creation and sustenance of an advisory committee is one vehicle for increasing support for an initiative. This provides instructors with an opportunity to assemble a cast of supporting players, each with specific expertise that can be used in the course of developing an enterprise.

Excellent Broker Skills

Self-interest is always a powerful motivator to get people involved in any initiative be it business or otherwise. Self-interest always seems to be a major factor in not only motivating individuals to engage but also to stay engaged over the long term. In essence, what can they get out of participating? Sometimes it may be the satisfaction of helping youth and communities. Other times there may be political gains to be made through participation. Yet other times there may be personal financial gain to be had from a community's transformation.

The ability for a teacher to identify self-interest and broker necessary commitments is a vital part of any social youth enterprise. Some would go so far as to argue that broker skills invariably are part of any successful businessperson's repertoire, so why shouldn't any successful teacher have those skills as well? Brokering skillfully requires many abilities, such as listening, communicating, and developing relationships.

Flexibility

The importance of flexibility goes beyond what is typically addressed in a standard curriculum—students must be prepared to learn from their successes and failures. Dees's (1998) observations of successful entrepreneurs note their high tolerance for ambiguity, ability to manage risks for themselves and others, and being able to treat failure of a project as a learning experience. Some may treat this failure as a personal tragedy; successful entrepreneurs do not. Thus, teachers must possess this flexibility and ability to create a learning experience regardless of enterprise outcome.

Rick's comments on flexibility (1999, p. 11) are directed at school-based enterprises (SBEs) but also hold relevance to youth enterprises with a set of social goals and principles: "The educator working with students in an SBE will need to be flexible. In certain situations, it will be important for the educator to retain control. For example, any SBE handling cash requires strict financial and teacher oversight, due to the legal and public relations importance of handling funds correctly. Other aspects of the enterprise may provide opportunities for students to exercise their own judgment once they have gained a basic understanding of the tasks. In these cases, an educator might provide some direct instruction and then take a more facilitative role. In general, it is important that the educator be comfortable with a range of roles and a variety of teaching methods." Rick (1999) has captured the importance of a teacher's having thorough knowledge of the field as well as the ability to help students succeed and, where applicable, allow students to make mistakes and learn from them.

CONCLUSION

The merging or integration of youth development and entrepreneurship to create social youth entrepreneurship is both exciting and challenging at the same time. Bringing together two fields that have historically not been thought of as sharing very much in common is not easy to accomplish. This marriage, so to speak, will require practitioners, academics, and researchers being willing to tolerate a high degree of ambiguity and possess significant flexibility in how they think about this new field. Further, when one of those fields has been historically equated with capitalism, the challenge is even more significant. However, social youth entrepreneurship does just that in this country and social youth entrepreneurship is a global phenomenon.

Who should be a social entrepreneur? Certainly not everyone as correctly observed by Dees (1998, p. 6): "Social entrepreneurship describes a set of behaviors that are exceptional. These behaviors should be encouraged and rewarded in those who have the capabilities and temperament for this kind of work. We could use many more of them. Should everyone aspire to be a social entrepreneur? No. Not every social sector leader is well suited to being entrepreneurial. The same is true in business. Not every business leader is an entrepreneur. . . . While we might wish for more entrepreneurial behavior in both sectors, society has a need for different leadership types and styles. Social entrepreneurs are one special breed of leader, and they should be recognized as such. This definition preserves their distinctive status and assures that social entrepreneurship is not treated lightly. We need social entrepreneurs to help us find new avenues toward social improvement as we enter the next century."

The potential of social youth entrepreneurship for youth and community transformation is only matched by its challenges. Successful social youth entrepreneurship requires cooperation between all of the major social domains in which youth participate, not least of which is school. The social dimension of social youth entrepreneurship grounds start-up businesses within a domain that has historically been foreign—namely, community. Community must not be thought of as merely a marketplace but as a target for service in the process of making profit.

Kourilsky (1995, p. 8) has issued a challenge on which it is appropriate to end this chapter because of its importance to the future of youth in this country: "Our country's economic growth will hinge on our ability to create new jobs through entrepreneurship. Successful entrepreneurship, in turn, will require well-trained, aspiring entrepreneurs willing to take the helm of venture creation. Effective initiatives in entrepreneurship education will be increasingly critical for expanding the flow of potential leaders from our school systems with the passion and the multiple skills needed not only to give birth to the inherently risky, entrepreneurial enterprise but also to guide it successfully through the initial growth phase, which is subject to both extremely high expectations and chance of failure."

PART III

Case Examples from the Field

Chapters 8 and 9 provide the reader with two social youth enterprise case examples drawn from the field of practice. Chapter 8 highlights the story of Food from the 'Hood, South Central Los Angeles. Chapter 9, in turn, tells the story of YA/YA (Young Aspirations/Young Artists) in New Orleans. Each of these two case studies utilizes an in-depth approach that provides sufficient details to help the reader develop a more comprehensive perspective on how these programs get operationalized and evaluated in the field. Both of these programs graciously agreed to participate in all facets of a field visit and provided free and unobstructed access to their meetings, records, and staff. Both of these case studies focus on urban-based programs that target youth of color.

CASE SELECTION METHODS

The two cases selected for inclusion in this book were screened through the following four-step process: (1) review of the literature (professional and mass); (2) Internet search; (3) key informant advice; (4) willingness to participate in all aspects of the case study design. Both had a history of sufficient length (minimum of five years) to offer lessons for others wishing to learn from their experiences.

There are many wonderful aspects about undertaking field case studies. They provide the author, and thereby the reader, with an opportunity to connect theory with practice. These case studies always, at least in my case, uncover new information and perspectives on the study being observed. There are times, however, when a case study's framework and questions are established prior to a field visit and then changed within individual cases and between cases. This flexibility is essential in order to capture idiosyncratic factors and circumstances. This, I might add, has certainly been the case with the two social youth enterprise programs addressed in this section. The reader, I believe, will benefit from this approach.

The case studies consist of the following sections: (1) Rationale for Case Selection; (2) Context and Historical Background (brief history of how the program originated and the factors leading to its creation); (3) Program-Specific Description; (4) Funding Sources; (5) Youth Development Foundation; (6) Lessons Learned (words of advice for others wishing to replicate the program); and (7) Final Comments. Each of the seven major categories will vary in content and detail between the two case studies addressed in this section. Each of these sections, however, provides readers with sufficient information to help them determine the feasibility of copying these enterprises, with necessary modifications, for their respective communities.

No case study, however, will satisfy the needs for all necessary information, and readers need to be warned of this limitation. Every effort has been made to maintain the initial broad categories. Nevertheless, the reader will soon notice that certain sections within each of these categories were emphasized and deemphasized to take into account unique aspects of the program and its history.

CASES SELECTED

Two case studies have been selected for the reader to develop a more in-depth understanding and appreciation of how social youth entrepreneurship has been conceptualized and implemented in the field. One of the cases involves a school-based enterprise entitled Food from the 'Hood, located in South Central Los Angeles. The second case involves a community youth organization called YA/YA (Young Aspirations/Young Artists) based in New Orleans, Louisiana, which uses the arts as a vehicle for achieving social entrepreneurship goals.

These case studies represent different types of enterprises, geography, setting, and products/services sold. Each case involves a different historical developmental path involving school-program collaboration and the broadening of the community they seek to reach for participants and to sell their products. These cases are by no means meant to be generalizable beyond the histories and activities of the organizations profiled. However, the cases do reflect on how principles, values, and local circumstances have created social youth enterprises in two of this nation's cities.

CHAPTER 8

Food from the 'Hood, Los Angeles

RATIONALE FOR SELECTION

The community of South Central Los Angeles has developed an everlasting national reputation based upon the Rodney King riots. Probably very few people in this country had ever heard of South Central prior to the riots. Unfortunately, probably very few adults in this country have an image of this community that is not related to the riots. These riots, captured by television cameras, left a profound impression on the nation. These same cameras, however, did not focus on the many positive attributes that can be found in this neighborhood. This community has been the source of inspiration and hope for countless other communities across the country. Miles Corwin's (1998) widely applauded book *And Still We Rise: The Trials and Triumphs of Twelve Gifted Inner-City High School Students* is based upon research at Crenshaw High School, the focus of this case study on Food from the 'Hood.

There were many reasons why the case of Food from the 'Hood was selected for inclusion in this book. However, its long and distinguished history and example of a school-based enterprise made it very appealing. The use of a community garden as a vehicle for undertaking a social economic enterprise was also very appealing to me. Contrary to common opinion, urban communities do not consist exclusively of brick buildings and paved sidewalks and streets. Land, sometimes not used for the betterment of a community, is available and lends itself for use in social enterprises. Further, it transforms public space from negative to positive uses, environmentally transforming a section of a community. Finally, one of the primary reasons for selection of Food from the 'Hood, however, centered on the public's image of South Central, which with some notable exceptions is quite negative.

CONTEXT AND HISTORICAL BACKGROUND

Food from the 'Hood began as a school-based enterprise in the South Central community in Los Angeles, California, in 1992. As a school-based organization, it has experienced many of the challenges of being connected to a low-income community, where economic and other resources such as space are limited. Overcrowding and other demands have historically taken priority for school funding. A social youth enterprise being based within a public school system increases the challenges because of a history of school systems neglecting entrepreneurial education in this country. However, the circumstances surrounding the birth of this enterprise are very much in this nation's psyche.

There is little question that Food from the 'Hood began with a passion. It was started in 1992 by Tammy Bird, a Crenshaw High School biology teacher, in response to the Rodney King beating and the subsequent uprisings resulting from the verdict vindicating the four Los Angeles police officers that had been captured on video and a desire to get food to her students. The lack of grocery stores in the immediate area severely limited the community's access to food. To many community residents the verdict once again illustrated the failure of the legal system to equitably dispense justice. Driven by frustration and hopelessness, what began as a protest turned into days filled with smoke and rampaging, as whole communities struggled to make sense of an event that defied any form of logic other than racism being allowed to emerge. The timing of this initiative worked well in its favor because of national attention on this community (Williams, 1998).

Located in the middle of South Central Los Angeles, Crenshaw High School students saw social injustice happening in their neighborhood and were moved to act in a constructive manner. Amidst the burning, looting, and violence, several Crenshaw High School students looked around and saw beyond the burned buildings and the looted stores and seized an opportunity to empower themselves and their community. There was an unused and weed-infested lot behind the school and, as a result of a vision and a lot of hard work, it became the first site for the Food from the 'Hood garden. The seeds were sown not just for another community garden, but also for an innovative new youth organization. The first harvest of the garden was given to the homeless and needy in the community, and the rest was sold at the Farmer's Market earning the workers a total of $150.

The youth who originally started Food from the 'Hood had to contend with numerous challenges usually associated with any business start-up. However, they also had to contend with being the butt of jokes from fellow Crenshaw High School students. Hoeing a small plot of land with six-foot high weeds in a distant corner of the campus was not the typical activity Crenshaw High School students were used to witnessing in their school and community (Educational Record, 1996; Williams, 1998). Overcoming these attitudes represented a critical step in getting broad acceptance of the enterprise inside and outside the school.

In the beginning, the focus was on grassroots organizing and contributing to the community. The program was driven by the founding students called the Original Gardeners (OGs) and their need to address their own emotional response to the Rodney King verdict. Disappointed by the judicial system and looking for a way to channel those energies, this group of Crenshaw High School students pulled together to harness their feelings and literally directed them into the earth. The cofounder, Melanie McMullen, who had a public relations background, was able to very quickly capture the vision students were trying to express. The two adult founders, McMullen and Byrd, were adept enablers who were able to take the ideas, emotions, and thoughts of the youth, capture their feelings of social injustice in communities of color, and find ways to mediate the anger and channel it more productively.

Although the Rodney King beating generated the emotional response that later became the initial spark for beginning the garden, the program did not exist until students decided to take the entrepreneurial route. It was still basically a community garden at first. However, when the students said, "Let's make money from this," things changed. The program sprung out of that. Food from the 'Hood netted $600 in the first year, and this profit motivated students because they saw the potential of this business (Educational Record, 1996). Eventually the business expanded beyond growing produce to manufacturing salad dressing, which was believed to have a higher profit margin. The salad dressing was called Straight Out 'the Garden Creamy Italian Dressing.

Food from the 'Hood's mission has five important dimensions: "(1) create jobs for youth; (2) show that young people can and do make a difference; (3) prove that business can be socially responsible, environmentally friendly, and profitable; (4) give back to the community; and (5) use this experience to prepare for the future." Further, Food from the 'Hood is committed to enhancing academic performance, business development, college preparation, and community building. Succeeding in each of these areas by themselves would be challenging. Succeeding at four, however, is extremely challenging!

The program, however, does not lose sight of the importance of youth being prepared for the world of career (Food from the 'Hood, 1997, p. 2): "This grassroots organization stresses the development of values, skills, self-discipline, and socially responsible business practices through the practicum of operating, managing, and maintaining a natural products line, as well as a quarter-acre organic garden. We strive to use independent growers and vendors located in enterprise development zones as our primary vendors."

PROGRAM-SPECIFIC DESCRIPTION

The program's mission, as already indicated, is to create jobs for youth and help them to develop social responsibility. Using real-world business experience, students learn how to prepare for the future, learn responsibility, and embrace the belief that young people can and do make a difference in a community and society. The program seeks to develop the idea of social empowerment within its participants by addressing the gaps that exist between education and career. As a result, the program focuses on four major areas: (1) community, (2) social development, (3) personal development, and (4) business skill development.

Not surprisingly, Crenshaw High School students encountered a disconnect between what they were learning in school and the knowledge and skills they needed to enter the career force. Thus, creating a meaningful and close connection between careers and school and providing inner-city youth who generally would not get an opportunity to learn business skills and real-life skills became increasingly important. School-based enterprises do not have the luxury of totally ignoring academic subjects. Instead, they need to find creative ways of integrating academic subjects into the enterprises and making the content of this subject matter relevant to day-to-day activities of the program. Through this program, students are exposed to math, English, and science, and these subjects take on new meaning when applied to real-life situations.

Like any good enterprise, this program is used as a vehicle to introduce and prepare students for the world they will eventually be entering by giving them the competencies, requisite attitudes, and experiences to be able to make the transition from school to career. In addition, the program not only provides an opportunity for students to learn about higher education, it also goes a step beyond, saying the opportunity is available, and helps them to actually access higher education. By getting the necessary skills to run a business, students get a real idea of what the real world is like. However, it is also important to get youth to pursue higher education, be it business-related or otherwise. The program's core focuses on entrepreneurial business-skill development, using business training and life skills development, such as presentation skills, responsible behavior, punctuality, signing in, and college preparatory classes. Although public announcements were made at school, students were generally not attending the college visits or picking up SAT information and were thus uninformed. As a result, staff members serve as coaches for business development, life skills, college preparation, team building, and leadership development.

The garden, however, for all intents and purposes signified community building, leadership networking, and teamwork (*Newsweek*, 1995, p. 29): "The goal was simple: to create a community garden that would bring life back to one of the city's most battered neighborhoods while giving the students some hands-on science experience. They planted flowers, herbs, lettuce, collard greens and other vegetables." The training core eventually evolved to embrace entrepreneurial content. However, that was not always the case. As the program evolved, its foci shifted and embraced more complex social and economic goals, one of the primary goals being students furthering their education upon graduation from Crenshaw High School.

Once students have been referred, there is a follow-up, and they are required to fill out an application and join the existing group at the garden, which is where the team building happens. Any screening out is minimal. There is no screening out based on either language or learning differences. However students must have a grade point average of "C" or better in order to participate in any school-connected program. The college placement rate for Food from the 'Hood participants has been outstanding, rivaling any youth-focused program anywhere in the country. All participants in Food from the 'Hood graduate from high school and over 95 percent go on to colleges throughout the country, although the state of California has a major share of the enrollees. In 2000 alone, 12 Food from the 'Hood alumni graduated from major universities across the country.

Most of the students participating in the program are not necessarily the cream of the crop or part of the magnet program. The program's original intent was to remain inclusive and, as a result, according to the executive director, "It's a replica of the garden—all kinds of fruits and vegetables." The primary advantage of having a diverse group of participants is that it prepares students to work with people of different backgrounds and abilities. Youth are always looking for a place they can belong and fit in. This program, as a result, understands the importance of space and place in the lives of youth and will not screen out youth because they do not meet rigid criteria for participation.

In 2002 the population involved in the program was primarily African American (80%) and Latino/a (17%). They were all Crenshaw High School students between the ages of 14 and 18. Students currently in the program primarily do referrals to the program. Most student owners are recruited into the company. Through student or program graduate referral, students invite other students, interview them, and then bring them in. On occasion students are recommended through teacher referrals.

Program participation is broad in scope. Student owners or interns are assigned to teams based on their abilities and interests, which are constantly evolving and changing during this developmental stage. Students take on progressively more important roles, interfacing with adults as equals rather than as subordinates. Staff members actively work to help participants increase their self-esteem. It is well accepted within the program that youth with low-self esteem do not have a high likelihood of achieving in this endeavor or in later efforts.

Youth have an established schedule that they follow on a weekly basis, carrying out specific tasks. Students have primary responsibility for carrying out and completing these tasks. On Fridays they usually listen to a speaker or do quality checks. Saturdays are devoted to tending to the garden. There are five teams of participants: (1) sales and marketing; (2) public relations; (3) advertising; (4) production; and (5) finance. The composition of each team is carefully thought out. Each team consists of a student intern (someone who has just entered the program, usually a freshman or a sophomore), a student owner (someone who has been in the program for at least a year and a half and knows the program), a graduate (someone who has graduated from the program), and a mentor (board member, volunteer, or an advisor).

The use of teams ensures that there is continuity if someone leaves the program. All students are involved in other parts of the program, such as research and development (i.e., products), accounting (but do not necessarily do the accounting), and office management (but do not manage the office). Initially, in the program's early history, there was no distinction in roles, but now there is an administrative team, which is primarily responsible for accounting and office management and most of whom are program alumni. The program, however, is now in the process of creating an infrastructure that will take the company to the next level.

Graduates run accounting and manage the office. Funding, however, wields a considerable amount of influence on staffing patterns. Funding for an administrative assistant is divided in half to fund two employees. Administrative assistants work 20 hours a week since each is expected to be in school. This program, in essence, can be conceptualized as an after-school program. When it was on campus, students who were in Ms. Byrd's biology class were running the program instead of studying conventional biology lessons. But the reality is that this is a business that is run after school. Students are primarily involved after school, on weekends, and during the summers. Now that the administrative part of the program is physically removed from the school, the program is now full time all year. Food from the 'Hood has evolved into a work-study program. This has resulted in more extensive staff coverage. Everyone works on Monday. In the afternoon everything is turned over to the students. One of the primary goals is to begin to tie in a real corporate structure into a community/grassroots organization.

The organization, in lieu of employing an operations manager, has a graduate overseeing daily production. Student interns and owners now interface with an operations manager and are very integrated. Student owners learn how to run office equipment, and an office manager is responsible for all other activities. This organizational change has resulted in staff helping participants with their math in order for them to be better able to do accounting. A student who is interested in a particular aspect of the organization has the opportunity to interface with students becoming interested in other dimensions of the enterprise. There is an onsite youth training specialist in Crenshaw High School, and efforts are under way to hire one for Dorsey and Audubon high schools. Staff members are very cognizant of minimizing the shock associated with moving from school to the real world.

Food from the 'Hood provides scholarship money for student participants. Since 1992 the program has raised over $200,000 and provided 77 scholarships to participants. On average, participants receive between $2,000 and

$3000 to cover college expenses. Fifty percent of all proceeds are reinvested into the program to cover expenses, and 50 percent goes directly into a scholarship fund. Twenty-five percent of all produce goes to feed the hungry of Los Angeles. A system was developed where student owners started checking in to get points for the work that they did. It's similar to using your time card. They use Quick Books to keep track of hours worked. Students arrive and check in and can tell how much work they did. They get 100 points for every hour. They calculate their time and get appropriate credit for time. However, the type of work done is also weighed (bonus points for particular jobs). One hundred points per hour determine a point's value. The board and the staff determine bonus points. At the end of the academic year, the points are totaled in order to determine the base from which to ascertain their value. Each student's total points are then divided into the pool of money to award the profits from the company.

Although youth feel tremendous satisfaction in working and providing a service to their community, their motivation to continue to participate in the program cannot rely solely on these factors. The potential for travel, particularly international travel, is a powerful motivator. Travel to other countries to show how Food from the 'Hood operates is a recent occurrence. In 2000 participants traveled to Germany to participate in the World's Fair, EXPO. Food from the 'Hood participated in a segment entitled More than Food, which featured natural food companies that have a strong social component such as giving food back to their communities.

Originally there was considerable parent involvement in the program. However, it is now considered very low. Parents who were initially involved in the program did so as a means of finding out more about what the program entailed. Now there is parent involvement but not to the same degree. Parents' knowledge of the program has proved to be a mixed blessing. Staff members have had a challenge convincing parents that they should still want to know more. Further, the attitude of parents in the school today is not considered optimal for active parental involvement. Thus, parental involvement is considered minimal.

Many parents are simply overwhelmed in meeting day-to-day requirements of life in Los Angeles and participating in program activities and events. The staff believes that parental attendance has become more of a job than a responsibility. For example, there is particularly low parental involvement among younger parents. Younger people are parenting, and their primary goal has essentially been to survive, directing much of their energy into their jobs with people other than biological parents—rearing a large number of students. Consequently, natural parents are not parenting a high number of their children. Parents see going to school the same way they view going to the dentist. They do not have the time, and the visit is not one that they would normally look forward to.

FUNDING SOURCES

In order to be eligible for community dollars, Food from the 'Hood needed to distance itself from the school. The program had to choose between being community based or school based. So the program needed to get into the empowerment zone, and in order to do that they needed to relocate. Although it is generally preferable for fund raising to generate cash, there are other forms of obtaining financial support. In addition to conventional sources for funding, Food from the 'Hood has obtained land from Crenshaw High School, a van donated by Prince Charles of Britain, who visited the program, water donated by the Los Angeles Fire Department, and advertising from a variety of sources in the private sector.

The institute is 90 percent supported by grants, which cover all staff salaries. The original $50,000 grant that led to the development of Food from the 'Hood came from Rebuild Los Angeles (RLA). In the beginning, the goal was to have 50 percent of the funding supported by grants and the other half from business enterprises. Much of the program's attention to product development went into the development of a salad dressing. However, with this increased attention it meant that marketing the new product suffered because there were no advertising dollars available for this purpose. Neither were youth out there moving the product and this caused economic hardships for the organization. The organization developed a ranch dressing and a "2 Thousand Island" (twice as good), boosting sales and amount of scholarships. Currently, the distribution of salad dressings is widespread, with over 2,000 grocery stores in California carrying the products, not including natural-food stores in 23 states (Griffin, 1996).

One of the central goals of the company is to become self-sustaining and, through growth, it is hoped that this goal can be achieved. Reliance on foundation and corporate grants have the potential to compromise the mission of Food from the 'Hood. Funders have to meet their criteria. Consequently, Food from the 'Hood hasn't shifted the way it does business. Fortunately, prior grants have not conflicted with the goals of the organization. However, the continual search for this type of funding takes valuable time away from other activities within the program. There is recognition that to change the current funding pattern, sales must be increased significantly and costs kept stable in the process.

Food from the 'Hood hired a grant writer in 2001. Grant procurement was originally the responsibility of the executive director. However, the executive director's time and energy was divided between generating funds and day-to-day operations. Now that there is a person whose prime responsibility is grant writing, the executive director is now able to pay greater attention to staff development, public relations, program evaluation, and recruitment of participants.

YOUTH DEVELOPMENT FOUNDATION

The question of how best to prepare students for life after graduation guided the formulation of the program's goals and activities. Youth participants must be guided and supported during the initial involvement in the program. At-risk youth encounter numerous challenges in the course of day-to-day living and are adjusting to a world that is often unpredictable. Staff members do not attempt to act as surrogate parents and instead view their role as collaborators with youth, a much more empowering perspective. The role of mentoring is well understood. Service to community, a critical element of any youth development inspired initiative, is well integrated into the program's mission and operation. Food from the 'Hood is a social youth enterprise well grounded in social values. Leadership development, in turn, has also found a prominent place within the organization.

Staff members see themselves as compassionate and able to help participants adjust to the outside world. Youth need to get better at documenting and communicating. Staff members teach students to get ready for real-life situations. This is accomplished through the use of outside trainers, role-playing, constructive criticism, anger management, and shyness control (inferiority, unknown). The program requires participants to get out and about in the community and undertake campaigns. One church campaign required youth to go out to different churches and give out press kits and practice public speaking. Food from the 'Hood requires that youth take ownership of their company. Many youth did not like to talk. They were put in teams with youth who enjoyed public speaking, who then taught those who didn't. Youth also had to learn phone etiquette, do demonstrations, community expositions, and bazaars, interface with the public, and go to homeless shelters and speak to the residents. Youth also had to develop the ability to work with peers and adults. Food from the 'Hood, in addition, sought to have them work with positive adult role models, who could help coach them through a school-to-career transition.

LESSONS LEARNED

Programs Evolve in Order to Take into Account Local-Specific Circumstances and Opportunities

Food from the 'Hood started as a school-based enterprise. However, social, economic, and political considerations necessitated that it relocate from a school base to a community base, a major transition in the history and development of the enterprise. Prior to 1992, although there was a business department, there was no focus on entrepreneurship at the school.

Curriculum has since evolved, but there is still no formal entrepreneurial business program, and even now there is very little vocational or school- to-career/real-world preparation. Program staff and participants believe that what the students are learning has had little or no relevance to their real-life goals. The science department was suffering before Food from the 'Hood was established. It did not have a science fair, and a lot of theoretical information was not translated into practical information.

When the program first began, it was still considered a project within the school—an extension of the science department's curriculum. As a result, the school basically left it alone, and the program was able to grow even though it was largely viewed as a little lab experiment. Many people were not even aware that there was a community garden in the backyard of the school. Possibly even fewer knew that there was a program attached to it or believed that the program would achieve as much national recognition as it has. Despite its national success, however, the product is conspicuously absent from both the Crenshaw High School cafeteria and the Los Angeles Unified School District's cafeterias. While the program itself was generated and housed on school property and run by Crenshaw High School students, there is a huge disconnect, which finally resulted in the program actually leaving its Crenshaw High School roots.

In 2001, the program was located about five minutes from the school. The site actually moved from the original site, which was at the back of the biology teacher's classroom, about a year ago. Prior to the relocation, everything from administration, to marketing, and product development happened in the same room. The program needed to expand its space. Students couldn't concentrate. Finally a decision was made by the former director and the board to begin the search for a place nearby. The decision was then made to relocate the administrative part of the program to an off-campus site.

The site chosen is at an enterprise incubator. There are only two sites in South Central Los Angeles, and they are now located at the site of the very first incubator in South Central, the Vermont/ Slauson business center, which is centrally situated in the empowerment zone. There are two major advantages to its new location: (1) it is now located in the middle of an empowerment zone and, as a result, the program can now benefit from empowerment zone funding; and (2) its new location now closely approximates a real-world business environment. Incubators have as a central goal the development of start-up enterprises and are able to access the resources, that is, space, workshops, and entrepreneurial courses sponsored by the incubator, including access to computers and a receptionist. It is a different setting from that of Crenshaw High School; there are clean bathrooms and no graffiti. This has resulted in the program moving away from being strictly an after-school program and developing more of its entrepreneurial goals and activities.

The original Crenshaw High School garden is also no longer affiliated with Food from the 'Hood because the site was not being utilized and was needed for another program with an ecology focus. Crenshaw Veterans Memorial Gardens offered the Food from the 'Hood program a space at Veterans Gardens in Westwood, which is now where the garden work occurs. Changes and shifts in program management meant those resources, including time, were used for other things. Most of the activity focused on the entrepreneurial goals. Although the garden is still very important for team building, there has not been any activity in the garden for a while. Food from the 'Hood was promised another space on campus, but the space never materialized. Crenshaw High School was already overcrowded, and space was limited. When a new principal was appointed to the school, Food from the 'Hood was given a classroom that became their on-campus program site.

The program is now considered a freestanding program and has evolved in part due to the fact that it is no longer physically tied to Crenshaw High School's campus. The business part of the program has always been growing, but because it was located on the Crenshaw High School campus it was subject to school regulations, bureaucracy, and problems, as well as break-ins, shutdowns, and lockdowns. Rather than contributing to or enhancing the program, the school atmosphere, it was felt, began to interfere with the program's goals and its ability to expand.

Running a business on a school campus became increasingly difficult because students could not make appointments to see their vendors, nor could vendors/visitors come to visit. In addition, getting on campus was difficult if there was a lockdown, which meant the program itself was not accessible during these periods. There are clear advantages to having an enterprise based within school grounds because of accessibility for students. However, there are also clear disadvantages.

Entrepreneurial Programs Must Successfully Address the Needs of the Community

The program seeks to address community issues at the micro- rather than a macrolevel. Staff members respond to issues affecting the community on a daily basis because poverty, racism, and discrimination affect the youth they work with directly and indirectly. The reality is that they are working with students who face these on a regular basis. The program helps students address these forces on an individual basis and does so in meetings as they arise. Crenshaw High School draws students from a geographical area where approximately 90 percent of the youth in foster care are special needs students, and grandparents or other relatives are rearing most of the children in the community.

The school is faced with a large proportion of students who have learning disabilities and/or are in ESL classes. Food from the 'Hood has been largely successful by pulling out a segment of this population, which is relatively representative of the community at large. There is no gang affiliation among this group, but there are students who experience emotional instability, have learning disabilities and, as a result, have low self-esteem. When asked how they would describe the program, one participant responded: "Not the grooviest people on campus, not the nerdy, kind of a hodgepodge. Music is a great way to get a sense of the group. Music tastes range from rap, rock, techno, R&Bs, oldies, to the classics. Music is one way to look at who currently makes up Food from the 'Hood." Being a place that is welcoming for all students is important in the life of any school or community, and nowhere is this more evident than in Crenshaw High School in South Central Los Angeles!

From the beginning stages in the program's history, the community has played a critical role in its development and existence. Salad dressing, for example, has stayed on the shelves in the stores even when the program went through a slow period and there was no active effort to market the product. Food from the 'Hood holds a prominent place in the community. Their product is not competitive with any other salad grower, and it is in community stores because people are saying they at least would like to try it. Leaders within the community speak well of the program, and the challenge is to ensure that the program stays in the forefront of their minds and meets the needs of the community.

Although Crenshaw High School students have been the predominant target group, there are plans to expand the program to other area schools because of a belief that the program needs to be part of a community-wide effort rather than be narrowly school defined. The director gave the following scenario: "[We] have to expand the program for several reasons. [We have] always been associated with just Crenshaw. What happens if you have a person who has always lived across the street from Crenshaw and then you go to another school or attend a parochial school? Are you not able to participate in this?"

Production Challenges

Making changes within a program is never for the faint of heart. However, it is widely acknowledged that any enterprise that lacks flexibility to respond to emerging opportunities is doomed to fail. Even some minor changes have tremendous implications for a program such as Food from the 'Hood, changing the size of a product being but one example. Nevertheless, in order for social youth enterprises to grow, they must be prepared to change in order to maximize their market for a product or service.

From a production standpoint the program wishes to broaden its market by changing the size of its product to include establishments. Salad dressings need to be packaged into larger sizes such as gallons. The packer they currently employ does not have this capacity, and Food from the 'Hood has had the same copacker for the last nine years. Thus, they will need to go to another packer who can package in gallons, which will then open up a market involving restaurants and companies that service the restaurant/food industry such as Smart, Final, and Costco.

Achieving Self-Sufficiency and Sustainable Development as Goals Is Arduous to Accomplish

Food from the 'Hood, at the time of the site visit, was in the process of putting together business plans to obtain commercial funding through venture capitalists and banks who have community development funds. Expanding the potential sources of grant funds, like expanding the market for products and services, is a reality in well-established social youth enterprise programs. Food from the 'Hood would like investment businesses to fund the social enterprise aspect of the program. This funding would facilitate Food from the 'Hood to expand its market for salad dressing by teaming up with other companies. The program needs funding to expand advertisement through television and billboards that can go on buses. Thus, the program perceives that it cannot develop without this additional infusion of capital. There is general agreement that there is lots of room to grow. Sales are currently projected at $250,000 a year, with potential to multiply severalfold with additional capital.

New Product Development Brings with It Advantages and Disadvantages for a Social Enterprise

The ever-constant search for new products to expand a business market brings with it excitement for youth and makes programs ever-vigilant for expansion into new markets. This search, as a result, requires youth to think strategically and practically. Finding the next hot product, however, has some inherent detractions and challenges. Development of a new product without a corresponding imaginative marketing plan is of limited use to social youth enterprises. New product development, in turn, must be done within the mission of the organization—namely, not sidetracking the organization into a totally new market.

Ironically, the expansion of salad dressings in the enterprise has essentially disconnected youth from the production of the new product and brought with it a set of challenges. The actual production of salad dressing is contracted out to Sweet Adelaide, so students are involved in the business enterprise, public relations, marketing, sales, but not the production of the product. They know it is bottled, and then it comes back. However, they really do not understand the whole process. Thus, the Executive Director suggested to the board that students be involved in the production side of the enterprise.

Development of new products or expansion of current production capacities require the hiring of new personal, possibly with skill sets that are new to the organization. Food from the 'Hood, as a result, is in need of a food chemist and a staff who can run the production and manage whole systems. Most students know that they bank their hours and that they get some money after four years if they meet the criteria. Unfortunately, most youth do not have a sense of how money can be invested and how it can grow—neither are they aware of how to start a checking account and other banking basics. Students get to know a great deal about business but personal finance is another matter altogether. Most youth programs have a tendency to lose youth who are seniors in high school because of their need to earn money to pay for the senior prom or to pay for entrance examinations for college. Students need money and most of them have parents who are not able to provide it.

Recruiting and Maintaining Political Support

Expanding recruitment efforts for participants, maintaining community support through constant talking to community leaders and educational leaders, and expanding support in the Los Angeles Unified School District (LAUSD) have been quite challenging. In addition, curriculum development, which is now being finalized, has been difficult. They are currently bonding the curriculum book together and working on an instructional video to accompany it. Food from the 'Hood solicited funding through the city's community development program.

Prior to the Rodney King riots, Los Angeles' urban renewal program divided the city into community development zones. Each zone, in turn, was further divided into regions. After the riots, the community catchment areas were changed, and Crenshaw High School was not considered a part of the community development zone. As a result the program at Crenshaw High School was ineligible for community development dollars. But a location two streets over from the school was considered to be in the zone. The community, however, advocated for the program. City officials said Crenshaw High School was not in the empowerment zone. The program needed to be in the empowerment zone in order to get funding.

Fundraising and Development Remain Major Challenges

The primary grant the program was receiving at the time of the site visit was from the Entrepreneurial Institute; however, to make the company sustainable there is a need to bring in best practices. In order to do that they need to attract personnel, and in order to accomplish that they need funding to pay the personnel. This has necessitated the initiation of an aggressive public awareness campaign with the goal of reminding the community why the program is important and why it was started.

Presenting the organization in a way that can facilitate its going after big grants can be quite labor intensive and thus challenging. It is relatively easy to access small grants in the amounts of $5,000, $10,000, and $15,000. However, to be eligible for greater funds Food from the 'Hood needs to have full financial statements and be able to hire an accountant to develop these statements and to pass requisite audits. "Got to do a whole lot to put yourself in a position to get the 200,000 and half million dollars bracket. We're grass-roots. Have to show successes of the program continuously despite the handicap of not having the dollars to be able to do the stuff they need to do. Building just a little bit at a time."

Maintaining a Social Enterprise Is Different from Operating Any Other Form of Enterprise

Food from the 'Hood is attempting to accomplish three major goals; it is a nonprofit with a for-profit enterprise. As a for-profit side of the enterprise, the staff members are trying to run the company like any other company. However, running the institute of the for-profit side, which has a training component, changes the focus. The organization needs program staff that not only can do training but can also engage in the operations aspects of the company. In essence, Food from the 'Hood needs to hire staff that have capabilities to not only impart knowledge and support youth, but also to operate the enterprise. Needless to say, these individuals are very special and not easy to come by.

Social youth enterprises must also be prepared to respond to the social expectations of youth and their communities. Balancing multiple responsibilities can be quite challenging for youth as well as adults. Obtaining funds to be able to do all aspects of the enterprise, for example, is a challenge. It often means that program staff must expand their vision of funding sources. Unfortunately, funding sources are invariably categorical in nature—for example, they may fund counseling but not product development.

Free Publicity Is an Excellent Form of Public Relations

Food from the 'Hood found out quickly that publicity translates well into marketing the program, participants, and products. This public exposure is hard to quantify into dollars and profits. However, there is little disputing that receiving local and national publicity has aided the program in marketing its products and obtaining foundation and corporation grants. Major newspapers and magazines such as the *Los Angeles Times*, *New York Times*, *Washington Post*, *People Magazine*, and *Newsweek* have spotlighted Food from the 'Hood.

Public relations also translates into bringing positive news coverage for the South Central Los Angeles neighborhood. Thus, Food from the 'Hood becomes a very attractive program to house and support because of its positive reputation, which also reflects on those organizations actively supporting it. It becomes a win-win situation for all participating parties. There can never be too much positive news.

FINAL COMMENTS

There is no question that this nation is in desperate need of youth programs inside and outside of school. Schools cannot be expected to meet every need youth have in any community and this need for youth programs takes on greater importance in undervalued communities. Programs such as Food from the 'Hood are needed to facilitate direct one-on-one relationships with students who can get lost in the shuffle. These programs take on the responsibility of tracking the development of students and advocating for them when needed. Any program that tracks the development of the students during their high school years provides continuity, which may not be available at home regardless of socioeconomic background. This is needed. It takes time. It doesn't happen overnight. It takes at least a year to two years to properly pull a program together.

Social youth enterprises must consist of multiple components that systematically address the business and social sides of youth and communities. The community has to be on board, and the task is labor intensive because involvement needs to be cultivated; further, involvement of both educators and parents is needed. The need for funding is always present. Social youth enterprises cannot be constantly worried about where the funding is going to come from. Youth very often face this challenge in the home and do not need to also constantly face it while participating in youth programs. Constant search for funding effectively detracts from the potentially positive experience youth can have in social youth enterprises.

CHAPTER 9

Young Aspirations/Young Artists (YA/YA), New Orleans

RATIONALE FOR SELECTION

Social youth enterprises can take many shapes and can easily adapt themselves to local circumstances, wide-ranging budgets, and community opportunities. No one-size-fits-all formula applies to these types of enterprises and any effort to standardize these types of enterprises is doomed to fail. The need for flexibility in conceptualization of these types of social enterprises makes comparisons between programs arduous. This need is clearly the case when comparing Food from the 'Hood with YA/YA, the subject of this case study. Further, an ability to evolve and expand the business aspect of the enterprise is usually a good indicator of social youth enterprises' ability to not only survive but also thrive in an ever-changing and demanding marketplace.

The prior case study of Food from the 'Hood focused on development of a product (vegetables and salad dressings). The enterprise has a strong history of school involvement, although this shifted. YA/YA, in turn, provides youth with an opportunity to engage in very different types of product development. Moreover, this enterprise does not require land. The artistic talents of youth of color have generally gone unnoticed in this society. All too often, American culture, primarily through its schools, has placed considerable value and emphasis on youth of color as athletes. YA/YA places emphasis on art. Art-centered enterprises, however, can be multidimensional in scope and can promote enterprise skill acquisition in addition to indigenous artistic talents. These types of enterprises can be large- or small-scaled, bringing a high degree of flexibility into how social youth enterprises focused on the arts can be conceptualized and operationalized on a daily basis.

CONTEXT AND HISTORICAL BACKGROUND

An artist, Jana, who also had extensive entrepreneurial skills and was very interested in youth activities and programs, founded YA/YA in 1988. Jana obtained permission from the principal of Reboutin Vocational High School to have 31 students (aged 15 to 20) attend painting classes that she was teaching. At the end of the contracted period, which was several months, she mounted an exhibition of the students' architectural paintings of historic New Orleans buildings and invited prominent people to their show. The paintings, priced between $12 and $20, sold out. The total amount raised was $1,800. Shortly afterward, Jana received a donation of secondhand chairs. She enlisted youth to paint them, and this was the spark that started YA/YA. The initial YA/YA group consisted of 25 students. Within one year, eight of the original group remained.

The organization at the time of this case study was in the process of growing more independent of Jana, who was still involved but not to the same degree as before. The program needed the charisma of an artist (which is what Rondell brings) with an artistic vision as well as a social vision. The codirectors, Anne and Rondell, have different foci that complement each other, and they share the responsibilities of director. Each has direct supervision, but they act as a backup for each other. Anne is directly responsible for Martha (financial assistant), and Rondell has direct responsibility for Coop (artistic director). Jana owned the building in which YA/YA was originally housed. YA/YA, however, has since moved across the street, and the building is being sold.

The space is a working studio/gallery. Smaller space is important because it defines this new generation of YA/YAs in a new and positive way. The move into a new setting has been beneficial to YA/YA for a variety of reasons. Space size and configuration can facilitate communication and group cohesion, and this certainly has been the case in the new setting. In the former space, the group wasn't as close; people could and did come and go without interacting with staff. The old space was large.

The name YA/YA was selected for a variety of very compelling reasons (Barker, 1996, p. 5): "YA/YA is an acronym for Young Aspirations/Young Artists. There is also a Yoruban word, ya-ya, meaning 'eldest daughter,' and in New Orleans, the food capital of the South, the term has developed a colloquial meaning through the phrase 'gumbo ya-ya,' a rich local soup. . . . So it fits, this odd-sounding name, on a variety of levels, to describe what Jana [founder] gave to her students. It means hope and art, food and family. It is local and international, Anglo and African. It is what the first eight YA/YA Guild members came to be called: the YA/YAs."

The name selected for a social youth enterprise program has a greater significance than probably for any other type of youth program. Social youth enterprises, unfortunately, are very rare across the country, compared to their social youth program counterparts, and what they name themselves must have strategic as well as symbolic meaning. Marketing and advertising play such an important role in youth enterprises, particularly in social youth enterprises.

The program is based upon a fundamental premise that youth have talents and that opportunities must be provided to allow them to identify and enhance these talents. If this is accomplished, youth can become self-sufficient through creative expression and artistic production. In the process of doing so, they can also learn the business side of art. Thus, YA/YA's primary mission is to open doors for inner-city youth in New Orleans through the creation of an environment that nurtures the participants and allows them to take advantage of other learning opportunities. Participants learn to work independently or in teams, whichever is necessary; to utilize their creativity and entrepreneurial skills in their communities; and to further their artistic talents in new forms. In essence, the successful YA/YA member is someone who is flexible, committed, and willing to work by himself or in a group when called upon.

YA/YA's hope for the future is well articulated in the following vision (Barker, 1996, p. 53): "Although we do not presume that YA/YA will cure America of its communication problems between people of different income levels, age, race, gender, or outlook, we do believe that the YA/YA's success has created a conversation about creativity and its origins that did not exist before." YA/YA's mission has always been for youth to develop a firm commitment to their present circumstances but also to look toward the future with some form of an art focus. There is also a recognition that youth must develop a better understanding of the world outside of their communities in order to better market their artwork.

YA/YA's mission has also been very much shaped by the context of the city of New Orleans (Goldsmith, 1997, p. 1): "The main goal of YA/YA . . . is to have graduates become professionally self-sufficient through creative expression, and we believe creative expression can take many forms. We're starting our second decade. We'd like to see New Orleans as a design center and YA/YA as the center of that." The city of New Orleans has a national and international reputation. Its architecture is unique, particularly within the French Quarter. Neighborhoods are generally not well defined geographically; mansions stand right next to public housing developments. This incredible proximity of neighborhoods brings a unique perspective to life in New Orleans for youth. Youth do not encounter many "don't-go-there" areas. People have a reputation for being genuinely friendly. The city's pace is not as fast as that in other major metropolitan areas of the country. New Orleans is a small enough city that it lends itself to residents being able to go relatively anywhere in the city proper in less than 15 minutes.

Although New Orleans has tremendous charm and resources, it, like other metropolitan areas of the country, has its set of challenges for youth. Young people find that they cannot go anywhere in New Orleans without running into someone they know, making it virtually impossible to be anonymous. A few years ago, New Orleans instituted a 9 P.M. curfew for youth under the age of 18, and this has created problems when a project has required late hours. YA/YA, as a result, had to obtain identification cards for participants in order for them to prove that they were working and had permission to be out after curfew.

The cost of living is relatively low for a major city. Housing is considered very affordable, with approximately 40 percent of residents owning their own homes. However, income levels are considered relatively low. According to the 2000 U.S. Census Bureau, African Americans are in the racial/ethnic majority; they represent 60 percent of the population. The city's population has been stable between 1990 and 2000. Two major festivals, Mardi Gras and Jazz Fest, are the major revenue producers in the city. New Orleans, as a result, relies heavily on tourism. The crime rate is high by most standards, and education and employment are also considered hot-button issues.

YA/YA's goals are multifaceted and address both youth and their community: (1) provide youth with an opportunity to develop their artistic talents; (2) open up possibilities for youth to continue their postsecondary education; (3) enhance New Orleans's reputation nationally as an artistic center; (4) develop in youth business and financial competencies that can be transferred into art and other aspects of their daily life; and (5) help to ensure that youths' socioemotional needs are met through participation in business enterprises.

The purchase of a YA/YA artwork can be conceptualized in a variety of ways. It can simply be viewed as the acquisition of an art piece for the home or business because of its esthetic value. Another reason to buy might be a social investment in youth (Barker, 1996, p. 45): "Most people who buy YA/YA artwork believe that they are making an investment in someone's future. So the real product is not the artwork; it is the young person who is creating it with his stories and images and sweat. But in order for most people to be able to see that, the artwork must be authentic, honest, and real."

YA/YA, like other social youth enterprises, has extensive community connections and actively embraces the importance of program-community relations. Community connections have occurred in a variety of ways and arenas. YA/YA, for example, annually has a craft booth at the Jazz Festival. At the time of this case study visit, students were currently working on completing projects that were especially developed for Jazz Fest. YA/YA partners youth with commercial art instructors for individual instruction in woodworking, painting, design, and fabric painting.

YA/YA, also at the time of the site visit, was in the process of negotiating with HUD to paint a mural for a housing development, which currently looks rather drab and uninspiring, in New Orleans. HUD is taking over the Housing Authority of New Orleans, and YA/YA is being contracted to work with community groups by using facilities in the housing development to design a new look for the development. YA/YA acts as a conduit by bringing the vision, ideas, and images of their clients together into a workable concept. Designs for community projects are client-driven and -inspired.

YA/YA has historically maintained an active set of community collaborations in an effort to more effectively carry out its mission. The following list
of community organizations highlight the type and range of collaborations
undertaken and completed over the past several years: KIDS CAFÉ helped
paint a mural for their dining room; KIDS museum; Hope HAVEN (group
home for troubled kids) helped them paint chairs for their center; Columbus,
OH MLK community Center painted a mural; Durham, Hitite Center
painted chairs, and showed them the process of design and prepping of chairs;
St John's Baptist Church painted mural; Cafe Du Monde painted mural.
These collaborations not only served to connect YA/YA with the community
but, in many cases, they also generated commissions for the project.

In the past, there hasn't been a great deal of collaboration between youth
organizations, although there has been extensive contact between these
types of organizations. Youth organizations generally come to visit because
they want to learn more about YA/YA and are not fully established programs.
YA/YA, however, has collaborated with Team Inspiration and hopes to develop
more collaborative ventures with youth organizations throughout New Orleans.

The Jazz Festival, although not a formal collaborative partner, represents
a form of community involvement. It is a juried event that YA/YA participates
in every year and that youth actively target as a major event. Four categories
of artists compete in this event: (1) contemporary crafts; (2) Louisiana Marketplace—artists from Louisiana; (3) Congo Square—African Diaspora (the
only area that allows a consortium of artists); and (4) Native Americans.

Artistic experience is not necessary for students to participate in YA/YA. In
fact, many students discover their artistic talents while involved in YA/YA.
Students are asked, however, to demonstrate their creativity via a design challenge required of every YA/YA member. Participants are required to main a
C average in order to be a member of YA/YA and a B average in order to
travel. This serves to encourage youth to not only stay in school but also to
do well enough to have options after graduation. Postsecondary education is
broadly defined and can consist of four-year institutions, community college,
art school, and apprenticeships with such organizations as Job Corps. Education is considered a vital part of self-sufficiency. Participants who elect not
to pursue higher education forfeit their savings to YA/YA. These funds, in
turn, pay for operating expenses (Fahey & Frickman, 2000).

Participants can attend YA/YA on a daily basis and on weekends when they
need to undertake large projects or work on individual commissions. Another
form of motivation for attending is that participants get a great deal of positive
recognition from inside and outside of the program (King, 2000, p. 5): "Since
the beginning of the organization, nonart journalists mentioned the names of
students. I believe giving them a personality and voice allowed the Guild to
survive through its lean and formative years. . . . Kids at YA/YA were given
responsibilities within the organization's structure. This accountability gave

YA/YA a source of pride and fulfillment in their lives that no one had ever given them before."

YA/YA's outreach efforts sought to accomplish two primary goals. Expanding the outreach efforts has had a significant impact on who participates in the program and has resulted in interesting other students in YA/YA. Rabouin Vocational High School was not considered one of the jumpiest schools (having a lot of educationally fun activities), and as a result youth thought there was not much going on there. YA/YA's other motivation was the desire to expand and reach more students. Opening YA/YA up to other students was initially successful, but eventually YA/YA ended up with roughly the same number of students. There are usually about 30 students, but only approximately 15 that show up on a daily basis. Daily attendance, as already noted, is not compulsory but influences decisions concerning commissions and travel.

There are usually more males than females involved; approximately six females participate in the program at any one time. Historically, this has always been the case, with males outnumbering females by a 3:1 ratio. Opening up YA/YA to other schools represented an effort to shift the gender balance and get more women involved in the program. Female students at Rabouin Vocational High School have historically enrolled in its cosmetology, nursing, and art programs. Anne suggests that the reason is that girls tend to be more focused than the boys and have more of an immediate and instrumental agenda such as finding service-industry jobs. Most, as a result, did not become involved in YA/YA to become artists or advance their artistic talents. They stayed involved because it was a fun thing to do after school, a way to pass the time, and a means of earning income.

Youth participant recruitment evolved over a period of time. Rabouin Vocational High School was originally the feeder school for YA/YA and the only school connected with YA/YA because of its proximity. It is literally around the corner from YA/YA. Interestingly, a few of YA/YA's participants went so far as to attend Rabouin Vocational High School simply because of YA/YA's ties to the school. However, students from other high schools in New Orleans are currently involved, making YA/YA a program for the city of New Orleans rather than for just one school.

Expansion into other schools had an interesting impact on inter-high school student relationships. Participants initially tended to identify strongly with their school, and there was little or no interaction between students from different high schools. YA/YA, however, has begun to break down that school social structure. Students in the program, as a result, are no longer exclusively tied to their school identities. Recruitment itself has not been formalized through active outreach or publicity activities and instead relies on peer efforts and community word-of-mouth.

A comment on YA/YA's board of directors is in order because of its makeup and its influential role in organizational development. YA/YA's board of directors is unique in many ways and highlights the potential of this resource for aiding social youth enterprises. The board of directors, like most boards, meets quarterly and consists of individuals from a variety of backgrounds: the current building landlord—he is also a lawyer; a proprietor of a specialty bookstore focusing on Louisiana/Southern writers and also a lawyer (nominally retired) and producer of an annual writer's festival; the associate producer of the Jazz Festival; a newspaper editor (board president); an alum from the program, currently a member of Why 5 (a spin-off, for-profit organization).

The board actively and effectively seeks to tie YA/YA into relationships/ connections with major institutions throughout the city in addition to providing expert advice and support. The composition of the board reflects the organizational needs of YA/YA. Having an alumnus as part of this governing body remains important.

The example of Tarrie Alexis illustrates the importance of a for-profit component to a social youth enterprise. Tarrie Alexis is a YA/YA alum and a board member of the organization. Tarrie has been involved for seven years; she was active in YA/YA as a student. Tarrie began in 1992. She read about the program in a local magazine (*Flip*) that was distributed for free at school when she was in junior high school. Her sister knew someone who was a participant in YA/YA. Further, she attended Rabouin Vocational High School, which was a requirement at the time to participate in YA/YA.

YA/YA also utilizes an advisory board as a way of introducing other people from different professions to YA/YA and getting them involved. The use of an advisory board provides YA/YA with the opportunity to tap resources that it currently does not have on the board of directors or that can supplement those on the board. This advisory group also provides YA/YA with the flexibility of initiating projects that can be supported by key persons and organizations on the advisory board.

YA/YA is a social enterprise that also provides a wide range of support for participants (Fahey et al., 2000, p. 42): "YA/YA promotes adolescent art. In addition, YA/YA functions unapologetically as an economic and social agency. YA/YA, like many other public art experiments . . . blurs boundaries. Like many projects that empower marginalized communities through cultural production, YA/YA's primary function is seen by many not as art but as social work." Social youth enterprises, when addressing marginalized youth, do not have the luxury of ignoring social dimensions in the lives of youth by totally focusing attention and resources on the enterprise side of the business. Both sides are essential in these types of enterprises, and this poses incredible challenges for program staff. The bridging of the social work and the business work is not just restricted to helping communities; participants also need to benefit in terms of expression and information.

YA/YA participants learn about the importance of deadlines, pricing, market assessment, client cultivation, proposals, balancing competing demands, prioritizing, and handling stress associated with a professional career in the arts. Participants, in addition to enhancing their artistic methods and learning about the business aspects of art, also take part in weekly classes on subjects such as conflict resolution, resume writing, and portfolio development. These topics are intended to address current issues as well as to prepare them for life postgraduation.

The lessons learned by YA/YA participants can easily be applied to other spheres in their lives (Barker, 1996, p. 109): "So our message in the YA/YA laboratory, to ourselves and to the students, is to use resources wisely— whether it is in the form of your own time, someone else's time, or the content of a brand new paint can—or you may not get any more. There is another kind of stewardship that is vital to YA/YA and is paramount in any endeavor whose focus is on young people. It goes beyond banking and bookkeeping, it is far more important than being written up in the newspaper, and it transcends the daily rules by which we run the organization. It is the careful stewardship of young people's souls. Sound awesome? It is?"

Although participants are not required to commit to attend higher education upon graduation from high school as a requirement for participating in YA/YA, conscious efforts are made to help youth make this type of decision. A variety of services are provided, such as assistance in obtaining application fee waivers and, in some instances, payment of the fee, tutoring, assistance in filling out applications, and guidance and counseling about the college process. Having former YA/YA graduates who attend or have graduated from college as staff also helps participants learn more about their options for higher education from someone who can certainly understand their concerns and insecurities as well as their strengths and dreams.

HIGHLIGHTS

One YA/YA alum, interviewed during the site visit, when asked to identify the key experiences he had while attending, noted the following as particularly standing out in his experience: (1) When he first arrived at YA/YA, there was no incoming cohort and he had to meld with either the group that entered before him or the one after. He was considered a fourth-generation YA/YA. Joining existing groups is never an easy task. However, experiences in doing so can prove quite rewarding in future situations. (2) Traveling was a great motivator for him. He had to maintain a B average in order to travel. Travel was the main motivation for participation. He went on to graduate with honors from high school. (3) Prior to arriving at YA/YA, he did not engage in painting. However, he learned to paint and draw during his participation. (4) He believed that the experience played a major role in helping him grow up and mature. He worked in the office and learned about business, clients, and the financial side of the enterprise. Internships had a great deal to do with this knowledge and skills acquisition. Internships provided financial assistance and opportunities to learn from senior-level staff and participants. Having to apply for internships helped him get "a feel for the business that way. Although they were not a requirement for participation, it was still a good way to get experience. Almost everyone did at least one of the internships. Just to get a feel."

The program relies heavily on voluntary student participation. The process of selection changes slightly over time, but a Guild system always selects students. As students advance up the Guild ladder, the level of commission changes. First- and second-year participants get 50 percent of their commissions, with 30 percent being set aside for a college fund and the remaining 20 percent used by YA/YA for operating expenses. Third-year members receive 80 percent, and 20 percent is reinvested in YA/YA. Most participants become Guild by the beginning of the 11th grade if they entered YA/YA by ninth grade. Guild is the highest level possible. Increased remuneration and responsibility as youth progress through the organization parallels a corporate model.

Guild levels determine how much youth earn from commissions and sales. Four levels exist in the Guild system:

1. Entry-level status. Most participants make entry-level within the first three months. At entry-level one takes home 50 percent of commissions, and 50 percent goes back to the company. Certain guidelines have to be completed before a person is eligible.

2. Apprentice status. Participants are really YA/YAs at this stage. They can travel, compete for commissions, and take home 50 percent of commissions.

3. Guild status. Participants need to be voted into the Guild by other Guild members and are expected to become Guild before graduating from high school. Entry into this level shows strong commitment. Guild members earn 80 percent of their commissions; they receive 50 percent up front, 30 percent is saved for college by YA/YA, and 20 percent goes back to the company. Guild members are expected to play greater leadership roles within the organization and plan and organize daily activities.

4. Alumni. Once members graduate from high school and enter a program of post-secondary education, they are elevated to senior Guild members. This fourth level is reserved for alumni. Alumni fulfill very important roles as mentors, program spokespersons, and advisors on commissioned projects. It is not unusual for program participants to establish lifelong relationships with other participants in the program, and this has certainly been the case with YA/YAs. A sense of family develops when participants don't just work together but also maintain contact outside of the program and after graduation.

All youth-focused programs face the challenge of how to keep participants motivated during periods when activities are not attractive or there is a lull in programming. Staff will often comment on the importance of youth developing the patience to endure during these periods. Lifelong lessons result for those who can maintain motivation during periods when the activities, or jobs, they are working on are not sufficiently challenging or satisfying.

YA/YA has identified and fostered mechanisms to keep youth engaged. In the past, internships were paid at an hourly rate, which answered the question of steady employment. Students used to come and just do artwork. The staff, in turn, would decide what the group projects would be. Current students now "own" more of their process. Now an outreach person keeps jobs available/job orders, which translates into more commissions. Prior to this change it was hard to keep youth motivated between commissions for jobs and it was not unusual to go two months before they received any money after a major project. Historically, commissions were presented to youth in a meeting, and a determination would be made concerning who would work on them based on level of interest.

Students are expected to compete for jobs and commissions and are also required to work with each other. A commission is considered a significant motivator because participants come from low-income families. An active level of participation in the program is expected. However, this is self-determined, and participants are not required to attend every day.

Free trips have been a great motivator for participants. One of the most important things about traveling was getting the opportunity to see how other people live. Participants have been to Singapore, Malaysia, Germany, Italy, Spain, and France as a result of being in YA/YA. Travel was probably one of the most motivating factors for participation, especially while the youth were in high school. This is a time when students are generally looking for clubs, something interesting that others are doing, some place to belong.

The level of participation students have shown is considered during trip participant selection. A committee looks at participation and grades in order to choose participants to go on field trips and community service projects. A conscious effort is made to include youth in the decision-making process, in partnership with adults. This selection committee consists of three students and two adult staff who determine job and travel assignments for youth. These travel assignments can be domestic as well as international.

FUNDING SOURCES

YA/YA has a budget of approximately $600,000 and serves a total of 40 youth, ages 15 to 21. Fifty percent of this budget is primarily derived from grants, with YA/YA generally obtaining 50 percent of its operating budget from commissions. The increased reliance in commissions for operating expenses, up from 13 percent in 1993 and 21 percent in 1994, for example, reflects expansion in its market. Grants, however, still play important roles in the life of the organization. In addition to helping pay for operating expenses, they have been used for project-specific needs, such as technology development (computers) and the establishment of a print studio in 1993.

The need for additional funding resulted in the creation of Why 5, the for-profit arm of YA/YA. It has been in existence since 2000. Youth, having graduated from YA/YA, were wondering what to do next. YA/YA needed a way to keep people connected. Further, since YA/YA was not able to market a product as a nonprofit organization, it needed a for-profit in order to license designs done at YA/YA.

Why 5 has since evolved into an enterprise involving four YA/YA alumni who are trying to create a graphic design business. Why 5 engages in illustration, book jacket design, textile design, surface design, web design, promotional material, package design, 2D/3D animation, and multimedia packages. Why 5 is the licensing agent for YA/YA. When YA/YA obtains really large jobs, Why 5 can come in and manage the project. This for-profit program will work almost like YA/YA in that it contracts out while offering opportunities for apprenticeships to YA/YA members. In many ways, Why 5 is the fruit of YA/YA's labor. There are other alumni art-related endeavors, but this is the first linked directly back to YA/YA. Why 5 is still very much in the developmental stages. Jana gave Why 5 the initial investment, but the partners want to totally own this business. They currently have their own office space around the corner from YA/YA.

YOUTH DEVELOPMENT FOUNDATION

YA/YA's program integrates numerous youth development principles and activities throughout all aspects of the enterprise. Involvement of youth in active and meaningful decision-making roles stands out. YA/YA evolved from an organization in which adults made key decisions to one where youth either make key decisions or share in this power. Decision making is a major element in ultimately allowing youth to own the program or enterprise.

Development of competencies in a wide range of areas that can easily transfer into other aspects of their lives is a hallmark of youth development programs. These competencies in the case of social youth enterprises, for example, involve marketing, presentation of self, knowledge of financial matters, good work habits, teamwork, effective communications skills, leadership, and service to community.

The increased significance given to community within the YA/YA mission and operations also reflects a growing trend within the field of youth development to reach out to communities. The involvement of community in all aspects of an enterprise, social or otherwise, has further grounded YA/YA within the broader New Orleans community, which has aided program development and expansion in a multitude of ways.

LESSONS LEARNED

Social Youth Enterprises and Schools

Social youth enterprises, schools, and communities have a relationship whether they like to admit it or ignore it. These relationships can either foster the mission or seriously undermine it. However, there is no denying the importance of social youth enterprises being actively supported by schools and communities.

Social youth enterprise relationships, however, should not be restricted to any one school or community. Instead, program participants can come from any school or community. Broadening participation serves to facilitate recruitment but also helps in development of a political constituency that can play influential roles in helping to obtain resources and access.

The development of positive partnerships necessitates having personnel with the patience and skills to enter schools and develop appropriate relationships. These relationships, further, must be fostered over an extended period of time. There is little question that when compared to community-based organizations, schools pose considerable challenges to social youth enterprises. Nevertheless, community-based organizations represent a critical dimension to any social youth enterprise, and the sooner this is acknowledged, the sooner partnerships can be created.

YA/YA Ties Its Future Growth to That of the City of New Orleans

The city's ability to project a national and international reputation as a creative arts center ultimately benefits programs such as YA/YA by expanding its base for commissions. It also facilitates receiving grants from national foundations. The desire to tie a social youth enterprise to a city's growth has many advantages, particularly a close working relationship with the city. There are limitations, however, that must be considered before attempting to do so.

Like many other youth-focused programs across the United States, YA/YA has faced or is facing a number of challenges. Some of these challenges are endemic to youth-focused programs be they social enterprise focused or otherwise. However, some of the challenges are the result of YA/YA's mission and place within the city of New Orleans.

Social Youth Enterprises and the Popular Media

Public relations serves to highlight a program's mission, bring positive attention to youth, serve as a venue for commissions, and play a vital role in recruitment of youth to the program. Although the concept of public relations is generally alien in most social types of programs, it is certainly well understood and embraced in the world of business. However, it takes on a different form when addressed within a social youth entrepreneurial perspective.

The development of something as simple and low labor intensive as a media packet, for example, can help programs disseminate the information, or message, that they wish to convey to the general public as well as to funding sources. These packets can contain testimonials from participants, description of services/products, concise histories of the program, contact persons, and newspaper clippings of previous stories about the program. These media packets, as a result, serve to provide an in-depth foundation for future interviews and stories.

Social youth enterprises, too, must prepare youth for their roles as interviewees. Participants are the best ambassadors for programs, and as ambassadors, they have to be prepared for this role. The use of role-playing and videotaping are excellent ways for youth to prepare. Having them observe interviews and then processing with them the experience is another way. Further, these leadership skills can easily be applied in other spheres of their lives.

Collaborative Partnerships and Growth of Social Youth Enterprises

Partnerships serve to strengthen a program's ties to the immediate and broader community. Further, these partnerships also create commissions and act as a source of potential referrals for program participants.

There are probably very few social youth enterprises that do not aspire to be self-sufficient. Nevertheless, achievement of this goal is elusive for a variety of reasons. It is necessary to develop a funding base involving a diverse set of funding sources, not to mention products/services. Food from the 'Hood, for example, actively seeks ways to obtain funding from banks with community development money and from venture capitalists. However, it is impossible to lose sight of the immediate needs of an enterprise. Food from the 'Hood recognizes the need for added capital to support and fund expansion of the business. Funding can be used to increase advertising efforts—television ads, bus ads, and billboards. As the labor force is constantly changing, due to graduation, this goal of self-sufficiency is difficult to achieve.

Social Youth Enterprises and At-Risk Youth

The general public tends to take the term at *risk* out of context. The primary problem with the phrase at *risk* is that people start thinking that students wouldn't have made it if they hadn't been in YA/YA. The public has focused on the *at risk* label in a manner that doesn't always apply. However, staff must endeavor to politicize this term for youth participants and not allow this label to negatively influence their self-image. The term at *risk* is generally used as a catchphrase for grant writing purposes.

Social Youth Enterprises Are Always Searching for Funding

Further, if these enterprises wish to involve graduates in meaningful and sustainable ways, they must be prepared to create new positions within the organization to achieve this goal. The development of for-profit programs has the potential to meet an increased proportion of an organization's funding needs.

The development of a for-profit aspect of youth enterprises is of critical importance for a variety of reasons: (1) it is a revenue source; (2) it provides an opportunity for program graduates to continue their involvement and professional growth without totally leaving the program; and (3) it expands the capability of the organization to receive commissions it would otherwise not be able to compete for locally and nationally.

There are probably few cities in the country that have a history of the arts as long and influential as New Orleans does. New Orleans is considered a very sophisticated city with extensive cultural resources. These resources have resulted in what many people would consider an active and thriving arts industry. This tradition and reputation has undoubtedly helped YA/YA get established and develop a national reputation.

A high level of support comes from people outside of New Orleans. Organizations outside of New Orleans, from New York City, for example are enthusiastic about YA/YA, possibly due in part to the press exposure it has received. YA/YA is a big name in community service. YA/YA is known because of its outreach program, having helped students design and paint murals in their schools.

Uniqueness of a Social Youth Enterprise

This uniqueness necessitates that programs consistently attempt to educate the public about their mission, a task that requires considerable time and energy. However, being unique does have its pluses. There are very few programs within a city or the country that have a particular mission, and YA/YA's statement of purpose facilitates getting attention from the media and money from foundations and corporations interested in funding creative projects.

It would be difficult for the average person to develop an accurate picture of what YA/YA is all about. The mix of artistic projects with enterprise development is different from many other youth-arts programs where the development of artistic talent is the primary mission. YA/YA has also tried to dispel stereotypes about youth participants. YA/YA does not draw from the wealthy uptown population, but participants are not necessarily at risk either. A better description of participants is youth who do not have extensive resources to explore or access to opportunities. However, they do have varying degrees of access, and some have limited economic resources.

Availability of Travel Opportunities

Social youth enterprises have tremendous appeal for youth since they can "have something positive to do," "learn," "contribute to community," "have fun," and "earn," while doing something they love to do. However, youth need additional incentives to enlist their continued commitment to an enterprise. Travel is such a motivator in the case of YA/YA.

The opportunity to travel nationally and internationally broadens the world for youth, particularly when they come from low socioeconomic households. Youth learn about other cultures and communities, knowledge that cannot but help broaden their perspective of life. Being able to travel with colleagues brings with it an inherent opportunity to share with each other the meaning of the adventure and solidifies the group in the process of doing so.

FINAL COMMENTS

New Orleans, like other major cities across the United States, is in desperate need for youth programs in general and social youth enterprises in particular. Although society can expect a great deal from its schools, it is not reasonable to expect them to do it all. YA/YA does a wonderful job of facilitating direct one-to-one relationships for students who can easily get lost in the shuffle of life in an inner-city community.

Engaging students while they are still in high school is a promising way of tracking and supporting them during their adolescence. This engagement helps to connect community life and school life for them. An enterprise based upon producing and marketing products is a natural mechanism for helping youth to express themselves and find a creative and positive vehicle for their talents and energy. However, engaging students in a meaningful manner necessitates that social youth enterprises are prepared to address a multitude of needs in their career force.

Human resources departments in industrialized nations have quickly understood the importance of having a career force without major problems. Providing a wide range of services within the organization or contracting out for these services helps to ensure that staff can operate to their maximum capabilities. Social youth enterprises in many ways are very similar except that they have as staff youth who are undoubtedly going through various challenging developmental phases.

CONCLUDING REMARKS TO THE CASE STUDIES

I certainly hope that the reader was as fascinated by these case studies as I was. Each of these case examples of social youth entrepreneurship serves to reinforce the need for the development of enterprises that have social and economic goals. Further, the cases reflect the ripple effect of having social youth enterprises actively reaching out to communities. It remains to be seen, however, how well youth participating in these ventures fare as a result of their experiences. Somehow I do not doubt that many of these youth, their families, and communities have benefited in some obvious and not so obvious ways when the evaluation results are finally generated.

PART IV

Lessons Learned and Recommendations

CHAPTER 10

Summary of Lessons from the Field

INTRODUCTION

Case studies, as already indicated, have the potential to generate a wealth of ideas, concepts, discussion, and excitement. The case studies of Food from the 'Hood and YA/YA, I believe, have succeeded in accomplishing the above goals. These cases, although very different types of social enterprises, nevertheless share a great deal in common. These common themes, in turn, help move the field forward. The field of practice as demonstrated by the two case studies has a tremendous amount of influence in shaping the future of social youth enterprises. Field examples bring theoretical concepts and constructs to life and at the same time challenge all those who profess a desire to shape this field. In addition, practice serves to inform or put on notice scholars and researchers by pointing out glaring gaps in knowledge and potential contradictions in commonly accepted truths.

This chapter culls the key practice implications from chapters 8 and 9 in an effort to highlight common themes and arena-specific themes that must be taken into consideration in addressing transition-to-work youth development activities and programs for youth that can be considered at-risk. As noted throughout this book, best practices have a way of providing practitioners with concrete advice, hope, and a positive sense of direction. Thus, their importance is almost unimaginable. The case studies of Food from the 'Hood and YA/YA have raised a series of practice considerations that should not be ignored.

The reader may well argue that two cases do not make a generalization and cannot possibly reflect the state of the field, and I agree. However, there are several observations that need to be made and briefly addressed as an initial step in creating a comprehensive and coherent picture of the field of social youth entrepreneurship. Unfortunately, the general extent of these observations may or may not be applicable to other social youth enterprises across the country, and only more extensive research can answer this. Nevertheless, several themes emerged from these two field studies and warrant attention and discussion in this chapter.

FUNDING

Finding operating funds is never an easy activity, particularly during the start-up phase of an enterprise. Pitching a mission to funders in a way that is realistic yet inspiring is quite a challenge. No enterprise wishes to overpromise nor does it want to sell short its noble mission. The importance of funding is well understood in both the for-profit and nonprofit worlds. If the financial status of Food from the 'Hood and YA/YA typifies the existence of other social youth entrepreneurial programs across the country, there is an ever-present need to create a constant source of income because self-sufficiency as a goal has not been feasible, and it may be many more years before it is.

Both case studies demonstrated the need for programs to have stable, non-grant sources of funding. Relying on grant funds for startup is critical, however. This necessity is very well understood by for-profit businesses and attests to the role and importance of venture capital. Social youth enterprises are no exception to this need. Nevertheless, the merging of social enterprises that generate money with grant support necessitates that programs have the personnel who can navigate both worlds. These two worlds are very different from each other, requiring expertise in staff that may be difficult to find, thus requiring recruitment of leadership staff. Further, grants are never given without some form of conditions that may compromise the central mission of a social youth enterprise.

If programs are to pay youth for their participation in ongoing activities, then a steady stream of funding is necessary. Having to wait for a project to be completed before participants are paid is particularly unrealistic in situations where youth are from marginalized economic communities. Further, regardless of economic status, having to wait an extended period of time to get paid is not considered a strong mechanism for maintaining participation regardless of the economic circumstances of participants. The concept of bonuses, however, was not mentioned in either program.

RECRUITMENT OF PARTICIPANTS

The recruitment of participants to the two programs followed distinctively different paths. Food from the 'Hood is closely tied to a school and a particular geographical area. YA/YA, in turn, recruits from throughout New Orleans after a history of relying on recruitment within a local school. Both programs had their origins as school-based enterprises—one located within (Food from the 'Hood) and one (YA/YA) outside but closely tied to one school. Both eventually expanded beyond their school origins in an effort to broaden their base for recruiting participants.

Interestingly, however, neither program has a stringent weeding out process for initial participation. This open-door policy, although challenging from a programmatic perspective, is nevertheless politically and socially very attractive. It seems that most youth programs have developed a set of criteria that participants must meet in order to enter a program. Making a program open to all wishing to participate provides a haven for youth who may have great difficulty fitting in somewhere else. An inclusive philosophy allows all youth a chance to make good.

By maintaining an open-door policy, programs such as the two featured in this book place a tremendous burden on the social side of the enterprise. This means that staff must be capable of handling a wide range of personal issues and problems faced by participants, a skill that may entail making appropriate referrals to outside services or employing staff with sufficient competencies in the interpersonal arena to address problems when they arise. Opening programs to all those who are interested, in turn, may well influence the enterprise goals of a program with much more time, effort, and resources being devoted to training and supporting youth than programs with stringent membership criteria.

HIGHER EDUCATION

School-to-career transition can encompass a variety of goals, with actual transition to the labor market being but one type. Although the importance of furthering a formal education was well articulated and encouraged in both programs, only Food from the 'Hood had developed a highly formalized program of activities and follow-up. Food from the 'Hood has particularly stressed this goal, evident not only in the number of activities emphasizing higher education but also in the evaluation reports issued by the program. Both programs, to their credit, have not defined higher education along very narrow parameters such as college or university.

Numerous other post high school training programs were also available to participants. A narrow interpretation of higher education can effectively screen out those participants who do not have a college degree as a legitimate goal or do not see themselves pursuing a college education in the immediate future. Further, not every participant can be expected to pursue postgraduate education immediately after completing his or her high school education. Therefore, a system is required that can effectively follow them after graduation and provide support as needed once they decide to continue their formal education.

SOCIAL YOUTH ENTERPRISES AND THEIR MISSION

The social dimensions of social youth enterprise programs necessitate that these types of ventures play close attention to needs that may be emotional, cognitive, physical, or social-relationship based. The social aspects of youth enterprises, in addition, do not have to be limited to helping communities. Youth participants invariably are themselves in need of social assistance. This type of assistance can be instrumental, expressive, or information-based; the assistance may also vary in duration. Some participants may experience a crisis while in the program or may be in need of long-term support.

Thus the conceptualization of social youth enterprises must also include a range of services and supports that do not typically fall within the umbrella of social enterprises. A holistic perspective on youth is needed, and this need has prodigious implications for the staffing and the services offered. Programs must develop the necessary protocols to help staff decide when to involve outside expertise in helping youth in crisis. A holistic approach also necessitates that staff undergo some form of training, in-house or outside, that will help them better handle crises when they occur.

IMPORTANCE OF HAVING A VIABLE PRODUCT

Both programs have extensive contact within their respective communities, which makes marketing to residents relatively easy and highly effective. However, venturing beyond community residents to external systems makes the goal of marketing more challenging. This invariably requires that someone, and in many cases this individual is a full-time staff person, assume the role of marketer. Youth are very limited in undertaking what many people in the field consider a full-time endeavor. School hours and homework systematically and quite dramatically limit the extent to which youth can serve in a marketing role.

However, this does not mean that youth cannot play an informed role in this aspect of an enterprise. It does mean, though, that training and mentoring opportunities must be systematically incorporated into staff-development activities. Youth act as a bridge between a social enterprise and the market (community) they are targeting. Their knowledge of the community needs to be increased through the use of such common techniques as key informant interviews and focus groups. Eventually youth can undertake these market research roles.

RESEARCH AND DEVELOPMENT IS AN INTEGRAL
PART OF ANY ENTERPRISE

Research and development has historically been viewed as an instrumental component of any enterprise with high ambitions. Social youth enterprises are no exception to this point. Research and development requires that social youth enterprises actively recruit members who have the creativity and the competencies to turn ideas into viable products and services. Further, it requires that these enterprises develop mechanisms that actively support research and development.

Product or service development does not take place within a social vacuum. Youth must play influential and critical roles within research and development, although adult staff may well play leadership or facilitative roles in this phase of a social youth enterprise. An organizational willingness and ability to stay ahead of the competition, so to speak, bodes well for product/service development, recruitment of youth participants, and the transference of specialized competencies to youth.

Research and development necessitates the investment of time, energy, and funds that cannot, as a result, be used in other aspects of a social enterprise. Thus, tempting as it may be to neglect this dimension of enterprises, it would be foolhardy to do so. Further, research and development cannot be neglected and then paid attention to at the whim of a program the way a faucet can be turned on and off. Either an enterprise has a commitment to research and development or it does not! If it does not, then it is only a question of time before the enterprise closes its doors!

A CLOSE RELATIONSHIP BETWEEN INCREASING
MARKET SHARE AND PUBLIC RELATIONS

As already noted, both Food from the 'Hood and YA/YA have benefited from the increased national and international exposure they have received as a result of public relations efforts on their behalf. Marketing, as a result, is just as strong a factor in the success of social youth enterprises as it is in the for-profit world. Public relations as an activity, however, requires particular expertise that is generally not fostered within the not-for-profit world. On the other hand, bringing in expertise from the for-profit world and then expecting these staff members to conduct public relations as usual with a social youth enterprise is not the answer either.

PLACES FOR ADULTS WITHIN SOCIAL YOUTH
ENTERPRISES

Adult staff must have a strong commitment to join together with youth participants to share the responsibilities and work needed to fulfill their mission, one that is both social and economic in nature. The relationship between adults and youth, however, cannot take the usual form of adults dictating major decisions within the organization. On the other hand, adults cannot stand by and allow youth to make serious mistakes that will doom an enterprise. The ability to discern what role adults need to play is one that I believe cannot be easily taught.

Jana, the founder of YA/YA, summed up the importance of adults quite well in the following statement (Barker, 1996, p. 110): "The key is having adults who know how to do something well, love what they do, and have the desire to share it with younger people. If you really have this, then everything else—the space, the money, the young people, even the product—falls into place." Jana's comments illustrate the importance of adults and youth engaging in a relationship that effectively taps the expertise of adults and the energy, drive, and commitment of youth.

BOTH PROGRAMS ACTIVELY SEEK TO INVOLVE ALUMNI IN VARIOUS LEADERSHIP ASPECTS

Social youth enterprises cannot afford to graduate youth from their programs and not actively seek to have them continue to contribute to the enterprise. Thus, any effort that can effectively tap their expertise, wisdom, and time cannot be overlooked. Food from the 'Hood and YA/YA have certainly tapped alumni for staffing key positions within their respective programs.

An explicit understanding exists of the role and importance of program graduates being a vital and instrumental part of an organization, and their contributions do not necessarily end when they officially graduate from these programs. Mechanisms that actively seek to continue graduate involvement postcompletion of a program are critical in the development of future social enterprises.

Graduates bring with them experience in the real world that can be tapped to mentor current participants. In all likelihood these mentors share a similar sociodemographic profile as the current participants, and this similarity serves to minimize barriers between mentor and mentee. Alum also benefit from continuing to participate in an active and meaningful way with the social youth enterprises of which they were once a part. They benefit from seeing how a program has evolved over the years, and reconnection provides them with an opportunity to impart their knowledge to participants who are often receptive to their wisdom.

EVALUATION OF SOCIAL YOUTH ENTERPRISES

Interestingly, neither Food from the 'Hood nor YA/YA had formal, ongoing evaluation mechanisms to help them better assess their achievements, document who benefited the most from participation, or how best to improve their programs. This does not mean, however, that neither program undertook many of the functions typically associated with program evaluation nor made evaluation efforts related to grant requirements.

The formal establishment of a program evaluation component fulfills a variety of important functions in addition to answering key questions: (1) it necessitates the development of data-generating systems that highlight the sociodemographic characteristics of participants, including those who leave prematurely; (2) it institutes a series of mechanisms that captures process as well as outcome objectives; (3) evaluation also serves to provide participants with research competencies that can be used in other areas of their lives; and (4) systematic establishment of evaluation procedures facilitates the development of final reports for grant-generated activities and helps in creation of fact sheets that are extremely useful in public relations functions.

PARENTAL INVOLVEMENT MUST FIND A WAY INTO SOCIAL YOUTH ENTERPRISES

How to motivate parents to become involved in social youth enterprise programs and their role when they do must be actively explored. Both programs acknowledged the importance of parents but also noted a challenge in getting and maintaining involvement. Neither program had seriously attempted to develop a parental advisory committee nor made special efforts to include parental representation on their boards of directors.

Parental involvement is also a theme in most youth development programs. Staff generally acknowledge its importance but also indicate a degree, and in some cases a high degree, of discomfort with parent participation in other than ceremonial events. However, parental recruitment and the role of parents need to be seriously considered. Parents can effectively support social youth enterprise goals within the home. Nevertheless, my experience in youth programs is that youth want parental involvement but not that of their own parents!

The recruitment of parents to social youth enterprises can be facilitated when services are available to assist them. Services such as ESL classes, as well as computer and other job-related training, among other forms of assistance, can entice parents to effectively be a part of social enterprises. However, their presence may divert enterprises from their primary goals and may inhibit youth participation.

CONCLUSION

There is little doubt that if social youth entrepreneurship is to thrive in this century that it must be strongly supported by government, foundations, educational institutions, community-based organizations, and ultimately by youth themselves. As noted by Slaughter (undated, p. 11) this comprehensive level of support will ensure the likelihood of these enterprises achieving success: "Priority consideration needs to be given to public policies which encourage entrepreneurship. . . . A nation in which each citizen can pursue his or her entrepreneurial dream and a school system which enlightens children to the opportunity to control this destiny by 'making a job' rather than just taking a job can."

Social youth enterprises may not be of interest to every youth. However, every youth can benefit from participation in these types of endeavors. Learning related to enterprise development, marketing, and evaluation of such endeavors, allows youth to integrate academic subjects in a meaningful and often fun manner. The lessons learned pertaining to work habits, communication, working in teams, and the value of seeking to provide a service to community will all come back to aid youth in their transition to adulthood, even if enterprises are not part of their future. Social youth enterprises are exciting ventures as evidenced by Food from the 'Hood and YA/YA. These two programs are indicative of a field that is ever-vibrant and evolving, yet with numerous challenges to be surmounted.

CHAPTER 11

Implications for Youth and Career Development: Field Practice, Professional Education, and Research/ Scholarship

INTRODUCTION

The future of social youth entrepreneurship will ultimately rest upon successful partnerships between field practice, professional education, and research/scholarship. This partnership of all three key components will help ensure that social youth enterprises thrive. There is little question that these types of enterprises will be practiced within and outside of school settings. However, for social youth enterprises to make the impact they are capable of making in this country, content on this subject must be addressed in the nation's classrooms at the secondary and postsecondary levels. Further, a body of research must be created that critically examines the influence of social youth enterprises on the lives of youth, their families, and their communities. In essence, the bottom line will ultimately guide the future development of these types of enterprises.

This chapter identifies a set of factors, activities, and principles and makes a series of recommendations that should guide the efforts of youth development staff in implementing programs that address work and social entrepreneurship in youth development settings. The field of youth development has not achieved its true potential, and, as a result, it can be expected to continue to expand and push traditional boundaries usually associated with this form of practice. The integration of career is but one example of the dynamic nature of the field.

IMPLICATIONS FOR FIELD PRACTICE

In examining the question of what must the field of practice do to embrace and sustain social youth entrepreneurship programs, it is necessary to separate out the field of practice from the field of professional education and research/ scholarship. Some would argue that such a separation is artificial because of the close relationship between the three. My experience contradicts this point. It seems that many times innovation in practice starts in the field and works its way into the curriculum of professional education and research/scholarship. Thus, the field of practice may be several years ahead of scholarship and research, that is, the cornerstones of any professional education curriculum. This perspective necessitates that one section to be devoted to the field of practice and two others, complementary in nature, of course, be devoted to professional education.

The following seven recommendations cover a variety of subjects that, when enacted together, have a positive synergistic effect on youth and their communities. It is tempting to pick and choose among these seven recommendations. However, they cannot be separated from each other, and any effort to bypass or minimize any one of the following recommendations will severely limit their potential for change:

1. It is not possible to achieve a quick fix. A long-term comprehensive system is needed that connects learning to career and employment, daunting as it may be for anyone in the field to try to undo years of neglect. This connection not only reinforces the importance and fun of learning but also transmits how learning can be practical and beneficial throughout a lifetime. Learning, however, does not have to be as formal as material covered in school-based curriculum. It can also be informally approached through a variety of methods outside of a school setting. The concept of community-connected learning mentioned earlier in this book captures the importance of contextualized learning in its broadest sense and captures both formal and informal approaches.

   Further, one of the primary challenges facing the field of social youth enterprises is bridging the worlds of school and community. These two worlds are too important in the lives of youth to not be connected. Fortunately, the emergence and wide acceptance of service-learning or contextual learning will facilitate collaboration between schools and communities. Social youth enterprises are natural mechanisms for youth engaging in pursuit of knowledge while concomitantly serving their communities. Youth and communities are not the only beneficiaries of this collaboration. Teachers and schools also benefit from the breaking down of barriers between these arenas.

   Consequently, the development of a long-term, comprehensive view of career education will require a commitment on the part of all interested parties to develop mechanisms to assure achievement of this goal. This goal, as a result, will necessitate that the worlds of school and community come closer together. The use of a social youth enterprise approach is an excellent vehicle for combining these two often-disparate worlds. More specifically, the use of a service-learning construct lends itself well to development of social youth enterprises.

2. New standards for measuring success that incorporate long-term follow-up are needed. There is a tendency by funding sources to focus on only immediate and highly recognizable changes. Such a perspective does more harm than good when

it involves youth and lends itself to eliminating problematic behaviors rather than enhancing assets. It is much easier to record elimination or reduction of problems than to record the prevention of a death, for example. Success, in turn, necessitates a consensus on performance standards. The inclusion of youth employment goals within a youth development paradigm requires that new thinking take place on goals and how to best measure them.

The experiences of the two case studies examined in chapters 8 and 9 bear out the importance of viewing social youth enterprises over an extended period of time rather than over a limited time. Start-up, for example, may take several years. This does not mean that youth engaged in social enterprises cannot benefit from their experiences during this phase. Nor does it mean that they cannot make meaningful and lasting contributions. However, it does mean that social youth enterprises undergo an evolutionary process that will involve youth in particular phases rather than the entirety of the experience—namely, youth participation may well be limited in time duration, and future generations may never come into contact with the initial generations of participants. Development of a system for capturing the history of a program, as a result, takes on added significance.

3. A comprehensive system at the community level should seek to foster long-term communication, partnership, and development. The introduction of community into a prominent place in the dialogue of youth development and employment opens up a vast array of possibilities for the development of collaborative partnerships between the private and public sector. Having a community focus, too, helps to ensure that youth employment initiatives not be conceptualized as individualistically focused and instead take into consideration community assets and needs. Nevertheless, achievement of this recommendation will prove quite challenging. We tend to romanticize community in this society. However, communities are never homogeneous, and every effort must be made to give voice to all sectors, a time-consuming and arduous process.

4. Efforts must be undertaken to identify, document, and connect islands of excellence. These are best practices that should be thoroughly evaluated, replicated, and their results disseminated as widely as possible. Best practices have a tremendous potential for helping others in the field. Unfortunately, many programs fail to disseminate the results of their projects, and the field loses as a result. Fortunately, there are many fine examples of model programs to draw upon. These efforts presuppose programs having clearly measurable processes and outcomes that allow for impartial evaluation efforts.

Development of case studies illustrative of various types of social youth enterprises will assist the field to better understand and assess the goodness of fit between types of enterprises and settings. Although the emphasis of these studies should be on success stories, there is also value and much to be learned from developing case studies of failures.

5. Creation of common definitions and a system of disseminating information to consumers and other providers is very much needed. The development of commonly accepted definitions is never an easy undertaking. The field of youth development, for example, has struggled with the development of a consensus definition and failed to arrive at common definitions of what is meant by youth, employment, social enterprise, and youth development, thus compounding the difficulty of evaluation.

Accessibility to this information represents an important aspect of increased accountability. In fact, best practices cannot be identified and replicated without clear and measurable standards of performance. Definitions with clear and widely accepted boundaries help to ensure that collaborative partnerships have a higher likelihood of success and are not burdened with setbacks because of misunderstandings of goals, strategies, or language/terms.

6. The development of incentives to keep youth actively involved in a program needs to go beyond the appeal of profits and pay. Financial incentives are important, particularly in the lives of youth from low-income families. However, experiences with both programs show how travel incentives can wield a tremendous amount of influence on participant attendance. YA/YA was relatively quick to recognize its importance. Food from the 'Hood, however, has only recently used this type of incentive. Travel opportunities for Food from the 'Hood youth may not be as readily available as for those participating in YA/YA. This may be due to the fact that the products (produce and salad dressings) do not lend themselves to travel. Nevertheless, opportunities for travel must be frequently offered to participants in social youth enterprises because of their value for motivation and learning.

The development of a career ladder with a requisite set of role qualifications, expectations, and rewards also provides participants with motivation to stay and succeed in social enterprises. Social youth enterprises in many ways are no different than their for-profit enterprise counterparts, in which promotions and perks are integrally related. Programs must systematically tap the interests of participants in order to provide them with outlets for creativity. This can be accomplished through development of program-specific reward systems.

7. There is a great need for the field of social youth entrepreneurship to share the wealth of its experiences with the general public and be willing to have scholars enter their programs to better learn the lessons of their success. This very point was articulated by YA/YA's founder (Barker, 1996, p. 110): "If we have learned anything through the YA/YA experience about working with talented youngsters, it is that whatever works should be shared. YA/YA can offer the world a model of how to take young people from one level to another."

As already noted, the field of practice will play an incredibly critical role in helping to shape curriculum and programs. Creation of collaborative partnerships between programs and university research and scholarship can be of benefit to both programs and universities. It is unreasonable to expect practitioners to undertake research and write scholarly articles; conversely, it is artificial for professors to write scholarly articles and books without meaningful contact and exchange with programs.

IMPLICATIONS FOR PROFESSIONAL EDUCATION

As noted earlier, the implications for using social youth enterprises to transform youth and their communities within professional education curricula is sufficiently different than that of practice to warrant a section of recommendations unto itself. This section, as a result, will draw conclusions and implications for how researchers, scholars, and professionals can best play a significant role in helping to transition marginalized youth from school-to-career.

Professional schools are slowly adopting youth development practice, and this movement is expected to continue into the twenty-first century (Parker, 2000). The trend toward the inclusion of youth development principles, theories, and goals within curricula holds much promise for the field of practice. However, the field of youth development cannot avoid addressing school-to-career transition and neither can professional educational programs in the nation's universities.

1. One of the many attractive features of social youth enterprises is that as a field it can easily find a home in any one of a multitude of professions. However, no profession should own the field of youth development or social youth entrepreneurship. The very nature of this field of practice is premised on the development of multiple partnerships within a community context. Thus, the ability of professions to communicate across traditional boundaries is very much dependent upon the development of common definitions and a commitment to providing a comprehensive system of service that no one setting or profession can possible provide.

   Further, the complex nature of the subject necessitates the creation of partnerships between professions and between professions and community. Having multiple perspectives on social youth enterprises helps to ensure a rich and in-depth understanding of how this field has evolved and can evolve to address a multitude of social and enterprise goals within organizations and communities.

2. The use of internships that are multidisciplinary in nature offers much promise for professional education. Development of these placements within ongoing social youth enterprises provides students with an opportunity to be a part of ongoing ventures. The lessons learned through this participation, in turn, can be carried back to the classroom through discussions and assignments.

   Internships within school settings are an excellent opportunity for students to establish working relationships with social youth enterprises. In addition, faculty advisors within sponsoring colleges and universities are provided access to these enterprises to provide youth with assistance where needed and requested; in addition, it facilitates the development of scholarship on social youth enterprises. In professions that use community settings for internships, such as in the social work field for instance, comparable opportunities exist to accomplish the same tasks as their school-based counterparts.

3. Professional educational conferences are ideal settings to bring together professionals to learn from each other and to display model programs that lend themselves to interdisciplinary collaborations. These conferences, it should be added, must also endeavor to bring youth participants into the sessions and discussions. Young people not only bring unique perspectives, they can also benefit from the experience of interacting with adults and other youth from throughout the country.

IMPLICATIONS FOR RESEARCH/SCHOLARSHIP

Much research and scholarship must be undertaken in the next decade to help guide the field of social youth entrepreneurship and help narrow the gap between practice and scholarship. Zeldin (1995, p. 12) identified the gap between scholars and practitioners as a key barrier for advancing youth development in the twenty-first century, and the same can be said for youth development and social youth entrepreneurship: "Scholars and funders of research will be able to refocus their efforts accordingly. A foremost challenge will be for scholars to tear down the artificial walls that exist between theory, research, and practice. . . . Until these shifts in research occur, a great deal of relevant information will remain in academic journals and in places not accessible to those who most need to use it."

Historically, a tremendous amount of distrust between the fields of practice and academia has existed. This lack of trust invariably manifests itself in all kinds of stereotypes and horror stories being perpetuated about each of these two worlds. Thus, closing the gap between the world of academia and practice will never be easy to achieve (Lakes, 1996). However, to say that because it is hard to achieve we must not strive to do so would be foolish. Social youth enterprises are sufficiently broad in scope to welcome a multidisciplinary perspective on the subject. Further, the service to community aspects of these ventures also lend themselves to bringing together business and community scholars to develop a language, concepts, and collaborative approaches to better inform the field. Everyone is destined to benefit from these partnerships; further, these partnerships will serve to spur collaborations in other arenas.

The following eleven research questions are by no means the only significant ones but ones that I believe, when answered, will move the field of social youth entrepreneurship forward in a significant manner:

1. How have participants been impacted over an extended period of time? This longitudinal study will also help better assess how schools and communities, too, have benefited.
2. What core elements (physical, emotional, cognitive, social, moral, and spiritual) are enhanced by participation, and how are they operationalized in the daily life of youth?
3. What are the sociodemographic characteristics of those youth who benefit the most and least from participation in social enterprises?
4. What organizational structures facilitate the integration of social and enterprise elements in social youth enterprises?
5. What are the most effective models for ensuring successful collaboration between social youth enterprises and community-based organizations?
6. To what extent are nonmonetary rewards such as field trips and foreign travel responsible for youth participation and commitment to programs?
7. Are there any significant differences in models and success of social youth enterprises when taking urban, suburban, and rural settings into consideration?

8. How does gender and type of product/service influence rates of success?

9. Finally, how is success conceptualized and measured when social goals combine with financial goals, and what measures are the most common in the field to record process and outcomes?

   It will take many years of active research and scholarship to advance the field of social youth enterprises in this country. However, it is imperative that we view the field, not from a narrow national perspective, but from one that is international in scope and influence. Research and scholarship within the United States can thus be infused with research and scholarship from abroad, helping to advance the field at home and in other countries throughout the world. Youth, it might be added, can play a critical role in planning and carrying out research and program evaluation (Delgado, under contract).

10. What is the frequency of social youth enterprises within distinct geographic entities such as inner cities? What level of representation of enterprises can be considered to foster development of more enterprises? The degree of representation of social youth enterprises within communities is unknown, particularly in marginalized and working-class communities.

CONCLUSION

The importance of professional education is too great within this country to not draw conclusions for how best to mobilize this resource in service to youth and their communities. Professional education serves many vital roles in helping educators and providers of services to develop new perspectives on youth with social youth entrepreneurship being but one example. Thus, to ignore the role of professional education is to seriously lose a portion of a vital formula. Without that missing segment, the desired outcome is impossible.

Professional education, as this chapter has highlighted, is multifaceted. Nevertheless, bringing a paradigm that incorporates youth development and social youth entrepreneurship into professional schools will not be easy, particularly if the hope is to introduce this paradigm in a comprehensive and sustained manner. Introducing youth development and social youth entrepreneurship in a reading or a course is not arduous. However, a set of readings or one course will not do justice to this topic though it may well be the easiest way to start with the hope of broadening content to also include other courses or to be integrated throughout the curriculum, with appropriate field placements where possible (Watkins & Iverson, 1998). It will no doubt require the same creativity for us in professional education that we require from youth in constructing social enterprises.

References

Abbott, J. (1995). Child needs communities—communities need children. *Educational Leadership, 52*, 6–11.

Abe, Y. (2001). Changes in gender and racial gaps in adolescent antisocial behavior: The NLSY97 versus the NLSY79. In R. T. Mitchel (Ed.), *Social awakening: Adolescent behavior as adulthood approaches* (pp. 339–378). New York: Russell Sage Foundation.

Academy for Educational Development. (1995). *School-to-work and youth development: Identifying common ground.* Washington, D.C.: Author.

Adams, A. C. (2000). Outrageous leadership: The work is a circus and you are the ringmasters. *CYD Journal Community Youth Development, 1*, 42–43.

Aldrich, H. E., & Baker, T. (1997). Blinded by the cites: Has there been progress in entrepreneurship research? In D. L. Sexton & R. W. Smilor (Eds.), *Entrepreneurship 2000* (pp. 24–26). Chicago: Upstart Publishing.

Allen, L., Hogan, C. J., & Steinberg, A. (1998). *Knowing and doing: Connecting learning & work.* Providence, RI: Education Alliance Lab, Brown University.

American Youth Policy Forum. (1997). *Some things do make a difference for youth: A compendium of evaluations of youth programs and practices.* Washington, D.C.: Author.

American Youth Policy Forum. (2000). *Looking forward: School-to-work principles and strategies for sustainability.* Washington, D.C.: Author.

American Youth Policy Forum. (2001). *High school of the millennium.* Washington, D.C.: Author.

Amit, R., Glosten, L., & Muller, E. (1993). Challenges to theory development in entrepreneurship research. *Journal of Management Studies, September,* 20–31.

Anderson, D. C. (1998). *Sensible justice: Alternatives to prison.* New York: W.W. Norton & Company.

Anderson, E. (1999). *Code of the street: Decency, violence, and the moral life of the inner city.* New York: W.W. Norton & Company.

Armistead, P. J., & Wexler, M. B. (1997). *Community development and youth development: The potential for convergence. Community & Youth Development series, Vol. 1.* Takoma Park, MD: The Forum for Youth Investment, International Youth Foundation.

Armistead, P. J., & Wexler, M. B. (1998). Community development and youth development: The potential for convergence. *New Designs for Youth Development, 14,* 27–33.

Astroth, K. (2000). Research and practice: Measuring your vibrancy index: A simple self-assessment tool. *CYD Journal Community Youth Development, 1,* 31–35.

Bachman, J. G., & Schulenberg, J. (1993). How part-time work intensity relates to drug-use, problem behavior, time use, and satisfaction among high school seniors: Are these consequences or merely correlates? *Developmental Psychology, 29,* 220–235.

Barker, C. (1996). *YA/YA! Young New Orleans artists and their storytelling chairs (and how to YA/YA in your neighborhood).* Baton Rouge: Louisiana State University Press.

Barling, J., Rogers, K. A., & Kelloway, E. K. (1995). Some effects of teenagers' part-time employment: The quantity and quality of work make the difference. *Journal of Organizational Behavior, 16,* 143–154.

Bartik, T. J. (2001). *Jobs for the poor: Can labor demand policies help?* New York: Russell Sage Foundation.

Barton, W. H., Watkins, M., & Jarjoura, R. (1997). Youths and communities: Toward comprehensive strategies for youth development. *Social Work, 42,* 483–493.

Bates, T. (1997). *Race, self-employment, and upward mobility.* Washington, D.C.: The Woodrow Wilson Center Press.

Benson, P. L., Scales, P. C., Leffert, N., & Roehlkepartain, E. C. (1999). *A fragile foundation: The state of developmental assets among American youth.* Minneapolis, MN: Search Institute.

Benz, M. R., Yovanoff, P., & Doren, B. (1997). School-to-work components that predict postschool success for students with and without disabilities. *Exceptional Children, 63,* 151–162.

Bernhardt, A., Morris, M., Handcock, M. S., & Scott, M. A. (2001). *Divergent paths: Economic mobility in the new American labor market.* New York: Russell Sage Foundation.

Bernstein, S. (2000, June). *Using the hidden assets of America's communities and regions to ensure sustainable communities.* Symposium on the Future of Local Government in Midland, MI.

Berryman, S. E., Hamilton, M. A., Hamilton, S. F., Rosenbaum, J. E., Stern, D., & Kazis, R. (1999). *Youth apprenticeship in America: Guidelines for building an effective system.* Washington, D.C.: American Youth Policy Forum.

Besharov, D. J. (Ed.). (1999). *America's disconnected youth.* Washington, D.C.: Child Welfare Press of America.

Bessemer, G., & Clinton, T. W. (1997). Developing delinquent youths: A reintegrative model for rehabilitation and a new role of the juvenile justice system. *Child Welfare, 76,* 665–716.

Black, P. (2000). Young entrepreneurs' organization. *Business Leader, 12,* 32.

Blank, R. M. (2001). An overview of trends in social and economic well-being, by race. In N. J. Smelser, W. J. Wilson, & F. Mitchell (Eds.), *America becoming: Racial trends and their consequences, Vol. 1* (pp. 21–39). Washington, D.C.: National Research Council.

Blum, R.W.M. (1998). Healthy youth development as a model for youth health promotion. *Journal of Adolescent Health, 22,* 368–375.

Bodnar, J. (2001, June). No kidding: For young entrepreneurs, there's no time like the present to get down to business. *Kiplinger's Personal Finance Magazine,* 110–113.

Bonacich, E., & Modell, J. (1980). The economic basis of ethnic solidarity: Small business in the Japanese American community. Berkeley, CA: University of California Press.

Booth, A., & Crouter, A. C. (Eds.). (2001). *Does it take a village? Community effects on children, adolescents, and families.* Mahwah, NJ: Lawrence Erlbaum Associates, Publishers.

Borman, G. D., & Rachuba, L. T. (2001). *Academic success among poor and minority students: An analysis of competing models of school effects.* Baltimore, MD: Center for Research on Education of Students, Johns Hopkins University.

Bornstein, D. (1999). The new social entrepreneurs. *Journal, 3,* 1–7.

Boschee, J. (1995). Social entrepreneurship. *Across the Board, 32,* 20–25.

Boston, T. D., & Ross, C. L. (Eds.). (1997). *The inner city: Urban poverty and economic development in the next century.* New Brunswick, NJ: Transaction Publications.

Bouvier, L. F., & Grant, L. (1994). *How many Americans? Population, immigration, and the environment.* San Francisco: Sierra Club Books.

Boyd, W. L., Crowson, R. L., & Gresson, A. (1997). Neighborhood initiatives, community agencies, and the public schools: A changing scene for the development and learning of children. *LSS Publication Series, No. 6.*

Boyd, W. L., & Shouse, R. C. (1997). The problems and promise of urban schools. In H. J. Walberg, O. Reyes, & R. P. Weisberg (Eds.), *Children and youth: Interdisciplinary perspectives* (pp. 141–165). Thousand Oaks, CA: Sage Publications.

Bradley, W. S. (1999). Lessons from Curitiba. *Educational Facility Planner, 35,* 17–18.

Breggin, P. R., & Breggin, G. R. (1998). *The war against children of color: Psychiatry targets inner city youth.* Monroe, ME: Common Courage Press.

Brierton, J. (2001, October 31). Welcome to economics with a social conscience. *The Scotsman,* p. 5.

Brinckerhoff, P. C. (2000). *Social entrepreneurship: The art of mission-based venture development.* New York: John Wiley & Sons, Inc.

Brown, B. V., & Emig, C. (1999). Prevalence, patterns, and outcomes. In D. I. Besharov (Ed.), *America's disconnected youth* (pp. 101–115). Washington, D.C.: Child Welfare League of America.

Brown, C. M. (1998). The business factory (community organizations help small businesses) (business opportunity). *Black Enterprise, 29,* 119–124.

Brown, D. E. (2000). *Advancing youth development under the Workforce Investment Act* (4, pp. 1–11). Washington, D.C.: National Governors Association Center for Best Practices.

Brown, M., Camino, L., Hobson, H., & Knox, C. (2000). Community youth development: A challenge to social justice. *CYD Journal Community Youth Development, 1,* 32–39.

Browne, I. (1999). Latinas and African American women in the U.S. labor market. In A. Browne (Ed.), *Latinas and African American women at work: race, gender, and economic inequality* (pp. 1–31). New York: Russell Sage Foundation.

Brumback, N. (2000). Ethnic markets growing up. *Brandmaking*, 7, 16–21.

Brundtland, G. H. (1987). *Our common future*. New York: Oxford University Press.

Brunelle, N., Brochu, S., & Cousineau, M. M. (2000). Drug-crime relations among drug-consuming juvenile delinquents: Tripart model and more. *Contemporary Drug Problems*, 27, 835–849.

Burgess, J. (2000). Youth and the future of community renewal. *National Civic Review*, 89, 27–30.

Burt, M. R., Resnick, G., & Novick, E. R. (1998). *Building supportive communities for at-risk adolescents: It takes more than services*. Washington, D.C.: American Psychological Association.

Butler, J. S. (1995, January 7). Race, entrepreneurship, and the inner city. *USA Today*, pp. 26–29.

Buttenheim, A. (1998). Social enterprise meets venture philanthropy: A powerful combination. *The Los Angeles Business Journal*, 20, 1–7.

Bygrave, W., & Minniti, M. (2000). The social dynamics of entrepreneurship. *Entrepreneurship Theory and Practice*, 24, 25–36.

Cahill, M. (1996). *Toward collaboration: Youth development, youth programs, and school reform*. Washington, D.C.: Academy for Educational Development.

Cahill, M. (1997). *Youth development and community development: Promises and challenges of convergence. Community and Youth Development Series. Vol. 2*. Takoma Park, MD: The Forum for Youth Investment, International Youth Foundation.

Caird, S. (1992). Problems with the identification of enterprise competencies and the implications for assessment and development. *Management Education and Development*, 23, 6–17.

Campbell, C. L., & Heck, W. W. (1997). An ecological perspective on sustainable development. In F. D. Muschett (Ed), *Principles of sustainable development* (pp. 47–67). Delray Beach, FL.: St. Lucie Press.

Camarillo, A. M., & Bonilla, F. (2001). Hispanics in a multicultural society: A new dilemma? In N. J. Smelser, W. J. Wilson, & F. Mitchell (Eds.), *America becoming: Racial trends and their consequences, Vol. 1* (pp. 103–134). Washington, D.C.: National Research Council.

Camino, L. (1995). Understanding intolerance and multiculturism: A challenge for practitioners, but also for researchers. *Journal of Adolescent Research*, 10, pp. 155–172.

Camino, L. (2000). Putting youth-adult partnerships to work for community change: Lessons from volunteers across the country. *CYD Journal Community Youth Development*, 1, 27–31.

Canadian Centre for Social Entrepreneurship. (2001). *Social entrepreneurship: Discussion paper No. 1*. Toronto: Author.

Capowich, G. E. (1995). Implementing positive youth development in juvenile justice. In *Contract with America's Youth: Toward a national youth development agenda* (pp. 54–55). Washington, D.C.: American Youth Policy Forum.

Carnegie Council on Adolescent Development. (1989). *Turning points: Preparing American youth for the 21st century*. New York: Carnegie Corporation of New York.

Carroll, M. E., et al. (1991). Classroom companies: The buck starts here. *Intervention in School and Clinic*, 27, 97–100.

Centers, N. L., & Weist, M. D. (1998). Inner city youth and drug dealing: A review of the problem. *Journal of Youth and Adolescence*, 27, 395–404.

Cervantes, J. M., & Ramirez, O. (1992). Spirituality and family dynamics in psycho-therapy with Latino children. In J. D. Koss-Chioino & L. A. Vargas (Eds.), *Working with Latino youth: Culture, development, and context* (pp. 103–128). San Francisco: Jossey-Bass.

Chalk, R., & Phillios, D. A. (Eds.). (1996). *Youth development and neighborhood influences: Challenges and opportunities.* Washington, D.C.: National Academy Press.

Chaplin, D., & Hanwa, J. (1996). High school enrollment: Meaningful connections for at-risk youth. Paper presented at annual meeting of the American Educa-tional Research Association, New York City.

Charner, I. (1996). *Study of school-to-work initiatives.* Washington, D.C.: U.S. Depart-ment of Education, Office of Educational Research and Improvement.

Checkoway, B. (1994). *Involving young people in neighborhood development.* Washington, D.C.: Academy for Educational Development.

Checkoway, B. (1998). Involving young people in neighborhood development. *Chil-dren and Youth Services Review, 20,* 765–795.

Cheshire, T. C., & Kawamoto, W. T. (2003). Positive youth development in urban American Indian adolescents. In F. A. Villarruel, D. F. Perkins, L. M. Borden, & J. G. Keith (Eds.), *Community youth development programs, policies, and practices* (pp. 79–89). Thousand Oaks, CA: Sage Publications.

Chigunta, F. (2002). *Youth entrepreneurship: Meeting the key policy challenges.* Paper pre-sented at the Youth Employment Summit, Civic Society Forum Agenda Con-ference, Alexandria, Egypt.

Children Today. (1993–1994). *Native youth businesses: Native American youth entrepre-neurship projects,* pp. 22, 24–26.

Chinyelu, M. (1999). *Harlem ain't nothin' but a third world country: The global economy, empowerment zones, and the colonial status of Africans in America.* New York: Mus-tard Seed Press.

Clay, E. S., & Bangs, P. C. (2000). Entrepreneurs in the public library: Reinventing an institution. *Library Trends, 48,* 606–615.

Cleland, R., Jemmott, F., & Angles, F. (2001). Helping ourselves to health: Youth lead wellness villages in California. *CYD Journal Community Youth Development, 2,* 7–13.

Cohn, M., & Greenberg, M. H. (2000). *Online content for low-income and underserved Americans: The digital divide's new frontier.* Santa Monica, CA: Author.

Collins, M. E. (2001). Transition to adulthood for vulnerable youth: A review of re-search and implications for policy. *Social Service Review, 75,* pp. 271–291.

Committee for Economic Development. (1997). *Connecting inner-city youth to the world of work.* Washington, D.C.: Author.

Connell, J. P., Aber, J. L., & Walker, G. (1999). *How do urban communities affect youth? Using social science research to inform the design and evaluation of comprehensive community initiatives.* Washington, D.C.: The Aspen Institute.

Connell, J. P., Gambone, M. A., & Smith, T. J. (2000). Youth development in com-munity settings: Challenges to our field and our approach. In *Youth development: Issues, challenges, and directions* (pp. 281–299). Philadelphia: Public/Private Ven-tures.

Connell, J. P., & Kubisch, A. C. (2001). Community approaches to improving out-comes for urban children, youth, and families: Current trends and future considerations. In A. Booth & A. C. Crouter (Eds.), *Does it take a village?*

Community effects on children, adolescents, and families (pp. 177–201). Mahwah, NJ: Lawrence Erlbaum Associates.

Cook, K. V. (2000). "You have to have somebody watching your back, and if that's God, then that's mighty big": The church role in the resilience of inner-city youth. *Adolescence, 35,* 717–727.

Corwin, M. (1997). *And still we rise: The trials and triumphs of twelve gifted inner-city high school students.* New York: William Morrow and Company.

Costello, J., Toles, M., Spielberger, J., & Wynn, J. (2000). History, ideology, and structure shape the organizations that shape youth. In *Youth development: Issues, challenges, and directions* (pp. 185–231). Philadelphia: Public/Private Ventures.

Covington, J. (1997). The social construction of the minority drug problem: Losing a generation: Probing the myths and reality of youth and violence. *Social Justice, 24,* 117–138.

Cowe, R. (2001, July 26). "Hard" finance for regeneration: Social enterprise—community banks are challenging received wisdom about risky loans. *Financial Times* (London), p. 13.

Crack at retail: Experiences of three former dealers. (1988, August 2). *New York Times,* p. A1.

Cutshall, S. (2001). STW successes. *Techniques, 76,* 22–25.

Dabson, B., & Kauffman, B. (1998). *Enterprising youth in America: A review of youth enterprise programs.* Washington, D.C: Corporation for Enterprise Development.

Danielson, R. (2000, April 26). Artist urges mix of charity, business spirit. *St. Petersburg Times,* p. 1B

Dawson, L. (1996). Women's role in sustainable development. *Green Teacher, 46,* pp. 27–30.

Dees, J. G. (1998). *The meaning of "social entrepreneurship."* Kansas City, MO: Kaufman Center for Entrepreneurship Leadership.

Dees, J. G. (1998a). "Enterprising nonprofits, what do you do when traditional sources of funding fall short?" *Harvard Business Review, Jan./Feb.,* 55–67.

Dees, J., Emerson, J., & Economy, P. (Eds.). (2001) *Enterprising nonprofits: A toolkit for social entrepreneurs.* New York: John Wiley & Sons.

De Jesus, E. (1997). Tales from the bright side: Conversations with successful graduates of youth employment programs. In A. Sum et al. (Eds.), *A generation of challenge: Pathways to success for urban youth* (pp. 57–71). Baltimore, MD: Sar Levitan Center for Social Policy, Johns Hopkins University.

Delgado, M. (1999). *Social work practice in nontraditional urban settings.* New York: Oxford University Press.

Delgado, M. (2000a). *Community social work practice in an urban context: The potential of a capacity enhancement perspective.* New York: Oxford University Press.

Delgado, M. (2000b). *New arenas for community social work practice with urban youth: Use of the arts, humanities, and sports.* New York: Columbia University Press.

Delgado, M. (2001). *Where are all of the young men and women of color? Capacity enhancement practice in the criminal justice system.* New York: Columbia University Press.

Delgado, M. (2002). *New frontiers for youth development in the twenty-first century: Revitalizing and broadening youth development.* New York: Columbia University Press.

Delgado, M. (under contract). *Social research and youth-involvement in community research and program evaluation.* Thousand Oaks, CA: Sage Publications.

Denner, J., Kirby, D., & Coyle, K. (2000). How communities can promote positive youth development: Responses from 49 professionals. *CYD Journal Community Youth Development, 1,* 31–35.

Despite its promises of riches. (1989, November 16). *New York Times,* p. A1.

Dickens, W. T. (1999). Rebuilding urban labor markets: What community development can accomplish. In R. T. Ferguson & W. T. Dickens (Eds.), *Urban problems and community development* (pp. 381–435). Washington, D.C.: Brookings Institution Press.

Dippo, D. (1998). An ethic of sustainability for work education. *Journal of Vocational Education Research, 23,* 325–338.

Dobson, J. (1993). *Taking over the asylum.* (http://www.newstartmag.co.uk/asylum.html)

Dominitz, J., Manski, C. F., & Fischhoff, B. (2001). Who are youth "at risk"? Expectations evidence in the NLSY97. In R. T. Michael (Ed.), *Social awakening: Adolescent behavior as adulthood approaches* (pp. 201–229). New York: Russell Sage Foundation.

Dorfman, L., & Schiraldi, V. (2001). *OFF BALANCE: Youth, race, and crime in the news.* Washington, D.C.: Building Blocks for Youth.

Dosher, A. (1996). Community youth development practice fields: National network for youth initiates new infrastructures of learning organizations. *New Designs for Youth Development, 12,* 11–13.

Dowdeswell, E. (1998). Lessons learned in sustainable development. *Northern Review: A Multidisciplinary Journal of the Arts and Social Sciences of the North, 18,* 57–63.

Dryfoos, J. (2000). The mind-body-building equation. *Educational Leadership, 57,* pp. 14–17.

Duncan, G. J., & Raudenbush, S. W. (2001). Neighborhoods and adolescent development: How can we determine the links? In A. Booth & A. C. Crouter (Eds.), *Does it take a village? Community effects on children, adolescents, and families* (pp. 105–136). Mahwah, NJ: Lawrence Erlbaum Associates.

Eccles, J., & Appelton, J. (Eds.). (2002). *Community programs to promote youth development.* Washington, D.C.: National Research Council.

Edelman, I. (2000). The riddle of community-based initiatives. *National Civic Review, 89,* 169–178.

Educational Record. (1996). Campus-business linkages: Food from the 'Hood and college, too, 77, pp. 56–57.

Elikann, P. T. (1996). *The tough-on-crime myth: Real solutions to cut crime.* New York: Plenum Press.

Elikann, P. T. (1999). *Superpredators: The demonization of our children by the law.* New York: Plenum Press.

Ellis, A. L. (1992). Urban youth economic enterprise zones: An intervention strategy for reversing the gang crisis in American cities. *Urban League Review, 15,* 29–40.

Ellwood, D. T., Blank, R. M., Blasi, J., Kruse, D., Niskanen, W. A., & Lynn-Dyson, K. (2000). *A working nation: Workers, work, and government in the new economy.* New York: Russell Sage Foundation.

Emerson, J., & Twersky, F. (1996). *New social entrepreneurs: The success, challenge, and lessons of nonprofit enterprise creation.* San Francisco: The Roberts Foundation Homeless Economic Development Fund.

ERIC Clearinghouse on Urban Education Digest. (2001). *Latinos in school: Some facts and findings.* New York: Author.

Essenberg, T. (2000). Urban community development: An examination of the Perkins model. *Review of Social Economy, 58,* 197–215.

Evanciew, C.E.P., & Rojewski, J. W. (1998). Skill and knowledge acquisition in the workplace: A case study of mentor-apprentice relationships in youth apprenticeship programs. *Journal of Industrial Teacher Education, 36,* 1–22.

Fahey, P., & Frickman, L. (2000). Fusing art, economics, and social reform: YA/YA's art as activism. *Art Education, 53,* 40–45.

Faris, S. (1999, December 27). *Youth entrepreneurship: An overview.* Kansas City, MO: Kauffman Center for Entrepreneurial Leadership.

Fassler, I. (1998). The voices of children and youth in the democratic process. *New Designs for Youth Development, 14,* 36–40.

Fawcett, J. T., & Gardner, R. W. (1994). Asian immigrant entrepreneurs and non-entrepreneurs: A comparative study of recent Korean and Filipino immigrants. *Population and Environment, January,* 28–39.

Feigelman, S., Stanton, B. F., & Ricardo, I. (1993). Perceptions of drug selling and drug use among urban youths. *Journal of Early Adolescence, 13,* 267–284.

Ferguson, R. F. (1994). How professionals in community-based programs perceive and respond to the needs of black male youth. In R. B. Mincy (Ed.), *Nurturing young black males* (pp. 59–92). New Brunswick, NJ: Rutgers University Press.

Ferguson, R. F., & Stoutland, S. E. (1999). Reconceiving the community development field. In R. F. Ferguson & W. T. Dickens (Eds.), *Urban problems and community development* (pp. 33–75). Washington, D.C.: Brookings Institution Press.

Ferrari, T. M. (2003). Working hand in hand: Community youth development and career development. In F. A. Villarruel, D. F. Perkins, L. M. Borden, & J. G. Keith (Eds.), *Community youth development: Programs, policies, and practices* (pp. 201–223). Thousand Oaks, CA: Sage Publications.

First Things First. (2000). *School improvement.* Kansas City, MO: Author.

Fitzpatrick, K., & LaGory, M. (2000). *The ecology of risk in the urban landscape: Unhealthy places.* New York: Routledge.

Food from the 'Hood. (1997). *Plant a seed and watch what happens . . .* Los Angeles: Author.

Fortier, S. (2001). *Building communities through youth leadership and teen-adult dialogues.* Pasadena, CA: Western Justice Center.

Freedman, M. (1993). *The kindness of strangers: Adult mentors, urban youth, and the new voluntarism.* New York: Cambridge University Press.

Freeman, R. B., & Holzer, H. (1986). The black youth employment crisis: Summary of findings. In R. B. Freeman & H. Holzer (Eds.), *The black youth employment crisis* (pp. 110–131). Chicago: The University of Chicago Press.

Frumkin, P., & Kim, M. T. (2000). *Strategic positioning and the financing of nonprofit organizations: Is efficiency rewarded in the contributions marketplace?* Cambridge, MA: The Kennedy School of Government, Harvard University.

Fuller, C. (1996, December 16). Urban spotlight: Notes on cities: Aiding youth can be good business. *The Atlanta Journal and Constitution,* p. A04.

Furstenberg, Jr., F. F., Cook, T. D., Eccles, J., Elder, Jr., G. H., & Sameroff, A. (1999).

Managing to make it: Urban families and adolescent success. Chicago: University of Chicago Press.

Gamble, D. N., & Weil, M. O. (1997). Sustainable development: The challenge for community development. *Community Development Journal, 32,* 10–22.

Gartner, W. B. (1988). Who is an entrepreneur? Is that the wrong question. *Entrepreneurship Theory and Practice, 13,* 47–48.

Gaum, W. G., & Van-Rooyen, H. G. (1997). Curriculum guidelines for a distance education course in urban agriculture based on an eclectic model. *International Journal of Environmental Education and Information, 16,* 347–366.

Gebreselassie, T., & Politz, B. (2000). Youth development and . . . series: A series of annotated quotations and excerpts from selected research on youth. (2ⁿᵈ ed.). Washington, D.C.: Center for Youth Development and Policy Research, Academy for Educational Development.

Gibbs, D. (1994). The implications of sustainable development for industry and employment in the 1990s. *Environmentalist, 14,* 183–192.

Giroux, H. A. (1997). *Channel surfing: Racism, the media, and the destruction of today's youth.* New York: St. Martin's Press.

Gittell, R., & Thompson, J. P. (1999). Inner-city business development and entrepreneurship: New frontiers for policy and research. In R. F. Ferguson & W. T. Dickens (Eds.), *Urban problems and community development* (pp. 473–520). Washington, D.C.: Brookings Institution Press.

Glover, J. (1995). Promoting youth development in a therapeutic milieu. In *Contract with America's youth: Toward a national youth development agenda* (pp. 22–23). Washington, D.C.: American Youth Policy Forum.

Goff, L. (1996, November 25). New immigrants discover how to create own jobs: Entrepreneurship replaces entry-level work. *Crains New York Business,* pp. 17, 20.

Goldberger, S., Keough, R., & Almeida, C. (2000). *Benchmarks for succession in high school education: Putting data to work in school-to-career education reform.* Providence, RI: The Lab at Brown University.

Goldsmith, S. S. (1997, March 2). YA/YA*** winning the world over. *The Baton Rouge Sunday Advocate,* p. 1.

Greenhouse, S. (2001, July 16). Hispanic workers die at higher rate: More likely than others to do the dangerous, low-end jobs. *New York Times,* p. A11.

Greenhouse, S. (2002, August 5). Government asked to act on teenagers' job security: Some work risks too high, advocates say. *New York Times,* p. A8.

Griffin, C. E. (1996). Growing up: Students learn real-life business lessons. *Entrepreneur.Com, January,* 1–2.

Grossberg, L. (1994). The political status of youth and youth culture. In J. S. Epstein (Ed.), *Adolescents and their music* (pp. 25–46). New York: Garland Press.

Grubb, W. N. (1989). Preparing youth for work: The dilemmas of education and training programs. In D. Stern & D. Eichorn (Eds.), *Adolescence and work: Influences of social structure, labor markets, and culture* (pp. 13–45). Hillsdale, NJ: Lawrence Erlbaum Associates.

Gruber, D. (1997). Creative resource development: An assessment of potential in selected cities. In A. Sum et al. (Eds.), *A generation of challenge: Pathways to success for urban youth* (pp. 87–121). Baltimore, MD: Sar Levitan Center For Social Policy Studies, Johns Hopkins University.

Gutierrez, L. M., & Lewis, E. A. (1999). *Empowering women of color.* New York: Columbia University Press.

Guynn, J. (2001, April 1). Web sites help Moraga, Calif.-area kids launch their own businesses. *Contra Costa Times*, pp. 1–2.

Guzman, H. R. C. (1997). The structure of inequality and the status of Puerto Rican youth in the U.S. In A. Darder, R. D. Torres, & H. Gutierrez (Eds.), *Latinos and education: A critical reader* (pp. 80–94). New York: Routledge.

Haddow, A. (1998). Wrestling for resources. *Current: The Journal of Marine Education, 15*, 44.

Halpern, S. (1999). *The forgotten half revisited: American youth and young families, 1988–2008.* New York: William T. Grant Foundation.

Hamid, J. A. (2001, February 8). Managing the knowledge path. *New Straits Times* (Malaysia), p. 7.

Hamilton, M. A., & Hamilton, S. F. (1997). When is work a learning experience? *Phi Delta Kappan, 78*, pp. 682–691.

Hamilton, S. F., & Hamilton, M. A. (1994). *Opening career paths for youth: What can be done? Who can do it?* Washington, D.C.: American Youth Policy Forum.

Hardesty, P. H., & Hirsch, B. J. (1992). Summer and school-term youth employment: Ecological and longitudinal analysis. *Psychological Reports, 71*, 595–606.

Harmsworth, J., & Sethna, A. (1994). Women's development: Strengthening institutions for change. *Convergence, 27*, 19–25.

Harris, A. S. (1994). Promoting a promising future. *Black Enterprise, 25*, 29.

Hasnain, R. (2001). *Entering adulthood with a disability: Individual, family, and cultural challenges.* Boston: Boston University School of Education Doctoral Dissertation.

Haveman, R., & Wolfe, B. (1994). *Succeeding generations on the effects of investment in children.* New York: Russell Sage Foundation.

Heath, S. B. (2000). *Making learning work.* Palo Alto, CA: Stanford University.

Heath, S. B., & McLaughlin, M. W. (1993). Ethnicity and gender in theory and practice: The youth perspective. In S. B. Heath & M. W. McLaughlin (Eds.), Identity & inner-city youth: Beyond ethnicity and gender (pp. 13–35). New York: Teacher's College Press.

Henry, T. (2001, January 25). Study: Latinas shortchanged by U.S. schools. *USA Today*, p. 8D.

Heredia, C., & Haddock, V. (2001, April 3). State's kids even more diverse than its adults. *The San Francisco Chronicle*, p. 1.

Hickens, M. (1999). Hot time in the city. In F. Siegal & J. Rosenberg (Eds.), *Annual edition of urban society, 10th edition.* Guilford, CT: McGraw-Hill/Dushkin.

High, R., & Collins, J. W. (1991–1992). High school employment: At what cost? *High School Journal, 75*, pp. 90–93.

Hill, P. T. (1999). Focus high schools. In D. I. Besharov (Ed.), *America's disconnected youth* (pp. 213–231). Washington, D.C.: Child Welfare League of America.

Hopkins, C., Damlamian, J., & Lopez Ospina, G. (1996). Evolving towards education for sustainable development: An international perspective. *Nature and Resources, 32*, pp. 2–11.

Horatio Alger Association. (1998). *The state of our nation's youth: 1998–1999.* Alexandria, VA: Author.

Horton, R. L., Hutchinson, S., Barkman, S. J., Machtmes, K., & Meyers, H. (1999).

Developing experientially based 4-H curriculum materials (4-H 897). Columbus: Ohio State University.

Hren, B. J., & Hren, D. M. (1996). *Community sustainability: A mini-curriculum for grades 9–12.* Gaithersburg, MD: Izaak Walton League of America.

Huebner, A. J. (1998). Examining "empowerment": A how-to guide for the youth development professional. *Journal of Extension, 36,* pp. 1–6.

Husain, D. D. (1999). Good news on the horizons. *Techniques, 74,* pp. 14–17.

Imel, S. (1995). School-to-work transition. *ERIC Clearinghouse on Trends and Issues Alert,* pp. 1–4.

In Focus. (2001, January). *Youth livelihoods and HIV/AIDS.* (http://www.pathfind.org/IN%20FOCUS/jan_2001.htm)

Jargowsky, P. A. (1997). *Poverty and place: Ghettos, barrios, and the American city.* New York: Russell Sage Foundation.

Jasso, G. (1997). *Immigrant children and work.* Paper presented to the Committee on the Health & Safety Implications of Child Labor. Department of Sociology, New York University.

Jeff, M.F.X. (1994). Afrocentrism and African American male youths. In R. B. Mincy (Ed.), *Nurturing young black males* (pp. 99–118). New Brunswick, NJ: Rutgers University Press.

Jickling, B. (1994a). Studying sustainable development: Problems and possibilities. *Canadian Journal of Education, 19,* 231–240.

Jickling, B. (1994b). Why I don't want my children to be educated for sustainable development. *Trumpeter, 11,* 1114–1116.

Johnson, C., Schweke, W., & Hull, M. (1999). *Creating jobs: Public and private strategies for the hard to employ.* Washington, D.C.: Corporation for Economic Development.

Johnson, R. S., & Smith, E. (1998). Banking on urban America. *Fortune, 137,* 129–133.

Kablaoui, B. N., & Paulter, A. J. (1991). The effects of part-time work experience on high school students. *Journal of Career Development, 17,* 195–211.

Kay, P., Estepa, A., & Desetta, A. (Eds.). (1998). *Things get hectic: Teens write about the violence that surrounds them.* New York: Touchstone Books.

Kazis, R., & Pennington, H. (1999). *What's next for school-to-career?* Boston: Jobs for the Future.

Ketcham, A. F., Taylor, F. A., & Hoffman, D. R. (1990). Entrepreneurial training for the disadvantaged. *Training and Development Journal, 44,* 61–63.

Kets de Vries, M.F.R. (1985). The dark side of entrepreneurship. *Harvard Business Review, Nov.–Dec.,* 8–19.

Kibel, B. M. (2001). Research and practice: Mapping journeys. *CYD Journal Community Youth Development, 2,* 43–48.

King, J. (2000). *YA-YA and the art of recycling.* (http.//home.sprintmail.com/kingjohn/ . . .)

Kipke, M. D. (Ed.). (1999). *Risks and opportunities: Synthesis of studies on adolescence.* Washington, D.C.: National Research Council.

Klein, K. K. (1998, February 18). Learning curve: Business lessons from Southern California. *Los Angeles Times,* p. D2.

Knox, V., Miller, C., & Gennetian, L. A. (2000). *Reforming welfare and rewarding work:*

A summary of the final report on the Minnesota Family Investment Program. Minneapolis, MN: Manpower Demonstration Research Corporation.

Konig, S. (2000, April 1). Cracking the Asian-American market: Merrill ace John Ong says language isn't a barrier, so long as you have the right mindset. *On Wall Street,* pp. 1–4.

Kouriloff, M. (2000). Exploring perceptions of a priori barriers to entrepreneurship: A multidisciplinary approach. *Entrepreneurship Theory and Practice, 24,* 59–79.

Kourilsky, M. L. (1995). *Entrepreneurship education: Opportunity in search of curriculum.* Kansas City, MO: Kauffman Center for Entrepreneurial Leadership.

Kourilsky, M. L., & Esfandiari, M. (1997). Entrepreneurship education and lower socioeconomic black youth: An empirical investigation. *The Urban Review, 29,* 205–215.

Kourilsky, M. L., & Walstad, W. B. (1998). Entrepreneurship and female youth: Knowledge, attitudes, gender differences, and educational practices. *Journal of Business Venturing, 13,* 77–88.

Kourilsky, M. L., & Walstad, W. B. (2000). *"The E generation": Prepared for the entrepreneurial economy.* Dubuque, IA: Kendall/Hunt Publishing Co.

Kressley, K. G., & Skelton, N. (1996). "Fully prepared": Weaving the work of youth and civic development. *Wingspread Journal, Autumn,* 1–4.

Krueger, N. F. (2000). The cognitive infrastructure of opportunity emergence. *Entrepreneurship Theory and Practice, 24,* 5–23.

Krueger, N. F., & Brazeal, D. V. (1994). Entrepreneurial potential and potential entrepreneurs. *Entrepreneurship Theory and Practice, 18,* 91–104.

Krumboltz, J. D., & Worthington, R. L. (1999). The school-to-work transition from a learning theory perspective. *The Career Development Quarterly, 47,* 312–322.

Kuhn, T. S. (1970). *The structure of scientific revolutions* (2nd ed.). Chicago: The University of Chicago Press.

LaGreca, A. J. (2000). *Urban youth.* Lincoln, NE: Heartland Center for Leadership Development.

Lakes, R. D. (1996a). *Youth development and critical education: The promise of democratic action.* Albany: State University of New York Press.

Lakes, R. D. (1996b). The new vocationalism: Community economic development. *Journal of Industrial Teacher Education, 33,* 66–69.

Larson, R. W. (2000). Toward a psychology of positive youth development. *American Psychologist, 58,* 170–183.

Lawrence, J.E.S., & Singh, N. (1996). *Sustainable livelihoods and employment: How are these concepts related?* Unpublished manuscript.

Lee, C. C. (1994). Assessing needs: Adolescent development. In R. B. Mincy (Ed.), *Nurturing young black males* (pp. 33–44). Washington, D.C.: Urban Institute Press.

Lee, J. A. (2001). *The empowerment approach to social work practice* (2nd ed.). New York: Columbia University Press.

Leffert, N., Saito, R. N., Blyth, D. A., & Kroenke, C. H. (1996). *Making the case: Measuring the impact of youth development programs.* Minneapolis, MN: Search Institute.

Lehrer, E. (1999, May 24). Finding markets near downtown. *Insight,* pp. 16–17.

Lerman, R. I. (1999). Improving links between high schools and careers. In D. J. Besharov (Ed.), *America's disconnected youth: Toward a preventive strategy* (pp. 185–212). Washington, D.C.: Child Welfare of America Press.

Lerman, R. I. (2000). *Are teens in low-income and welfare families working too much?* Washington, D.C.: Urban Institute.

Lerner, R. M. (1995). *America's youth in crisis: Challenges and options for programs and policies.* Thousand Oaks, CA: Sage Publications.

Lerner, R. M., & Galambos, N. L. (1998). Adolescent development: Challenges and opportunities for research, program, and policies. *Annual Review of Psychology, 49*, 413–436.

Lerner, R. M., Ostrom, C. W., & Freel, M. A. (1997). Preventing health-compromising behaviors among youth and promoting their positive development: A developmental contextual perspective. In J. Schulenberg, J. L. Maggs, & K. Hurrelmann (Eds.), *Health risks and developmental transitions during adolescence* (pp. 498–521). New York: Cambridge University Press.

Lewis, A. (1992). Urban youth in community service: Becoming part of the solution. *ERIC Clearinghouse on Urban Education Digest, 81*, 1–5.

Li, X., & Feigelman, S. (1994). Recent and intended drug trafficking among male and female urban African American early adolescents. *Pediatrics, 93*, 1044–1099.

Liederman, D. S. (1995). *Don't forget young people in foster care! In Contract with America's youth: Toward a national youth development agenda* (pp. 52–53). Washington, D.C.: American Youth Policy Forum.

Light, I., & Rosenstein, C. (1995). *Race, ethnicity, and entrepreneurship in urban America.* New York: Aldine De Gruyter.

Lindner, J. R., & Cox, K. J. (1998). Youth entrepreneurship. *Journal of Extension, 36*, 1–6.

Linn, D. (1998, April 13). *Preparing students for the twenty-first century issue brief.* Washington, D.C.: National Governor's Association.

Lobsenz, A. (1991). Kids teach capitalism to economic revolutionaries. *Public Relations Journal, April*, 1–2.

Lopez, B., Nerenberg, L., & Valdez, M. (2000). Migrant adolescents: Barriers and opportunities for creating a promising future. In M. Montero-Sieburth & F. A. Villarruel (Eds.), *Making invisible Latino adolescents visible: A critical approach to Latino diversity* (pp. 289–307). New York: Falmer Press.

Lynch, R. L. (2000). *New directions for high school career and technical education in the 21st century.* Columbus: Ohio State University.

MacDonald, G. B., & Valdivieso, R. (2000). Measuring deficits and assets: How we track youth development now, and how we should track it. In *Youth development: Issues, challenges, and directions* (pp. 149–184). Philadelphia, PA: Public/Private Ventures.

Madden, S., & Bowen, M. (1996). *Design for success: Young Aspirations/Young Audiences.* Washington, D.C.: National Endowment for the Arts.

Magruder, J. (2000, March 16). Kids want fulfillment from jobs, study says. *The Arizona Republic*, p. A1.

Maimson, J., Hersey, A., & Silverberg, M. (1999). *Building blocks for a future school-to-work system: Early national implementation results.* Princeton, NJ: Mathematica Policy Research.

Males, M. A. (1996). *Scapegoat generation: America's war on adolescents.* Monroe, ME: Common Courage Press.

Males, M. A. (1999). *Framing youth: 10 myths about the next generation.* Monroe, ME: Common Courage Press.

Malveaux, J. (1999). Black dollar power. *Essence, 30,* 88–95.

Mangum, S., & Waldeck, N. (1997). Investments in people matter. In A. Sum et al. (Eds.), *A generation of challenge: Pathways to success for urban youth* (pp. 45–55). Baltimore, MD: Sar Levitan Center for Social Policy Studies, Johns Hopkins University.

Mann, P. H. (1992). *Entrepreneurship and the world of small business.* San Francisco: UMI Information Store..

Manning, W. D. (1990). Parenting employed teenagers. *Youth & Society, 22,* 184–200.

Mariani, M. (1994). The young and the entrepreneurial. *Occupational Outlook Quarterly, 38,* 2–9.

Martinez, A. L. (1999). Cambios: A Spanish-language approach to youth development. *SIECUS Report, 27,* 9–10.

Maselow, R. E. (1995). *How little tykes become big tycoons.* San Francisco: UMI Information Store.

Maser, C. (1997). *Sustainable community development: Principles and concepts.* Delray Beach, FL: St. Lucie Press.

Matthews, C. (1995). Family background and gender: Implications for interest in small firm ownership. *Entrepreneurship and Regional Development, Oct.–Dec.,* 13–20.

Mayo, E., & Ramsden, P. (2001, March 26). Time to take stock of the inner city: Fast-drowning enterprises in the inner cities could receive a big boost from a financial index being launched later this year. *New Statesman, 130,* xvii.

McKenzie-Mohr, D., & Smith, W. (1999). *Fostering sustainable behavior: An introduction to community-based marketing.* British Columbia, Canada: New Societies Publisher.

McLaughlin, M. W. (1993). Embedded identities: Enabling balance in urban contexts. In S. B. Heath & M. W. McLaughlin (Eds.), *Identity & inner-city youth: Beyond ethnicity and gender* (pp. 36–68). New York: Teacher's College Press.

Meyer E. C., & Nauta, T. (1994). *Four approaches to entrepreneurship II.* San Francisco: UMI Information Store.

Millstein, S. G., Petersen, A. C., & Nightingale, E. O. (Eds.). (1993). *Promoting the health of adolescents: New directions for the twenty-first century.* New York: Oxford University Press.

Mincy, R. B. (1994a). Why this book? In R. B. Mincy (Ed.), *Nurturing young black males* (pp. 1–29). New Brunswick, NJ: Rutgers University Press.

Mincy, R. B. (1994b). Conclusions and implications. In R. B. Mincy (Ed.), *Nurturing young black males* (pp. 187–203). New Brunswick, NJ: Rutgers University Press.

Mitchael, R. T. (2001). A lens on adolescence: The 1997 national longitudinal survey of youth. In R. T. Mitchael (Ed.), *Social awakening: Adolescent behavior as adulthood approaches* (pp. 1–22). New York: Russell Sage Foundation.

Montero-Sieburth, M. (2000). Demystifying the images of Latinos: Boston-based case studies. In M. Montero-Sieburth & F. A. Villarruel (Eds.)., *Making invisible Latino adolescents visible* (pp. 155–201). New York: Falmer Press.

Morino, M. (1998). Point of view: Technology as a social benefit tool. *Next Generation.* Reston, VA: Morino Institute.

Moss, P., & Tilly, C. (2001). *Stories employers tell: Race, skill, and hiring in America.* New York: Russell Sage Foundation.

Murdock, S. H. (1995). *An America challenged: Population change and the future of the United States.* Boulder, CO: Westview Press.

Murphy, R. (1995a). *Definitions, language, and concepts for strengthening the field of youth development work.* Washington, D.C.: Academy for Educational Development.

Murphy, R. (1995b). *Training for youth workers: An assessment guide for community-based youth-serving organizations to promote youth development.* Washington, D.C.: Academy for Educational Development.

Muschett, F. D. (Ed.). (1997a). *Principles of sustainable development.* Delray Beach, FL: St. Lucie Press.

Muschett, F. D. (1997b). An integrated approach to sustainable development. In F. D. Muschett (Ed.), *Principles of sustainable development* (pp. 1–45). Delray Beach, FL: St. Lucie Press.

Nakanishi, D. T. (2001). Political trends and electoral issues of the Asian Pacific American population. In N. J. Smelser, W. J. Wilson, & F. Mitchell (Eds.), *America becoming: Racial trends and their consequences, Volume 1* (pp. 170–199). Washington, D.C.: National Research Council.

National Center for Social Entrepreneurs. (2001). *Merging mission, market & money: A nonprofit's guide to social entrepreneurship.* Minneapolis, MN.: Author.

National Collaboration for Youth. (1997). *Credentialing activities in the youth development field.* Washington, D.C.: Author.

National Collaboration for Youth. (1997). *Youth community service and service learning.* Washington, D.C.: Author.

National Collaboration for Youth. (1998). *Positions for youth: Public policy statements of the National Collaboration for Youth.* Washington, D.C.: Author.

National Collaboration for Youth. (1999). *Positions for youth: Public policy statements of the National Collaboration for Youth.* Washington, D.C.: Author.

National Employer Leadership Council. (1994). *Work and America's youth: Lessons from the National Panel on Work and America's Youth.* Washington, D.C.: Author.

National Research Council. (1993). *Losing generations: Adolescents in high-risk settings.* Washington, D.C.: Author.

National Research Council. (1998). *Protecting youth at work: Health, safety, and development of working children and adolescents in the United States.* Washington, D.C.: National Academy Press.

National School-to-Work Learning and Information Center. (1996). *Incorporating a youth development perspective into school-to-work systems.* Washington, D.C.: Author.

National School-To-Work Learning and Information Center. (1996a). *School-to-work opportunities for out-of-school-youth.* Washington, D.C.: Author.

National School-to-Work Learning and Information Center. (1997). Involving community-based organizations in school-to-work. *Resource Bulletin, August,* 1–8.

National Technical Information Service. (1991). *Youth development program models.* Washington, D.C.: U.S. Department of Commerce.

National Youth Employment Coalition. (1995). *Toward a national youth development system: How we can better serve youth at-risk.* Washington, D.C.: Author.

Neal, P. (1995). Teaching sustainable development. *Environmental Education, 50,* 8–9.

Nesdale, D., & Pinter, K. (2000). Self-efficacy and job-seeking activities of unemployed ethnic youth. *The Journal of Social Psychology, 140,* 608–614.

Newman, K. S. (1995). Dead-end jobs: A way out. *Brookings Review, 13*, 24–28.

Newman, K. S. (1999). *No shame in my game: The working poor in the inner city.* New York: Russell Sage Foundation.

Newman, R. P., Smith, S. M., & Murphy, R. (2000). A matter of money: The cost and financing of youth development. In *Youth development: Issues, challenges, and directions* (pp. 81–124). Philadelphia, PA: Public/Private Ventures.

Neumark, D. (Ed.). (2000). *On the job: Is long-term employment a thing of the past?* New York: Russell Sage Foundation.

Nixon, C. (1996, September 17). Program teaches teens how to start own business. *Antelope Valley* (News Section), p. 1.

O'Connor, A., Tilly, C., & Bobo, L. D. (2000). *Urban inequality: Evidence from four cities.* New York: Russell Sage Foundation.

O'Connor, A. (1999). Swimming against the tide: A brief history of federal policy in poor communities. In R. F. Ferguson & W. T. Dickens (Eds.), *Urban problems and community development* (pp. 77–137). Washington, D.C.: Brookings Institution Press.

O'Donnell, J., Michalak, E. A., & Ames, E. B. (1997). Inner-city youths helping children: After-school programs to promote bonding and reduce risk. *Social Work in Education, 19*, 231–241.

Ogbu, J. U. (1989). Cultural boundaries and minority youth orientation toward work preparation. In D. Stern & D. Eichorn (Eds.), *Adolescence and work: Influences of social structure, labor markets, and culture* (pp. 101–140). Hillsdale, NJ: Lawrence Erlbaum Associates.

Ogbu, J. U. (1997). Understanding the school performance of urban schools. In H. J. Walberg, O. Reyes, & R. P. Weisberg (Eds.), *Children and youth: Interdisciplinary perspectives* (pp. 190–222). Thousand Oaks, CA: Sage Publications.

Olive, E. (2003). The African American child and positive youth development: A journey from support to sufficiency. In F. A. Villarruel, D. F. Perkins, L. M. Borden, & J. G. Keith (Eds.), *Community youth development programs, policies, and practices* (pp. 27–46). Thousand Oaks, CA: Sage Publications.

Organisation for Economic Co-operation and Development. (2000). *From initial education to working life: Making transitions work.* Paris, France: Author.

Organisation for Economic Co-operation and Development. (2001). *Social enterprise: A primer on economic and social co-operation.* Paris, France: Author.

Osterman, P. (1989). The job market for adolescents. In D. Stern & D. Eichorn (Eds.), *Adolescence and work: Influences of social structure, labor markets, and culture* (pp. 235–256). Hillsdale, NJ: Lawrence Erlbaum Associates.

Padilla, F. M. (1994). *The gang as an American enterprise.* New Brunswick, NJ: Rutgers University Press.

Panayiotopoulos, P., & Gerry, C. (2000). Small enterprise promotion targeting youth: Experience from state-sponsored programmes. *Papers in International Development.* (http://www.swansea.ac.uk/eds/devres/pubs/pid22.htm)

Paquin, T. P. (1991). A school-based enterprise: The Saint Pauls, North Carolina experience. *Rural Special Education Quarterly, 10*, 26–28.

Parker, M. (2000). The way it could be. In D. Hellison, N. Cutforth, J. Kallusky, T. Martinek, M. Parker, & J. Stiehl (Eds.), *Youth development and physical activity: Linking universities and communities* (pp. 17–27). Champaign, IL: Human Kinetics.

Patillo, M. E. (1998). Sweet mothers and gangbusters: Managing crime in a black middle-class neighborhood. *Social Forces, 76*, 747–763.

Pauly, E., Hilary, K., & Haimson, J. (1995). *Home-grown lessons: Innovative programs linking school and work.* San Francisco: Jossey-Bass Publishers.

Pennsylvania State University. (2000). *Family/youth resiliency & policy: Community youth development.* Happy Valley, PA: Department of Family & Consumer Sciences.

Perez, S. M., & Salazar, D. D. (1997). Economic, labor force, social implications of Latino educational and population trends. In A. Darder, R. D. Torres, & H. Gutierrez (Eds.), *Latinos and education: A critical reader* (pp. 45–79). New York: Routledge.

Phillip, M. C. (1995, September 7). Entrepreneurship education. *Black Issues in Higher Education*, p. 5.

Phillips, T. (1999). *Foundation information: Most teens want to start own business.* Kansas City, KS: Kauffman Foundation.

Pierret, C. R. (2001). The effect of family structure on youth outcomes in the NLSY97. In R. T. Michael (Ed.), *Social awakening: Adolescent behavior as adulthood approaches* (pp. 25–48). New York: Russell Sage Foundation.

Pike, A. (2001, May 31). A helping hand for women entrepreneurs. *Financial Times* (London), p. 15.

Pines, M., & Spring, B. (1997). Moving into the mainstream: Making connections for disconnected youth. In A. Sum et al. (Eds.), *A generation of challenge: Pathways to success for urban youth* (pp. 123–142). Baltimore, MD: Sar Levitan Center for Social Policy Studies.

Pittman, K. J. (1991). *A new vision: Promoting youth development.* Washington, D.C.: Academy for Educational Development.

Pittman, K. J. (2000). Balancing the equation: Communities supporting youth, youth supporting communities. *CYD Journal Community Youth Development, 1*, pp. 33–36.

Pittman, K. J., Irby, M., & Ferber, T. (2000). Unfinished business: Further reflections on a decade of promoting youth development. In *Youth development: Issues, challenges and directions* (pp. 17–64). Philadelphia, PA: Public/Private Ventures.

Pittman, K. J., & Zeldin, S. (1994). From deterrence to development: Shifting the focus of youth programs for African American males. In R. B. Mincy (Ed.), *Nurturing young black males* (pp. 32–36). New Brunswick, NJ: Rutgers University Press.

Pittman, K. J., & Zeldin, S. (1995). *Defining the why, what, and how of promoting youth development through organizational practice.* Washington, D.C.: Academy for Educational Development.

Planting seeds, harvesting scholarship: Food from the 'Hood. (1995, May 29). *Newsweek*, 29.

Poerkson, U. (1993). *Plastic words.* Ontario, Canada: CBC.

Pomerantz, M. (2000). Social investing helps create sustainable nonprofits. *Business Magazine, 22*, 12–14.

Prestegard, S. (1997). Learning by doing. *Marketplace Magazine, 8*, 31–32.

Public/Private Ventures. (Eds.). (2000). Introduction and overview. Youth development: Issues, challenges, and directions (pp. 1–7). Philadelphia, PA: Author.

Purdue, D. (2001). Neighbourhood governance: Leadership, trust and social capital. *Urban Studies, 38*, 2211–2224.

Quater, J., & Richmond, B. J. (2001). Accounting for social value in nonprofits and for-profits. *Nonprofit Management & Leadership, 12*, 75–85.

Quinn, J. (1994). Traditional youth service systems and their work with young black males. In R. B. Mincy (Ed.), *Nurturing young black males* (pp. 119–162). New Brunswick, NJ: Rutgers University Press.

Quinn, J. (1999). Where need meets opportunity: Youth development for early teens. *The Future of Children, 9*, 96–116.

Quinones-Mayo, Y., Wilson, K. B., & McGuire, M. V. (2000). Vocational rehabilitation and cultural competency for Latino populations: Considerations for rehabilitation counselors. *Journal of Applied Rehabilitation Counseling, 31*, 19–30.

Rauner, D. M. (2000). *The role of caring in youth development and community life: "They still pick me up when I fall."* New York: Columbia University Press.

Reingold, D. A. (1999). Social networks and the employment problem of the urban poor. *Urban Studies, 36*, 1907–1931.

Reskin, B. F. (1999). Occupational segregation by race and ethnicity among women workers. In I. Browne (Ed.), *Latinas and African American women at work: Race, gender, and economic inequality* (pp. 183–204). New York: Russell Sage Foundation.

Reynolds, P. D., Hay, M., & Camp, S. M. (1999). *Global entrepreneurship monitor: 1999 executive report.* Kansas City, MO: Kauffman Center for Entrepreneurial Leadership.

Ricardo, I. (1994). Life choices of African American youths living in public housing. *Pediatrics, 93*, 1055–1059.

Rick, L. (1999). *Who's minding the store? A guide for educators working with school-based enterprises.* Berkeley, CA: National Center for Research in Vocational Education, University of California, Berkeley.

Ries, E. (2000, April 1). Owning their education. *Techniques, 75*, 26–29.

Robinson, M. (1992). Linking distance education to sustainable community development. In D. Wall & M. Owens (Eds.), *Distance education and sustainable community: Selected articles from a conference on distance education and sustainable community development* (pp. 80–87). Edmonton, Alberta, Canada: Canadian Circumpolar Institute, University of Alberta.

Rodriguez, C. E. (Ed.). (1997). *Latin looks: Images of Latinas and Latinos in the U.S. media.* Boulder, CO: Westview Press.

Rodriguez, M. C., Morrobel, D. & Villarruel, F. A. (2003). Research realities and a vision of success for Latino youth development. In F. A. Villarruel, D. F. Perkins, L. M. Borden & J. G. Keith (Eds.), *Community youth development programs, policies, and practices* (pp. 47–78). Thousand Oaks, CA: Sage Publications.

Rogoff, B., & Lave, J. (Eds.) (2001). *Everyday cognition: Development in social context.* Cambridge, MA: Harvard University Press.

Rosenbaum, J. E. (1997). Schools and the world of work. In B. A. Weisbrod & J. C. Worthy (Eds)., *The urban crisis: Linking research to action* (pp. 100–128). Evanston, IL: Northwestern University Press.

Rosenblum, S. B. (1998, December 21). Cities urged to link youth jobs and education to community building. *Nation's Cities Weekly*, 11.

Rossman, J. (2000). *Promoting small businesses: The new face of community development.* Richmond, VA: Federal Reserve Bank of Richmond, Community Affairs Office.

Roth, J., Brooks-Gunn, J., Murray, L., & Foster, W. (1998). Promoting healthy adolescents: Synthesis of youth development program evaluations. *Journal of Research on Adolescence, 8,* 423–459.

Roy, M., & Turner, J. (1996). *Information for sustainable development project.* Winnipeg, Canada: International Institute for Sustainable Development.

Ruben, B. (1995). Common ground. *Environmental Action, 27,* 26–28.

Ruhm, C. J. (1998). Is high school employment consumption or investment? *Journal of Labor Economics, 113,* 285–317.

Sampson, O. (2000, November 30). The price of work/high-school students who hold part-time jobs bang into downside of earning extra cash. *The Gazette,* p. 3.

Sampson, R. J. (1999). What "community" supplies. In R. F. Ferguson & W. T. Dickens (Eds.), *Urban problems and community development* (pp. 241–292). Washington, D.C.: Brookings Institution Press.

Sampson, R. J. (2001). How do communities undergird or undermine human development? Relevant contexts and social mechanisms. In A. Booth & A. C. Crouter (Eds.), *Does it take a village? Community effects on children, adolescents, and families* (pp. 3–30). Mahwah, NJ: Lawrence Erlbaum Associates.

Sandefur, G. D., Martin, M., Eggerling-Boeck, J., Mannon, S. E., & Meier, A. M. (2001). An overview of racial and ethnic demographic trends. In N. J. Smelser, W. J. Wilson, & F. Mitchell (Eds.), America becoming: Racial trends and their consequences, Vol. 1 (pp. 40–102). Washington, D.C.: National Research Council.

San Diego County Office of Education. (1997). *School-to-career transition.* San Diego, CA: Author.

Santiago, A. M. (2000). The impact of growing up poor or welfare-dependent on the economic status of young adults. In M. Montero-Sieburth & F. A. Villarruel (Eds.), *Making invisible Latino adolescents visible: A critical approach to Latino diversity* (pp. 29–60). New York: Falmer Press.

Sarason, Y., & Koberg, C. (1994). *Hispanic women small business owners.* San Francisco, CA: UMI Information Store.

Sarver, D., Johnson, E., & Verma, S. (2000). A tool to assess the worth of a youth organization. *Journal of Extension, 38,* 50–56.

Schemo, D. J. (2002, September 5). Education study finds Hispanics both gaining and lagging. *New York Times,* p. 30.

Scherzer, A. (2000, January 13). Program gets kids down to business. *The Tampa Tribune,* pp. 1–2.

Schwartz, R. G. (2000). Juvenile justice and positive youth development. In *Youth development: Issues, challenges, and directions* (pp. 233–279). Philadephia: Public/Private Ventures.

Schwartz, W. (1995). School dropouts: New information about an old problem. *ERIC Clearinghouse on Urban Education Digest, 109,* 1–5.

Seidman, E., & French, S. E. (1997). Normative school transitions among urban adolescents: When, where, and how to imagine. In H. J. Walberg, O. Reyes, & R. P. Weisberg (Eds.), *Children and youth: Interdisciplinary perspectives* (pp. 166–189). Thousand Oaks, CA: Sage Publications.

Shaffer, R. (1995), Achieving sustainable economic development in communities. *Journal of the Community Development Society, 26*, 145–154.

Shaklee, H. (2000). Inventing adolescence: 20th century concepts of youth development. *Journal of Family & Consumer Sciences, 92*, 11–16.

Shanahan, M. J., Finch, M. D., Mortimer, J. T., & Ryu, S. (1991). Adolescent work experience and depressive affect. *School Psychology Quarterly, 54*, 299–317.

Shannon, M. J. (1992). *Education-based community development.* Waltham, MA: Civic Practice Network, Heller School for Advanced Studies in Social Welfare.

Shaw, L. (2001, July 9). Summer tech program rises from partnership public, private hands create low-cost camp. *The Seattle Times*, p. B1.

Sheehy, Jr., A. M., Oldham, E., Zanghi, M., Ansell, D., Correia III, P., & Copeland, R. (2000). *Promoting practices: Supporting transition of youth served by the foster care system.* Baltimore, MD: Annie E. Casey Foundation.

Skinner, C. (1995). Urban labor markets and young black men: A literature review. *Journal of Economic Issues, 29*, 47–59.

Slaughter, M. P. (undated). *Seven keys to shaping the entrepreneurial organization.* Kansas City, MO: Kauffman Center for Entrepreneurial Leadership.

Slaughter, M. P. (1996). *Entrepreneurship: Economic impact and public policy implications: An overview of the field.* Kansas City, MO: Kauffman Center for Entrepreneurial Leadership.

Small, S., & Supple, A. (2001). Communities as systems: Is a community more than a sum of its parts? In A. Booth & A. C. Crouter (Eds.), *Does it take a village? Community effects on children, adolescents, and families* (pp. 161–174). Mahwah, NJ: Lawrence Erlbaum Associates.

Smilor, R. W. (1996). *Entrepreneurship and philanthropy.* Kansas City, MO: Kauffman Center for Entrepreneurial Leadership.

Smilor, R. W. (1997). *Entrepreneurship and community development.* Kansas City, MO: Kauffman Center for Entrepreneurial Leadership.

Smith, C. L., & Rojewski, J. W. (1993). School-to-work transitions: Alternatives for educational reform. *Youth & Society, 25*, 222–250.

Smith, K. (1996, August 23). Snacks offer youth taste for business; Entrepreneurs: Morgan State program turns summer stand into educational experience. *The Baltimore Sun*, p. 1B.

Social Enterprise London. (2001). *Social enterprises explained.* London: Author.

Solomon, B. (1976). *Black empowerment.* New York: Columbia University Press.

Solomon, B., & Gardner, H. (2000). The origins of good works: Getting kids, parents, and coaches on the same page. *CYD Journal Community Youth Development, 1*, 36–41.

A sporting chance. (1998, February 18). *Los Angeles Times*, p. 1.

Stanton, B., & Galbraith, J. (1994). Drug trafficking among African American early adolescents: Prevalence, consequences, and associated behaviors and beliefs. *Pediatrics, 93*, 1039–1043.

Starr, E. (1997). The changing workforce and workforce outcome. (http://wwwsbanet. uca.edu/docs/proceedings/95sbac01.txt).

Stein, J. (2000). *Youth and family development concept paper: Youth contributions to community.* (http://www.extension.umn.edu/capacity/yfd/components/youth_community_concept.html).

Steinberg, L., Fegley, S., & Dornbusch, S. M. (1993). Negative impact of part-time work on adolescent adjustment: Evidence from a longitudinal study. *Developmental Psychology, 29*, 171–180.

Stern, D. (2000). *School-to-work policy insights from recent international developments.* Berkeley: University of California National Center for Research in Vocational Education.

Stern, D., & Eichorn, D. (Eds.). (1989). *Adolescence and work: Influences of social structure, labor markets, and culture.* Hillsdale, NJ: Lawrence Erlbaum Associates.

Stern, D., Stone III, J., Hopkins, C., McMillion, M., & Crain, R. (1994). *School-based enterprises: Productive learning in American high schools.* San Francisco: Jossey-Bass Publishers.

Stevens, J. W. (2002). *Smart and sassy: The strengths of inner-city black girls.* New York: Oxford University Press.

Stone, C., Doherty, K., Jones, C., Ross, T. (1999). Schools and disadvantaged neighborhoods: The community development challenge. In R. F. Ferguson & W. T. Dickens (Eds.), *Urban problems and community development* (pp. 339–380). Washington, D.C.: Brookings Institution Press.

Stoutland, S. E. (1999). Community development corporations: Mission, strategy, and accomplishments. In R. F. Ferguson & W. T. Dickens (Eds.), *Urban problems and community development* (pp. 193–240). Washington, D.C.: Brookings Institution Press.

Sum, A., Fogg, N., & Fogg, N. (1997). Confronting the demographic challenge: Future labor market prospects of out-of-school young adults. In A. Sum et al. (Eds.), *A generation of challenge: Pathways to success for urban youth* (pp. 13–44). Baltimore, MD: Sar Levitan Center for Social Policy Studies, Johns Hopkins University.

Sum, A., Mangum, S., deJesus, E., Walker, G., Gruber, D., Pines, M., & Spring, W. (Eds.). (1997). *A generation of challenge: Pathways to success for urban youth.* Baltimore, MD: Sar Levitan Center for Social Policy Studies, Johns Hopkins University.

Swanson, D. P., Spencer, M. B., 'Angelo, T. D., Harpalani, V., & Spencer, T. R. (2002). Identity processes and the positive development of African Americans: An exploratory framework. In R. M. Lerner, C. S. Taylor, & A. V. Eye (Eds.), *New directions for youth development: Pathways to positive development among diverse youth* (pp. 73–99). San Francisco: Jossey-Bass Publishers.

Taylor, C. S., et al. (2002). Stability of attributes of positive functioning and of developmental assets among African American adolescent male gang and community-based organization members. In R. M. Lerner, C. S. Taylor, & A. V. Eye (Eds.), *New directions for youth development: Pathways to positive development among diverse youth* (pp. 35–55). San Francisco: Jossey-Bass Publishers.

Taylor, E. H. (2000, March 7). Hard work, tough studies. *Star Tribune* (Minneapolis, MN), p. 1E.

Taylor, R. B. (2001). On Mount and Fayette: Implications for comprehensive youth development approaches. In A. Booth & A. C. Crouter (Eds.), *Does it take a village? Community effects on children, adolescents, and families* (pp. 203–210). Mahwah, NJ: Lawrence Erlbaum Associates.

Terpstra, D. E., & Olson, P. R. (1993). Entrepreneurship start-up and growth: A classification of problems. *Entrepreneurship Theory and Practice, 17*, pp. 5–20.

Theobald, P., & Nachtigal, P. (1995). *Culture, community, and the promise of rural education*. Unpublished manuscript.

Thorton, R. (2001). Trends among American Indians in the United States. In N. J. Smelser, W. J. Wilson, & F. Mitchell (Eds.). *America becoming: Racial trends and their consequences* (pp. 135–169). Washington, D.C.: National Research Council.

Total buying power of African Americans expected to reach $682 billion in 2006. (2001, November 26). *PR Wire*, 1–2.

U.S. Census Bureau. (1997). *1997 economic census of minority- and women-owned businesses in the United States*. Washington, D.C. Author.

Useem, J. (1996, December). The virtue of necessity. *Inc., Magazine Archives*, 1–7.

Valdes, I., & Seoane, M. (Eds.). (1999). *Hispanic market handbook*. Detroit, MI: Gale Publications.

Villarruel, F. A., Perkins, D. F., Borden, L. M., & Keith, J. G. (Eds.). (2003). *Community youth development: Programs, policies, and practices* (pp. 201–223). Thousand Oaks, CA: Sage Publications.

Virgil, J. D. (1993). Gangs, social control, and ethnicity: Ways to redirect. In S. B. Heath & M. W. McLaughlin (Eds.), *Identity & inner-city youth: Beyond ethnicity and gender* (pp. 94–119). New York: Teacher's College Press.

Waldinger, R., Aldrich, H., & Ward, R. (1990). *Ethnic entrepreneurs: Immigrant businesses in industrial societies*. Newbury Park, CA: Sage Publications.

Walker, E. M., & Sutherland, M. E. (1993). Urban black youths' educational and occupational goals: The impact of America's opportunity structure. *Urban Education, 28*, 200–220.

Walker, G. (1997). Out of school and unemployed: Principles for more effective policies and programs. In A. Sum et al. (Eds.), *A generation of challenge: Pathways to success for urban youth* (pp. 73–86). Baltimore, MD: Sar Levitan Center for Social Policy Studies, Johns Hopkins University.

Walker, G. (2001). *The policy climate for early adolescent initiatives*. Philadelphia, PA: Public/Private Ventures.

Walstad, W. B., & Kourilsky, M. L. (1998). Entrepreneurial attitudes and knowledge of black youth. *Entrepreneurship Theory and Practice, 23*, pp. 5–18.

Walstad, W. B., & Kourilsky, M. L. (1999). *Seeds of success: Entrepreneurship and youth*. Kansas City, MO: Kauffman Center for Entrepreneurial Leadership.

Wang, M. C., Haertel, G. D., & Walberg, H. J. (1997). Fostering educational resilience in inner-city schools. In H. J. Walberg, O. Reyes, & R. P. Weisberg (Eds.), *Children and youth: Interdisciplinary perspectives* (pp. 119–140). Thousand Oaks, CA: Sage Publications.

Watkins, M., & Iverson, E. (1998). Youth development principles and field practicum opportunities. In R. R. Greene & M. Watkins (Eds.), *Serving diverse constituencies: Applying the ecological perspective* (pp. 167–197). New York: Aldine De Gruyter.

Way, N. (1998). *Everyday courage: The lives and stories of urban teenagers*. New York: New York University Press.

Weisman, G. K. (1993). Adolescent PTSD and the development consequences of crack dealing. *American Journal of Orthopsychiatry, 63*, 553–561.

Wentling, R. M., & Waight, C. L. (1999). Barriers that hinder the successful transition of minority youth into the workforce. *Journal of Vocational Education Research, 24*, 165–183.

Wentling, R. M., & Waight, C. L. (2000). School and workplace initiatives and other factors that assist and support the successful school-to-work transition for minority youth. *Journal of Industrial Teacher Education, 37* (2), 5–30.

Werner, E. E. (1989). Adolescents and work: A longitudinal perspective on gender and cultural variability. In D. Stern & D. Eichorn (Eds.), *Adolescence and work: Influences of social structure, labor markets, and culture* (pp. 159–187). Hillsdale, NJ: Lawrence Erlbaum Associates.

White, J. (1999). *Five capacities that build communities, and 10 things funders can do to support them.* Ontario, Canada: Ontario Trillium Foundation.

Whitehead, T. L., Peterson, J., & Kaljee, L. (1994). Socioeconomic deprivation, urban drug trafficking, and low-income African American male gender identity. *Pediatrics, 93,* 1050–1054.

Williams, D. A. (1998, October 13). Simple garden blossoms into student-owned business in L. A: Food from the 'Hood raises money to send participants to college. *Peoria Journal Star,* pp. 1–2.

Williams, L. S. (2001). City kids and country cousins: Rural and urban youths, deviance, and labor market ties. In R. T. Mitchell (Ed.), *Social awakening: Adolescent behavior as adulthood approaches* (pp. 379–413). New York: Russell Sage Foundation.

Wilson, W. J. (1996). *When work disappears.* New York: Alfred J. Knopf.

Wilson, W. J. (1999). The plight of the inner-city black male. In D. J. Besharov (Ed.), *America's disconnected youth: Toward a preventive strategy* (pp. 31–48). Washington, D.C.: Child Welfare League of America Press.

Worley, L. P. (1995). Working adolescents: Implications for counselors. *School Counselor, 42,* 218–223.

Working Group on Youth Entrepreneurship. (1996). *Catching the wave: Framework for youth entrepreneurship success.* Toronto, Canada: Author.

Worthington, R. L., & Juntenen, C. L. (1997). The vocational development of non-college-bound youth: Counseling psychology and the school-to-work movement. *Counseling Psychologist, 25,* 323–363.

Youniss, J., & Yates, M. (1997). *Community service and social responsibility in youth.* Chicago: University of Chicago Press.

Youth Venture. (2002). Youth ventures. (http://www.youthventure.org/ventures.asp).

Zeldin, S. (1995a). *School-to-work and youth development: Identifying common ground.* Washington, D.C.: Academy for Educational Development.

Zeldin, S. (1995b). *Making research relevant to community mobilization efforts for youth development.* Washington, D.C.: Academy for Educational Development.

Zeldin, S. (1995c). *Preparing youth for adulthood: Common grounds between the school-to-work and youth development fields.* Washington, D.C.: Academy for Educational Development.

Zeldin, S., & Camino, L. (1998). Nothing as theoretical as good practice: Improving partnerships with researchers. *New Designs for Youth Development, 14,* 34–36.

Zeldin, S., Kimball, M., & Price, L. (1995). *What are the day-to-day experiences that promote youth development? An annotated bibliography of research on adolescents and their families.* Washington, D.C.: Academy for Educational Development.

Zhou, M. (2001). Contemporary immigration and the dynamics of race. In N. J. Smelser, W. J. Wilson, & F. Mitchell (Eds.), *America becoming: Racial trends and their consequences* (pp. 200–242). Washington, D.C.: National Research Council.

Zhou, M., & Bankston III, C. L. (1998). *Growing up in America: The adaptation of Vietnamese adolescents in the United States*. New York: Russell Sage Foundation.

Zuckerman, A. (2000). The more things change, the more they stay the same: The evolution and development of youth employment programs. In *Youth development: Issues, challenges and directions* (pp. 301–324). Philadelphia, PA: Public/Private Ventures.

Zuniga, M. M. de (2001). *Companies must innovate to reach diverse Hispanic communities*. Madrid: The Spain-U.S. Chamber of Commerce.

Name Index

Abbott, J., 29, 32, 33, 34, 77, 185
Abe, Y., 68, 185
Aber, J. L., 189
Adams, A. C., 28, 185
Aldrich, H. E., 93, 99, 185, 206
Allen, L., 8, 185
Almeida, C., 79, 80, 88, 193
Ames, E. B., 32, 200
Amit, R., 99, 185
Anderson, D. C., 5, 185
Anderson, E., 62, 185
'Angelo, T. D., 4, 205
Angles, F., 24, 189
Answell, D., 20, 204
Appleton, J., 8, 20, 191
Armistead, P. J., 29, 122, 186
Astroth, K., 20, 186

Bachman, J. G., 85, 186
Baker, T., 99, 185
Bangs, P. C., 112, 189
Bankston, C. L., 93, 208
Barker, C., 152, 154, 158, 174, 180, 186
Barkman, S. J., 36, 186
Barling, J., 86, 186
Bartik, T. J., 57, 70, 186
Barton, W. H., 32, 186

Bates, T., 92, 186
Benson, P. L., 20, 21, 34, 186
Benz, M. R., 80, 82, 186
Bernhardt, A., 55, 70, 186
Berstein, S., 46, 186
Besharov, D. J., 5, 78, 87, 186
Bessemer, G., 186
Black, P., 110, 186
Blank, R. M., 70, 97, 186, 191
Blasi, J., 70, 191
Blum, R.W.M., 24, 187
Blyth, D. A., 26, 196
Bobo, L. D., 55, 57, 200
Bodar, J., 123, 187
Bonacich, E., 93, 187
Bonilla, F., 97, 188
Booth, A., 11, 187
Borden, L. M., 19, 206
Borman, G. D., 61, 187
Bornstein, D., 98, 99, 187
Boschee, J., 112, 187
Boston, T. D., 20, 187
Bouvier, L. F., 98, 187
Boyd, W. L., 11, 84, 109, 187
Bradley, W. S., 51, 187
Brazeal, D. V., 99
Breggin, G. R., 62, 187

Breggin, P. R., 62, 187
Brierton, J., 109, 117, 187
Brinckeroff, P. C., 106, 187
Brochu, S., 188
Brooks-Gunn, J., 21, 203
Brown, B. V., 87, 187
Brown, C. M., 91, 187
Brown, D. E., 37, 187
Brown, M., 28, 187, 197
Browne, I., 57, 187
Brumback, N., 120, 121, 188
Brundtland, G. H., 45, 188
Brunelle, N., 188
Burt, M. R., 29, 188
Butler, J. S., 93, 188
Buttenheim, A., 124, 188
Bygrave, W., 70, 99, 188

Cahill, M., 122, 188
Caird, S., 99, 188
Camarillo, A. M., 97, 188
Camino, L., 20, 28, 32, 55, 187, 188, 207
Camp, S. M., 98, 202
Campbell, C. L., 50, 188
Capowich, G. E., 24, 188
Carroll, M. E., 101, 114, 188
Centers, N. L., 69, 188
Cervantes, J. M., 73, 188
Chalk, R., 29, 189
Chaplain, D., 86, 189
Charner, I., 63, 105, 189
Checkoway, B., 26, 29, 30, 32, 189
Cheshire, T. C., 4, 189
Chigunta, F., 99, 100, 189
Children Today, 189
Chinyelu, M., 62, 189
Clay, E. S., 112, 189
Cleland, R., 24, 189
Clinton, T. W., 186
Cohn, M., 24, 189
Collins, J. W., 85, 194
Collins, M. E., 24, 189
Connell, J. P., 16, 20, 24, 29, 189
Cook, K. V., 73, 90, 192
Cook, T. D., 5, 29, 192
Copeland, R., 24, 204
Correia, P., 24, 204

Corwin, M., 135, 190
Costello, J., 20, 24, 190
Cousineau, M. M., 188
Covington, J., 69, 190
Cowe, R., 117, 190
Cox, K. J., 85, 86, 110, 197
Coyle, K., 27, 28, 191
Crain, R., 112, 205
Crouter, A. C., 11, 187
Crowson, R. L., 11, 108, 187
Cutshall, S., 126, 190

Dabson, B., 124, 190
Damlamian, J., 52, 194
Danielson, R., 190
Dawson, L., 50, 190
Dees, J. G., 13, 99, 107, 109, 110, 129, 190
DeJesus, E., 62, 79, 90, 205
Delgado, M., 8, 14, 19, 20, 23, 26, 32, 33, 43, 44, 55, 62, 73, 94, 108, 114, 119, 120, 190–91
Denner, J., 27, 28, 191
Desetta, A., 56, 195
Dickens, W. T., 84, 191
Dippo, D., 52, 70, 191
Dobson, J., 109, 191
Doherty, K., 61, 84, 87, 205
Dominitz, J., 83, 191
Doren, B., 80, 82, 186
Dorfman, L., 67, 191
Dornbusch, S. M., 85, 204
Dosher, A., 24, 33, 191
Dowdeswell, E., 51, 191
Dryfoos, J., 31, 191
Duncan, G. J., 27, 29, 191

Eccles, J., 5, 8, 20, 29, 34, 38, 191, 192
Economy, P., 190
Edelman, I., 29, 191
Eggerling-Boeck, J., 97, 203
Eichorn, D., 62, 205
Elder, G. H., 5, 29
Elikann, P. T., 5, 191
Ellis, A. L., 11, 59, 90, 119, 191
Ellwood, D. T., 70, 191
Emerson, J., 9, 78, 108, 118, 190, 192
Emig, C., 87, 187

Esfandiari, M., 102, 104, 126, 196
Essenberg, T., 116, 192
Estepa, A., 56, 195
Evanciew, C.E.P., 95, 192

Fahey, P., 155, 157, 192
Faris, S., 123, 192
Fassler, I., 21, 192
Fawcett, J. T., 91, 192
Fegley, S., 85, 204
Feigelman, S., 58, 192
Ferber, T., 4, 28, 58, 60, 201
Ferguson, R. F., 26, 29, 192
Ferrari, T. M., 24, 30, 34, 192
Finch, M. D., 86, 204
Fischoff, B., 83, 191
Fitzpatrick, K., 11, 192
Fogg, N., 62, 98, 205
Fortier, S., 9, 192
Foster, W., 21, 203
Freedman, R. B., 196
Freel, M. A., 24, 197
French, S. E., 85, 203
Frickman, L., 155, 157, 192
Frumkin, P., 97, 192
Fuller, C., 192
Furstenberg, F. F., 5, 29, 192

Gailbraith, J., 58, 204
Galambos, N. L., 197
Gamble, D. N., 50, 193
Gambone, M. A., 16, 20, 24, 189
Gardner, H., 30, 204
Gardner, R. W., 91, 192
Gartner, W. B., 99, 193
Gaum, W. G., 50, 193
Gebreselassie, T., 24, 32, 193
Gennetian, L., 24, 195
Gerry, C., 104, 200
Gibbs, D., 45, 193
Giroux, H. A., 193
Gittell, R., 92, 193
Glosten, L., 99, 185
Glover, J., 24, 193
Goff, L., 92, 193
Goldberger, S., 79, 80, 89, 193
Goldsmith, S. S., 153, 193
Grant, L., 98, 187

Greenberg, M. H., 24, 189
Greenhouse, S., 64, 65, 193
Gresson, A., 11, 108, 187
Griffin, C. E., 142, 193
Grossberg, L., 3, 193
Grubb, W. N., 62, 193
Gruber, D., 79, 193, 205
Gutierrez, L. M., 30, 193
Guynn, J., 124, 194
Guzman, H.R.C., 67, 194

Haddock, V., 66, 194
Haddow, A., 52, 194
Haertel, G. D., 85, 206
Haimson, J., 85, 86, 201
Halpern, S., 59, 60, 194
Hamid, J. A., 194
Hamilton, M. A., 79, 82, 96, 194
Hamilton, S. F., 79, 82, 96, 124
Handcock, M. S., 55, 70, 186
Hanwa, J., 86, 189
Hardesty, P. H., 86, 194
Harmsworth, J., 50, 194
Harpalani, V., 4, 205
Harris, A. S., 125, 126, 194
Hasnain, R., 72, 194
Haveman, R., 68, 86, 194
Hay, M., 98, 202
Heath, S. B., 31, 69, 194
Heck, W. W., 50, 188
Henry, T., 194
Heredia, C., 66, 184
Hersey, A., 85, 197
Hickens, M., 194
High, R., 85, 194
Hilary, K., 86, 201
Hill, P. T., 87, 194
Hirsch, B. J., 86, 194
Hobson, H., 28, 187
Hoffman, D. R., 101, 119, 195
Hogan, C. J., 8, 185
Holzer, H., 67, 192
Hopkins, C., 52, 112, 194, 205
Horton R. L., 36, 194
Hren, B. J., 51, 195
Hren, D. M., 51, 195
Huebner, A. J., 30, 195
Hull, M., 88, 195

Husain, D. D., 94, 195
Hutchinson, S., 36, 194

Imel, S., 8, 195
In Focus, 35, 119, 195
Irby, M., 4, 28, 53, 60, 201
Iverson, E., 183, 206

Jargowsky, P. A., 20, 195
Jarjoura, R., 32, 186
Jasso, G., 65, 195
Jeff, M.F.X., 21, 195
Jemmott, F., 24, 189
Jickling, B., 52, 195
Johnson, C., 88, 195
Johnson, E., 25, 203
Johnson, R. S., 112, 195
Jones, C., 61, 84, 87, 205
Juntensen, C. L., 81, 207

Kablaoui, B. N., 86, 195
Kaljee, L., 69, 207
Kauffman, B., 124, 190
Kawamoto, W. T., 4, 189
Kay, P., 56, 195
Kazis, R., 8, 81, 82, 195
Keith, J. G., 9, 206
Kelloway, E. K., 86, 186
Keough, R., 79, 80, 88, 193
Ketcham, A. F., 101, 119, 195
Kets de Vries, M.F.R., 127, 195
Kibel, B. M., 20, 195
Kim, M. T., 97, 192
Kimball, M., 64, 81, 207
King, J., 155, 195
Kipke, M. D., 29, 195
Kirby, D., 27, 28, 191
Klein, K. K., 102, 111, 195
Knox, C., 28, 187
Knox, V., 24, 187, 195
Koberg, C., 203
Konig, S., 121, 196
Kouriloff, M., 99, 102, 103, 104, 196
Kourilsky, M. L., 91, 92, 115, 126, 131, 196, 206
Kroenke, C. H., 26, 196
Krueger, N. F., 113, 114, 196
Krumboltz, J. D., 81, 196

Kruse, D., 70, 191
Kubisch, A. C., 29, 189
Kuhn, T. S., 22, 196

LaGory, M., 11, 192
LaGreca, A. J., 72, 98, 196
Lakes, R. D., 9, 32, 95, 182, 196
Larson, R. W., 36, 196
Lave, J., 33, 202
Lawrence, J.E.S., 50, 196
Lee, C. C., 57, 58, 196
Lee, J. A., 30, 196
Leffert, N., 26, 34, 186, 196
Lehrer, E., 92, 196, 197
Lerman, R. I., 66, 67, 81, 87, 95, 196
Lerner, R. M., 24, 32, 197
Lewis, A., 32, 39, 197
Lewis, F. A., 30, 119, 194
Li, X., 58, 197
Liederman, D. S., 24, 197
Light, I., 93, 197
Lindner, J. R., 85, 86, 110, 197
Linn, D., 79, 197
Lobsenz, A., 114, 197
Lopez, B., 63, 65, 197
Lopez-Ospina, G., 52, 194
Lynch, R. L., 94, 197
Lynn-Dyson, K., 70, 191

MacDonald, G. B., 24, 27, 197, 198
Machtmes, K., 36, 194
Madden, S., 197
Magruder, J., 86, 197
Maimson, J., 85, 197
Males, M. A., 62, 197
Malveaux, J., 93, 198
Mangum, S., 7, 62, 198, 205
Mann, P. H., 101, 198
Manning, W. D., 85, 198
Mannon, S. E., 97, 203
Manski, C. F., 83, 191
Mariani, M., 98, 101, 177, 198
Martin, M., 97, 203
Martinez, A. L., 63, 198
Maselow, R. E., 101, 114, 198
Maser, C., 43, 45, 51, 198
Matthews, C., 57, 91, 198
Mayo, E., 93, 122, 198

McGuire, M. V., 72, 202
McKenzie-Mohr, D., 51, 198
McLaughlin, M. W., 69, 194, 198
McMillion, M., 112, 205
Meier, A. M., 97, 203
Meyer, E. C., 127, 198
Meyers, H., 26, 194
Michalak, E. A., 32, 200
Miller, C., 24, 195
Millstein, S. G., 24, 198
Mincy, R. B., 58, 198
Minniti, M., 70, 99, 188
Mitchael, R. T., 55, 198
Modell, J., 93, 187
Montero-Sieburth, M., 67, 198
Morino, M., 118, 198
Morris, M., 55, 70, 186
Morrobel, D., 4, 202
Mortimer, J. T., 86, 204
Moss, P., 6, 55, 56, 57, 198
Muller, E., 99, 185
Murdock, S. H., 71, 98, 199
Murphy, R., 21, 22, 23, 25, 35, 199, 200
Murray, L., 21, 203
Muschett, F. D., 43, 49, 199

Nachtigal, P., 50, 206
Nakanishi, D. T., 97, 199
Nauta, T., 127, 198
Neal, P., 46, 199
Nerenberg, L., 63, 65, 197
Nesdale, D., 55, 198
Neumark, D., 5, 200
Newman, K. S., 4, 6, 32, 47, 56, 57, 60, 83, 84, 200
Newman, R. P., 71, 200
Nightingale, E. O., 24, 198
Niskanen, W. A., 70, 191
Nixon, C., 118, 200
Novick, E. R., 29, 188

O'Connor, A., 55, 57, 87, 200
O'Donnell, J., 32, 200
Ogbu, J. U., 61, 84, 200
Oldham, E., 24, 204
Olive, E., 4, 200
Olson, P. R., 99, 205

Osterman, P., 47, 200
Ostrom, C. W., 24, 197

Padilla, F. M., 59, 200
Panayiotopoulos, P., 104, 200
Paquin, T. P., 101, 114, 119, 200
Parker, M., 181, 200
Patillo, M. E., 68, 69, 201
Paulter, A. J., 86, 195
Pauly, E., 86, 201
Pennington, H., 8, 81, 82, 195
Perez, S. M., 66, 67, 201
Perkins, D. F., 19, 206
Petersen, A. C., 24, 198
Peterson, J., 69, 207
Phillios, D. A., 29, 189
Phillip, M. C., 92, 98, 201
Phillips, T., 96, 104, 201
Pierret, C. R., 70, 201
Pike, A., 117, 201
Pines, M., 62, 80, 201, 205
Pinter, K., 55, 199
Pittman, K. J., 2, 20, 23, 25, 28, 32, 53, 60, 201
Poerkson, U., 28, 201
Politz, B., 24, 32, 193
Prestegard, S., 106, 201
Price, L., 64, 81, 207
Purdue, D., 117, 202

Quater, J., 117, 202
Quinn, J., 21, 24, 202
Quinoes-Mayo, Y., 72, 202

Rachuba, L. T., 61, 187
Ramirez, O., 73, 188
Ramsden, P., 93, 122, 198
Raudenbush, S. W., 27, 29, 191
Rauner, D. M., 29, 188
Reingold, D. A., 100, 122
Reskin, B. F., 57, 202
Resnick, G., 29, 188
Reynolds, P. D., 98, 202
Ricardo, I., 69, 192, 202
Richmond, B. J., 117, 202
Rick, L., 117, 129, 130, 202
Ries, E., 202
Robinson, M., 50, 202

Rodriguez, C. E., 67, 202
Rodriguez, M. C., 4, 202
Roehlkepartain, E. C., 34, 186
Rogers, K. A., 86, 186
Rogoff, B., 33, 202
Rojewski, J. W., 95, 192, 204
Rosenbaum, J. E., 84, 202
Rosenblaum, S. B., 11, 202
Rosenstein, C., 93, 197
Ross, C. L., 20, 87, 187
Rossman, J., 203
Roth, J., 21, 203
Roy, M., 46, 203
Ruben, B., 50, 203
Ruhm, C. J., 86, 203
Ryu, S., 86, 204

Saito, R. N., 20, 21, 26, 196
Salazar, D. D., 66, 67, 201
Sameroff, A., 5, 29, 192
Sampson, O., 85, 203
Sampson, R. J., 28, 88, 203
Sandefur, G. D., 97, 203
Santiago, A. M., 55, 60, 203
Sarason, D., 203
Sarver, D., 25, 203
Scales, P. C., 34, 186
Schemo, D. J., 63, 203
Scherzer, A., 113, 203
Schiraldi, V., 67, 191
Schulenberg, J., 85, 186
Schwartz, R. G., 203
Schwartz, W., 24, 62, 203
Schweke, W., 88, 195
Scott, M. A., 55, 70, 186
Seidman, E., 85, 203
Seoane, M., 120, 206
Sethna, A., 50, 194
Shaffer, R., 204
Shaklee, H., 64, 204
Shanahan, M. J., 86, 204
Shannon, M. J., 105, 204
Shaw, L., 107, 108, 204
Sheehy, A. M., 24, 204
Sherraden, M., 26
Shouse, R. C., 84, 187
Silverberg, M., 85, 197
Singh, N., 50, 196

Skinner, C., 58, 204
Slaughter, M. P., 90, 98, 103, 106, 204
Small, S., 28, 204
Smilor, R. W., 9, 89, 90, 98, 99, 100,
    102, 103, 110, 111, 115, 204
Smith, C. L., 95, 204
Smith, E., 112, 195
Smith, K., 204
Smith, S. M., 71, 200
Smith, T. J., 16, 20, 24, 189
Smith, W., 51, 198
Solomon, B., 30, 204
Spencer, M. B., 4, 205
Spencer, T. R., 4, 205
Spielberger, J., 20, 24, 190
Spring, B., 62, 80, 201, 205
Stanton, B., 58, 192
Stanton, B. F., 58, 204
Starr, E., 89, 90, 125, 204
Stein, J., 7, 29, 32, 38, 204
Steinberg, A., 8, 185, 204
Steinberg, L., 85, 204
Stern, D., 62, 82, 94, 100, 101, 112,
    114, 205
Stevens, J. W., 26, 205
Stone, C., 61, 84, 87, 112, 204, 205
Stoutland, S. E., 29, 88, 205
Sum, A., 62, 98, 205
Supple, A., 28, 204
Sutherland, M. E., 206
Swanson, D. P., 4, 205

Taylor, C. S., 4, 24, 205
Taylor, E. H., 83, 205
Taylor, F. A., 101, 119, 195
Taylor, R. B., 8, 205
Terpstra, D. E., 99, 205
Theobald, P., 50, 206
Thompson, J. P., 92, 193
Thorton, R., 97, 206
Tilly, C., 6, 55, 56, 57, 198, 200
Toles, M., 20, 24, 190
Turner, J., 24, 203
Twersky, F., 78, 192

Useem, J., 92, 114, 206

Valdes, I., 120, 206
Valdez, M., 63, 65, 197

Valdivieso, R., 24, 27, 197
Van-Rooyen, H. G., 50, 193
Verma, S., 25, 203
Villarruel, F. A., 4, 19, 202, 206
Virgil, J. D., 69, 206

Waight, C., 60, 86, 206, 207
Walberg, H. J., 85, 206
Waldeck, N., 7, 198
Waldinger, R., 93, 206
Walker, E. M., 206
Walker, G., 3, 7, 55, 57, 62, 189, 205, 206
Walstad, W., 91, 92, 96, 103, 104, 196, 206
Wang, M. C., 85, 206
Ward, R., 93, 206
Watkins, M., 32, 183, 186
Way, N., 5, 56, 206
Weil, M. O., 50, 193
Weisman, G. K., 58, 206
Weist, M. D., 69, 188
Wentling, R. M., 60, 86, 206, 207

Werner, E. E., 57, 207
Wexler, M. B., 29, 122, 186
White, J., 27, 207
Whitehead, T. L., 69, 207
Williams, D. A., 207
Williams, L. S., 68, 136, 207
Wilson, W. J., 20, 69, 207
Wilson, K. B., 72, 202
Wolfe, B., 68, 86, 194
Worley, L. P., 86, 207
Worthington, R. L., 81, 196, 207
Wynn, J., 20, 24, 190

Yates, M., 9, 32, 207
Yourniss, J., 9, 32, 207
Yovanoff, P., 80, 82, 186

Zanghi, M., 24, 204
Zeldin, S., 20, 23, 24, 25, 31, 34, 35, 37, 64, 81, 182, 201, 207
Zhou, M., 93, 97, 207, 208
Zuckerman, A., 36, 37, 74, 208
Zuniga, M. M., 120, 208

Subject Index

Academy for Educational Development, 3, 34, 35, 88, 185

Adolescents: barriers, 60; development, 27, 85; employment, 32; exposure to business, 104; meta-analysis, 85; national experiences, 3; national study, 86; normative tasks, 58; older, 65; race and ethnicity, 69; volunteers, 32; youth entrepreneurship, 110

Advisory boards, 129

African-Americans/Blacks, 22, 26, 58, 60, 62, 63, 67, 68, 72, 84, 92, 93, 103, 121, 139

Afrocentric perspective, 22

Alaskan natives, 92

American Youth Policy Forum, 20, 34, 42, 80, 81, 82, 185

Amish, 92

Aquariums, 120

Asians and Pacific-Islanders, 92, 120–21

Atfort Solutions, 116

At-risk label, 115

Banks, 112, 114, 117

Blaming the victim, 5, 10

"Call to arms," 5

Canadian Centre for Social Entrepreneurship, 98, 99, 109, 188

Case studies, 133–34, 165–66, 169

Childhood programs, 4

Chinese, 93

Collaboration: community-based organizations, 80, 87; profits and nonprofits, 117

Committee for Economic Development, 6, 43, 57, 87, 189

Community: benefits, 11; building, 9; businesses, 80; construct, 28; context, 28; definitions, 49; entrepreneurial history, 70; importance, 69; initiatives, 28; marginal, 5, 6; markets, 11; support, 32

Community-based organizations, 15, 32, 45, 80, 120

Community capacity enhancement: all encompassing, 43; broad reach, 44; career, 8; community-based organizations, 15; definition, 43; education, 44, 45; elements, 44; emphasis, 43; funding, 45; interconnectedness, 44; literature, 44;

newness, 8; open-space, 43; philosophy, 45; premise, 43; urban, 44

Community-connected learning, 8, 178

Community development corporations, 9, 29, 116

Community-food security, 49

Community-individuals interactions, 28

Community service, 32

Countries: Australia, 82; Canada, 98, 109; Ecuador, 83; England, 82, 142; France, 82, 160; Germany, 82, 141, 160; Italy, 160; Japan, 82; Korea, 82; Malaysia, 160; Mexico, 83; Netherlands, 82; Scotland, 82; Singapore, 160; Spain, 82, 160; Sweden, 82; United States, 3, 6, 52,62, 64, 69, 70, 83, 84, 88, 89, 90, 91, 92, 93, 94, 96, 97, 98, 105, 121, 125, 162, 165

Crenshaw High School (L.A.), 135, 136, 138, 139, 140, 142, 144, 145, 146, 148

Crenshaw Veterans Memorial Gardens (L.A.), 144–45

Delancy Street Foundation, 108

Disconnectedness, 5

Ecological perspective, 61

Economic inactivity, 68, 86

Economic self-sufficiency, 10, 69

Economic well-being, 106, 82

Economists, 99

Educational record, 136, 137

Educational reform, 5, 70

Employment: benefits, 86; dangers, 85; dead-end, 84; deaths, 64; detriments, 86; English proficiency, 63; federal law, 64; gainful, 79; grades, 85; growth, 78; injuries, 65; lack of, 53; racial-ethnic distinctiveness, 66; retention, 5; trends, 64, 78; underemployment, 62; unemployment, 2, 66, 67; window of opportunity, 78

Empowerment, 30, 44, 110, 118, 122, 138, 142

Enterprise zones, 137

Entrepreneurial Development Institute, 124, 148

Entrepreneurialship: appeal, 99; barriers, 102; benefits for community, 101; benefits for youth, 100, 101; case examples, 100; catalyst, 98; challenges, 102, 104, 131; classification, 99; community, 100; community development, 101; community history, 70; community service, 102; definition, 99; dream, 110; ecological perspective, 99–100; education, 101, 102, 104, 105; egalitarian nature, 102; examples, 98; field, 99; force, 115; ideal age, 101; innovation, 100; interest, 78; international, 104; interventions, 104; learning context, 99, 105; literature, 100; multidisciplinary, 99; potential, 97; process, 103; secret weapon, 99; skills, 78; social relationships, 101; SROI, 97; success, 103, 131; teaching, 101; youth, 99, 103; youth receptivity, 103; venture philanthropy, 97; vision, 109

Entrepreneurs: optimists, 99; youth, 100

ERIC Clearinghouse on Urban Education Digest, 63, 192

ESL, 145, 175

Europe, 93

Fairfax County Public Library, 112

First Things First, 34

Five Elements greeting cards, 113

Food from the 'Hood: academic subjects, 138; administrative assistant, 140; adults, 137; advertising, 147; afterschool, 140; ages, 139; alumni, 139, 140; at-risk, 143; attitudes, 136–37; career transition, 137; challenges, 136; church campaign, 143; community dollars, 142; community needs, 145; community role, 136; communication skills, 144; compassion, 143; competencies, 138;

core, 138; curriculum, 143–44; disabilities, 145; distribution, 142; empowerment, 138; enterprise zone, 137, 142, 148; ESL, 145; evaluation, 175; executive director, 137, 147; expo, 141; farmer's market, 136; foster care system, 141; founder, 137, 174; funding, 148–49; fundraising, 147, 169; future, 138; garden, 136, 138, 139, 145; goals, 137, 149; grades, 139; graduates, 139, 174; grantwriter, 142; higher education, 138, 139, 171; history, 136, 143–44, 146, 151; homeless, 136; inclusiveness, 139; incubators, 91; independent growers, 137; interns, 140; leadership development, 143; location, 136, 144, 148; marketing, 144; mentoring, 140; mission, 137, 172; national attention, 136; new product development, 147–48; Original Gardeners (OGs), 137; parental involvement, 141, 148; participants, 139; points, 141; political support, 148; production challenges, 146–47; products, 137, 147; profits, 137; public image, 135; public relations, 137, 148, 149, 173; public speaking, 143; recruitment, 139, 148, 170–71; referrals, 139; reinvestments, 141; Rodney King verdict, 137, 148; salad dressing, 137, 142, 147, 151; sales, 147; SAT, 138; schedule, 139; scholarships, 140; screening, 171; self-sufficiency goals, 147; service, 143; social values, 143; speakers, 139; staff, 143, 149; teams, 139–40, 143; teamwork, 138; travel, 141; work study, 140; World's Fair, 141; youth development, 143
Forgotten Half, 59, 60
For-profit businesses, 106, 120, 124, 173
Fortune 500, 89
From the Students, For the Students, 123
Full-service schools, 31–32

Gallup Poll, 103
Gangs, 59, 90
GED, 62
Gender: females, 26, 50, 100, 108, 119; identities, 4; males, 9, 26
Global competition, 90

High school, 35, 85, 87, 103, 165
High school graduates, 62, 78, 139
Housing Authority of New Orleans, 154

Illegal business, 59
Informal education, 105
Innova Apparel, 121
International Institute for Sustainable Development, 46
Internet/Web sites, 61, 118, 133
Intrapreneur, 129

Japanese, 93
Job shop, 57
Jobs Corp, 155
Joint work, 31

Kauffman Foundation, 104
Kibibi Stationary, 115
Kids on the Hill, 36
Koreans, 93

Language, 93
Latin artists, 37
Latinos, 60, 62, 63, 65, 66, 67, 72, 84, 120, 139
Learning community, 77, 80
Libraries, 61, 120
Lifestyle entrepreneurs, 90
Livelihood, 35–36, 46
Los Angeles Fire Department, 142
Los Angeles Housing Authority, 111
Los Angeles Times, 102, 149
Los Angeles Unified School District, 144, 148

Mack Knick Knack Boxes, 115
Mannatez Corporation, 125
Mentorship, 83
Microenterprise, 112

Migrant workers, 63
Museum, 120

National Center for Social
   Entrepreneurs, 99, 117, 199
National Collaboration for Youth, 32,
   62, 85, 199
National Employer Leadership
   Council, 78, 96, 199
National Foundation for Teaching
   Entrepreneurship, 124, 125
National Research Council, 5, 64, 65,
   66, 85, 199
National School-to-Work Learning and
   Information Center, 24, 66, 87, 199
National Technical Information
   Service, 24, 199
National Youth Employment Coalition,
   37, 199
Native American, 93
New Careers, 10
Newcomer youth: dangers, 83, 84;
   hours of employment, 83, 84;
   remittance to family, 83, 84;
   schooling, 83, 84; work ethic, 83, 84
Newsweek, 138
New York Times, 58, 149
New Youth Entrepreneur (NYE), 126
Nontraditional settings, 43, 94

Organisation for Economic Co-
   operation and Development, 110,
   200

Paradigms: assets, 7, 8, 9; boundaries,
   8, 20–21, 22; challenges, 8;
   community, 43; consensus, 22;
   deficits, 42; definition, 22, 24;
   evaluation, 42; guidance, 42, 53;
   importance, 16, 22, 35, 42; role, 41,
   42; shifts, 53; theoretical
   underpinnings, 22, 41; youth, 9
Pennsylvania State University, 23, 201
People magazine, 149
Political systems, 7
Prince Charles, 142
Prison, 62
Private/public ventures, 4, 19, 105, 201

Professional education, 180–81
Psychologists, 99

Rainbow Technologies, 124
Rebuild Los Angeles, 142
Resiliency, 85
Roberts Foundation, 108
Rodney King riots, 135, 148

San Diego County Office of Education,
   78, 88, 89, 203
Santa Clara River Valley Hometown
   Creations, 118
School-based enterprises, 112, 117, 138
School success, 39
School-to-career: academic
   achievement, 79; academic subjects,
   81; active-learning, 81; barriers, 60;
   benefits, 81; challenges, 83;
   collaboration, 80; community-based
   organizations, 8; ecology, 84–85,
   100; elements, 80; enhancement, 78;
   higher education, 96; history, 14;
   human capital, 81; initiatives, 80; key
   transition points, 85; lifelong
   learning, 8; movement, 81; national
   attention, 96; school-based
   enterprises, 80; self-sufficiency, 8;
   shift, 80; stakeholders, 8; strategic
   initiatives, 78; terms, 8; vocational
   education, 82; work-based learning,
   80; window of opportunity, 78
School-to-career transition: barriers,
   86; career preparation, 82;
   challenges, 73, 83, 84; community-
   based organizations, 87;
   competencies, 88; complexity, 73;
   comprehensive perspective, 86;
   contextual learning, 89; creativity,
   57; ecological perspective, 84–85;
   factors, 56, 88, 89; foundation skills,
   88; frame, 74; future, 87–88; goals,
   15; human capital, 81; impetus for,
   14; initiatives, 34; international, 82;
   key transition points, 85; learning,
   89; mentors, 83; national attention,
   82; principles, 82; school-based
   enterprises, 53; schools, 89;

substitution, 8; success, 81; universities, 14; youth development, 53, 86; youth of color, 83, 86; work ethic, 83

School-to-Work Opportunities Act: engagement, 80; funding, 79; goals, 80; history, 79; impact, 82; learning arenas, 80; reform, 82; search institute, 34; Secretary of Labor's Commission on Achieving Necessary Skills, 88; stakeholders, 81

Self-efficacy, 113

Service-learning, 39

Small businesses: administration, 90; Amish businesses, 92; bias against, 90; communities of color, 91–92, 94; community-based organizations, 90; economic development, 59; employment, 96; entry-level jobs, 90; Fortune 500, 89; hiring trends, 89; impact, 89–90, 92; importance to country, 89, 90, 91, 96; incubators, 91; international, 104; labor intensive, 96; literature, 91; markets, 92; needs, 93; net job growth, 90; opportunities, 96; ownership, 125; plans, 116; potential, 89–90; social policy, 94; strategic role, 92; typical size, 90; urban, 92–93; workforce, 89

Smith-Hughes Act, 94

Social arenas, 84

Social capital, 42, 61, 116, 117

Social Enterprise London, 107, 111, 204

Social entrepreneurs, 13

Social entrepreneurship: adults, 121; afterschool, 115; behaviors, 130; benefits, 117; blurring of sectors, 107, 109; case examples, 111; change agents, 110; concept, 108; definition, 109, 110, 130; distrust of business sector, 108; empowerment, 118; encompassing nature, 9; engaging youth, 113–14; factors, 111; funding, 108, 114; goals, 8, 107, 108; history, 9, 107; homelessness, 107; indigenous driven, 109, 114–15;

information technology, 118; institution driven, 113–14; integration, 9; intervention strategy, 108; language, 107; markets, 107, 117; mission, 117; myths, 114; origins, 118; popularity, 109; principles, 117; problem-solving, 110; process, 110, 111; role, 9; school-based, 125; social aims, 107; social-dimension, 131; social mission, 117; starting social enterprises, 111–12; sustaining social enterprises, 111–12; "Third Way," 109; venture capital, 124; youth, 13

Social Security, 97

Social work, 9, 14, 15, 19, 157

Social youth entrepreneurship: adaptation to local circumstances, 151; afterschool, 115; appeal, 98; arts, 151; assumptions, 116; athletes, 151; behavior, 130; benefits, 11; best practices, 179; boundaries, 20, 107, 177, 181, 182; capital, 117; career, 177, 178, 180; challenges, 52, 176; circulation of capital, 117; collaboration, 180; community benefits, 9, 108, 109; community context, 11; components, 150; concept, 108, 116, 123; conceptual frame, 11; connected-learning, 178; considerations, 123–25; context, 107; curriculum, 180; definition, 179; ecology, 11; economics, 5; education, 15, 19, 106, 125; elements, 122–23; emergence, 38; empowerment, 122; engagement, 113; field-based, 15; fields, 12, 15, 107, 178; flexibility, 151, 177; framework, 36; funding, 150; global, 130; goals, 19, 107, 116; history, 14, 33, 179; impact, 115; importance, 17; incentives, 180; inclusiveness, 118–19; innovative practice, 107; internships, 105, 181; investments, 115; knowledge of community, 121, 172; language of, 107; lessons, 180; literature, 118; marginal youth, 56; market, 107; measures, 178–79; mentors, 38;

merger, 74; mission, 172; motivation, 36; opportunity, 38, 107; paradigm, 19, 183; parental involvement, 175; potential, 9, 10, 15, 16, 19, 98, 130, 181; premise, 115; pride, 120–21; principles, 118–22; process, 121; professional education, 180–81; programs, 17; rehabilitation, 15; reinvestment, 121; research and development, 173; roots, 98; rules, 118–19; scholarship, 182–83; self-efficiency, 113; service-focus, 118, 119, 120; social aims, 98; social work, 15; sociology, 15; support, 176; values, 116, 119; vocational education, 52; youth development, 38, 130, 181; youth of color, 98

Sociologists, 99

States: California, 63, 66, 124, 136, 139, 142; Florida, 13; Louisiana, 155, 157; Maryland, 58; Massachusetts, 64; Minnesota, 83; New York, 113, 123; North Carolina, 64; Virginia, 56, 112

St. John's Baptist Church, 155

Street Souljahwear, 56

Street Sport Fashion, 122

Substance abuse, 53, 68

Sugar and Spice, 108

Sustainable community development: agriculture, 50; boundaries, 49; challenges, 52; classroom activities, 52; concepts, 52; curriculum, 51, 52; definition, 45, 52; ecology, 50; economic criteria, 50; economics section, 45; education, 51–52; elements, 49–50; environment, 40, 49, 52; environment section, 45; facilitating factors, 50; funding, 51; future, 51; goals, 49; hindering factors, 50; history, 51; influence, 51; international, 51; lifespan, 46; limitations, 52; livelihood, 46; people section, 45; popularity, 51; principles, 50; reach, 51; relevance, 50; rural, 50; schools, 51; strengths, 52; success, 50; technology section, 45;

universities, 51; urban, 46–49; vocational education, 52; women, 50

Teacher preparation: broker skills, 129; flexibility, 129; knowledge of community, 128; personality, 128; qualities, 126–27; supportive advisory board, 129

Transition to adulthood: complexity, 7, 79; challenges, 77, 79, 95, 96; hiatus, 78; marginal youth, 96; outreach, 78

Twins Angeles Designs, 119

Unemployment, 62

United Nations, 98

Urban areas: Albany, N.Y., 123; Arlington, Va., 56; Baltimore, Md., 36, 58; Chicago, Ill., 46; London, England, 107; Los Angeles, Calif., 111, 133, 134, 135, 136, 141, 142, 148; Minneapolis, Minn., 83; New Orleans, La., 133, 134, 151, 152, 153, 154, 164; New York, 36, 37, 57, 108, 125, 164; Ossining, N.Y., 113; San Diego, Calif., 78, 88; San Francisco, Calif., 102, 108; Tampa, Fla., 113; Washington, D.C., 157, 119

Urban labor markets, 58

Urban Youth Enterprise Zones, 59

U.S. Census Bureau, 65, 91, 154, 206

U.S. Department of Labor, 78, 88

Vietnamese, 93

Vocational education: benefits, 94; dumping grounds, 95; educational reform, 96; equipment, 95; history, 94; industrial revolution, 94; U.S. history, 94; vision, 95

Washington Post, 149

YA/YA: adults, 160; alumni, 157, 158, 159, 174; animation, 61; at-risk, 163; artistic director, 152; artistic expression, 155, 156, 164; artwork, 154; attendance, 155, 160; board of directors, 156–57; budget, 160; business side of art, 153; career ladder, 159; career skills, 158; chairs, 152, 155; challenges, 159, 162, 165; collaborative partners, 155, 163; commissions, 155, 160; community, 154; competencies, 157, 161; computers, 160; context, 153; curfews, 153; empowerment, 157; evaluation, 175; expenses, 160; field-trips, 160; for-profit unit, 160–61; founder, 151, 152, 174; French Quarter, 153; fundamental premise, 153; funding, 163–64, 169; future, 162; goals, 153, 154; grades, 155, 160; grants, 160; guild, 159; higher education, 155, 158, 171; history, 152–53; internships, 158; Jazz Festival, 154, 155; job corps, 155; lessons, 158, 159; Mardi Gras, 154; marketing, 160, 161; media, 162–63; mentors, 159; mission, 153, 162, 164, 172; motivation, 160; murals, 155; origins of name, 152; outreach, 156; participants, 156; print studio, 160; projects, 157; public relations, 173; Reboutin Vocational High School, 152, 156, 157; recruitment, 156, 170–71; rules, 158; schools, 161–62; screening, 159, 171; selection process, 159; social enterprise, 157; staff, 160; success, 153; supervision, 152; team inspiration, 155; travel, 158, 160, 165; uniqueness, 164; Yea Café, 58; youth development, 161; youth knowledge, 165; youth organizations, 155

Youth: adults, 3; artistic talents, 151; at-risk, 15; bias, 3; business, 11, 117; capital, 4; career development, 6, 18; challenges, 4, 55, 56, 57; community, 29; community building, 9; community transformation, 11; competencies, 4; complexities, 3, 77; courts, 5; decision-making, 31; definition, 10; demographics, 65; developmental age, 78; disconnectness, 87; diversity, 56; economic fabric of community, 4;

employment programs, 10, 85; empowerment, 30; energy, 121; experiences, 22, 64; failure, 5; fears, 4; focus, 77; future, 6; historical perspective, 42; initiatives, 53; knowledge base, 5; labels, 22; literature, 32; media, 5; needs, 77; newcomers, 65; paradigm, 8; policies, 3; preserve, 4; programs, 7; promise of, 6, 16; resources, 29; sexual orientation, 3; systems, 3; unemployment, 62; virtues, 5; waivers to adult court, 5; work-force, 6

Youth assets, 30, 41, 124; cognition, 33; merging, 30

Youth development: adults, 22, 29; advocates, 21, 29, 35, 37, 40; arts, 14, 26; attention, 19; blurring of distinctions, 11, 15, 28; boundaries, 15, 22–23, 24, 25, 40; broadness, 16, 20, 40; capital, 7; career development, 30, 108; cautions, 16; challenges, 20, 21, 24, 38; commitment, 21, 25; community, 11, 23, 24, 27, 38; community development, 14, 29; community service, 30, 32; competencies, 33; comprehensive initiatives, 8, 21; conceptual, 14; context, 20, 21, 22; core elements, 22, 70, 71; critics, 28, 70; data, 27; definition, 11, 20, 21, 23, 40; ecology, 11; economic self-sufficiency, 29, 35; employment, 35, 37, 74; empowerment, 30, 31; environment, 28; evaluation, 20; evolution, 38; exurbia, 21; families, 22, 23, 24, 27, 38, 40, 71; field, 15; focus, 11; fostering, 28; gap between theory and practice, 20, 21; goals, 25, 28, 37, 38, 124; higher education, 14; history/evolution, 20, 30, 37, 38, 40; HIV/AIDS, 35; importance, 17, 24, 25; key elements, 86; knowledge construction, 33; learning, 11, 33; literature, 25, 26; livelihood, 35; long-term commitment, 38, 52; marginal youth, 16; measurement,

27; motivation, 36; new arenas, 14; newcomers, 29; new frontier settings, 14; paradigm, 11, 19, 35, 86, 108; participation, 31; peers, 22, 40; popularity, 23; potential, 19, 38; premier paradigm, 42; premise, 26; principles, 25; productive member, 79; recreation, 14; rural, 21; safety, 33; scholarship, 21, 34; schools, 38, 39; school-to-career, 34, 35; school-to-work, 35; social network, 22; thin-line, 24; transition to adulthood, 10; urban, 21; vibrancy, 19; work force development, 36

Youth Livelihood Movement, 35–36, 46

Youth of Color Aspirations, 85

Youth policies, 3

Youth venture, 36, 37, 56, 58, 108, 115, 116, 119, 121, 122, 123, 125

Zoos, 120

About the Author

MELVIN DELGADO is a faculty member and chair of Boston University's Macro-Practice Department at the School of Social Work, where he specializes in issues of youth development in urban communities. He has written several books and publishes extensively in the areas of social work practice in nontraditional settings. Recently, Dr. Delgado was awarded a grant by the National Institute on Drug Abuse, to establish the Boston University Social Work Minority Research Center for Research and Training in Urban Communities of Color.